The
Psychology
of Baseball

The
Psychology
of Baseball

Inside the Mental Game
of the Major League Player

Mike Stadler

GOTHAM BOOKS

GOTHAM BOOKS
Published by Penguin Group (USA) Inc.
375 Hudson Street, New York, New York 10014, U.S.A.
Penguin Group (Canada), 90 Eglinton Avenue East, Suite 700, Toronto,
Ontario M4P 2Y3, Canada (a division of Pearson Penguin Canada Inc.);
Penguin Books Ltd, 80 Strand, London WC2R 0RL, England;
Penguin Ireland, 25 St Stephen's Green, Dublin 2,
Ireland (a division of Penguin Books Ltd);
Penguin Group (Australia), 250 Camberwell Road, Camberwell,
Victoria 3124, Australia (a division of Pearson Australia Group Pty Ltd);
Penguin Books India Pvt Ltd, 11 Community Centre,
Panchsheel Park, New Delhi –110 017, India;
Penguin Group (NZ), 67 Apollo Drive, Mairangi Bay,
Auckland 1311, New Zealand (a division of Pearson New Zealand Ltd);
Penguin Books (South Africa) (Pty) Ltd, 24 Sturdee Avenue,
Rosebank, Johannesburg 2196, South Africa

Penguin Books Ltd, Registered Offices: 80 Strand, London WC2R 0RL, England

Published by Gotham Books, a division of Penguin Group (USA) Inc.

First printing, April 2007
10   9   8   7   6   5   4   3   2   1

Gotham Books and the skyscraper logo are trademarks of Penguin Group (USA) Inc.

LIBRARY OF CONGRESS CATALOGING-IN-PUBLICATION DATA HAS BEEN APPLIED FOR.

ISBN 978-1-592-40275-5

Printed in the United States of America
Set in Minion   •   Designed by Elke Sigal

While the author has made every effort to provide accurate telephone numbers and Internet addresses at the time of publication, neither the publisher nor the author assumes
any responsibility for errors, or for changes that occur after publication. Further, the
publisher does not have any control over and does not assume any responsibility for author or third-party Web sites or their content.

For Brandi

CONTENTS

INTRODUCTION

ONE OF MY FAVORITE SPORTS ARTIFACTS IS AN ISSUE OF *SPORTS Illustrated* from October 1954, which includes Roger Kahn's account of that year's World Series. Part of the story is a series of five photos taken in rapid succession. Bit by bit, they show the Willie Mays miracle known in baseball simply as "The Catch." With the first game of the series tied 2–2 in the eighth inning, and the heavily favored Cleveland Indians threatening to score with none out and two runners on base, Vic Wertz hit a pitch deep to center field and it appeared, at least for a time, that both runners would score easily. But Willie Mays performed one of the most memorable athletic feats of the century: at a full sprint, with his back to home plate, he caught Wertz's drive, then whirled around to throw the ball back to the infield, preventing even one run from scoring. The Giants went on to win both the game and the World Series.

Baseball is heralded as the national pastime, and those Giants of the early 1950s are evidence of this: third baseman Bobby Thomson's "shot heard round the world" won the National League pennant in 1951, and the Giants' improbable victory three years later (which featured The Catch) over an Indians team that had won 111 of 154 regular-season games are salient bits of U.S. sports lore. Kahn's reporting of the Giants victory in the World Series reveals another of our favorite recreations, armchair psychology. The story relates a series of questions put to Indians manager Al Lopez by another reporter, each question pressing Lopez again and again to identify the "turning point" in the series. In a purely objective sense, the Indians were the same team after losing the World Series that they had been before. Athletic ability is not so evanescent that it changes much in a mere four games (barring injuries, of course). But that persistent reporter was fishing for a more psychological account—what changed in the Cleveland psyche, and when did it change? An angry Lopez finally snapped at the reporter, cutting off the questions. Knowing perhaps better than anyone how exceptional his team was, Lopez could not grasp how it was that they had not only lost, but been trounced.

The reporter who hectored Lopez with those questions about turning points was doing what we all do at times: trying to explain why someone did what he did in a particular situation. In life, we ask questions like "Why did I think one word and type another?" In baseball, we ask, "Why did the hitter freeze at that third-strike fastball right down the middle of the plate?" Baseball fans are baseball psychologists: like psychologists, they attempt to explain human behavior and they invoke various mental forces as they craft a theory. One of the attractions of baseball and other sports is that they afford the opportunity to offer our own analysis. Very few can play the game at a high level, but everyone can think the game (especially in retrospect).

Baseball is impossible without psychology: impossible to play, and impossible to appreciate fully as a fan. The physical demands of the game are intense and the physical abilities of the players, as extraordinary as they are, cannot by themselves meet those demands. Working alone, even the fastest reflexes would be insufficient—the reflexes must be supported by the player's intellect. The player's intellect, in turn, is shaped by those cognitive and emotional forces that are the province of psychology.

We marvel at the athletic prowess, the quickness on display when a great hitter turns on a fastball or when a shortstop makes one of those plays that we see for weeks on the highlight shows. We are intrigued and amazed by the physical constraints on the game, the way a pitcher manipulates the influence of wind resistance on the ball to fashion a slow curve or a biting slider. And then there is the mental game: the responses a nervous system must generate in order to hit a 90mph fastball, the fielder calculating the ballistics of a ball in flight, the baffling failures of players known to possess great physical prowess, or the influences of pressures like impending free agency, a lengthening hitting streak, or the mounting tension of a tie score during a high-stakes game. Psychology mediates between the demands imposed by the physics of the game and the capabilities afforded by the athletic ability of those who play it.

The importance of psychology to baseball is evident in the game's culture. Listen to any radio or television broadcast of a baseball game, and with the play-by-play, statistics, and beer commercials you get a liberal dose of psychology. The announcers, at least one of whom is invariably a former player or coach, try to read the minds of the players on the field to make known their motives and struggles. These analysts offer their guesses about what a player might be thinking, and how that might lead to the action we see on the field.

Fans are just as adept at using psychology to understand what they see on the field. Indeed, in everyday life, we all make all kinds of attributions about the psychology of others around us: we explain their behavior in terms of beliefs and goals. The psychology we get from baseball analysts is that same common-sense, intuitive psychology. To get the *uncommon* sense, a deeper reading from psychological science is required. Our intuitions are limited. Evidence of these limits comes from all over psychology. Psychologists study phenomena ranging from optical illusions to depression, from false memory to stereotyping, all of which appear to involve distortions of thought and belief. In all of psychology's subdisciplines there is evidence of how limited our intuitive understanding of the world really is. Much of what we see and hear and believe is illusory. We have enough of an intuitive sense of physics that we can navigate the world easily, but we also fail miserably when asked to describe and explain some of the most trivial of physical phenomena. Our intuitions about the relative likelihood of different events are often wildly erroneous. Even our intuitive explanations of our own behavior have been shown to be faulty and incomplete. And recent research has shown that we hardly even understand what will make us happy or unhappy, and by how much.

It should thus be no surprise that our intuitive explanations of other people's behavior are marked by consistent and common errors, and that this can occur in baseball as much as in any other aspect of life. For example, one such tendency, known as the fundamental attribution error, is our inclination to attribute the causes of another's behavior more to the actor and less to the situation than is appropriate. We believe that the strikeout is due more to the mastery of the pitcher and less to the law of averages, or the home run is more the pitcher's fault and less due to the wind blowing from behind home plate. Certainly the pitcher plays a role in these situations, but we tend to overemphasize that role and underemphasize the influence of other factors. These and many other related phenomena demonstrate that our intuition is limited, limited by what we have the ability to name, limited by what we are aware of, and limited by our native cognitive capacities and patterns of thinking.

Even the sports psychologist in the dugout is focused only on part of what the field of psychology as a whole has to offer. Students in introductory psychology courses at colleges and universities are often surprised to find that there is more to psychology than Sigmund Freud and profiling serial killers for the FBI. Students of the game of baseball may be surprised to find that psychology has more to offer than concepts like "staying in the zone." Perhaps the most well-known baseball psychologist is Harvey Dorfman, who has worked with the Oakland A's, the World Series–winning 1997 Florida Marlins, and for baseball superagent Scott Boras and his clients. In an article for the professional journal *Sport Psychologist,* Dorfman lists the ways he helps players with performance issues by using the "techniques of concentration, relaxation, visualization, control of arousal levels, and positive self-talk," and also discusses his role in helping with a range of other personal issues, or "off-field performance inhibitors." Those are obviously important psychological issues, but there is much more psychology in baseball than that list of services reveals.

We can see and understand many aspects of the physical forces at work in baseball using common sense. But physics can tell us more: why a curveball curves, why fly balls follow the trajectories they do, and why, as a matter of physics, it hardly matters that Sammy Sosa corked his bat. We can sense and understand many aspects of the psychological forces at work using common sense, too. But psychology can tell us more.

Yogi Berra is reported to have said, "Baseball is 90 percent mental; the other half is physical." To be sure, much of what we see in baseball owes to speed and strength and quickness of reflex. But watch any game, and most of what you see is thinking: the pitcher readying his pitch, the defense alert, the hitter anticipating that pitch.

Few people realize how much psychological research has been applied to baseball. From early experiments done on Babe Ruth to virtual-reality batting simulations in today's psychological laboratories, psychology has examined the vision, the reflexes, the psyches, the motivations, of the baseball player. As a result of this research, psychology can probe more thoroughly the minds of the best players to understand what makes them the best of the best. And because of this research, psychology can also help answer (or at least come close to answering) some of the questions that baseball fanatics have debated endlessly— questions such as "Do baseball players really have streaks and slumps, and if so, why?" and "Is it true that players play better right before they become free agents?" In addition, psychology is now in a position to dispel some of baseball's most entrenched myths, such as the popular myth that some power pitchers throw fastballs that rise, or the belief that thinking too much impairs a player's performance. The commonsense view, the conventional wisdom, is often wrong. Psychology can explain why. And when the conventional wisdom *is* correct, psychology often can explain why, which is often not the reason that people assume. Psychology can also help describe what we see on the field:

- How can a player hit a ball that is going 95mph, a ball that is going so fast that you and I would be hard pressed to see it, let alone hit it?

- How do pitchers throw with more accuracy than is needed to hit the bull's-eye on a dartboard?
- How do outfielders easily figure where a fly ball (a ballistic object) will land when rocket scientists armed with computers have not yet been able to build a system that reliably intercepts missiles?

This book is organized around two broad principles: the nature of skill and the nature of variability in performance. The skills that have been investigated most are hitting, catching fly balls, and throwing, so the first section of the book will focus on each of these in turn. The second section of the book will consider why the outcome of a given event (getting a hit during an at bat, catching a fly ball, throwing a pitch for a strike) varies from one occasion to the next. There are two fundamental forms this variability in outcomes takes, variability between individuals (from one player to another) and variability within an individual (from one occasion to another). These will be considered in turn. And finally, the book takes a look at the psychology of the fan—why do we become fans, and what shapes our fanaticism? What factors affect the ways that we perceive and think about the game?

CHAPTER ONE

Hitting Is 50 Percent Mental

BEFORE THE "JUICED" ERA THAT BEGAN IN THE 1990S, THE YEAR of the Hitter had to be 1941, not so much because of a league-wide offensive explosion, but because two of the greatest hitters in history turned in their most memorable seasons. Joe DiMaggio was voted the American League MVP after hitting .357 with thirty home runs and 125 RBI on a foundation laid by his famous fifty-six-game hitting streak (which was followed immediately by a sixteen-game streak, giving him hits in seventy-two of seventy-three consecutive games). Were it not for DiMaggio's streak, Ted Williams might have won the MVP—his 1941 season was the last in which a hitter would finish with a batting average over .400. Williams missed the Triple Crown by just 5 RBI with his .406 average, thirty-seven homers, and 120 RBI (he would win the Triple Crown in '42 and '47, years in which he also led the American League in runs scored). In 1941, Williams led the American League with an incredible .553 on-base percentage (a mark that stood as the all-time highest until Barry Bonds put up .582 and .609 in 2002 and 2004) and a .735 slugging percentage (in 1941, the tenth highest all-time—most of the season totals ahead of his were compiled by Babe Ruth).

That's not all: DiMaggio and Williams hardly ever struck out. DiMaggio struck out only thirteen times in 541 at bats! Williams had just twenty-seven strikeouts, and both players had fewer strikeouts than home runs and more than five times as many walks as strikeouts. Over their careers, DiMaggio had more home runs than strikeouts in seven of his thirteen seasons, and Williams in three of his nineteen. Williams's 1.285 OPS (on-base percentage plus slugging percentage) in 1941 beat the second-place DiMaggio's by .202, and DiMaggio's beat the third-place Charlie Keller's by .087. It wasn't until Barry Bonds led the league with a 1.379 OPS to Sammy Sosa's 1.174 in 2001 that the first-place finisher outpaced the next hitter by such a wide margin.

1941 hitting statistics for DiMaggio and Williams.											
	AB	R	H	HR	RBI	BB	SO	BA	OBP	SLG	OPS
DiMaggio	541	122	193	30	125	76	13	.357	.440	.643	1.083
Williams	456	135	185	37	120	145	27	.406	.551	.735	1.285

DiMaggio's was just one of several streaks that the Yankees put together that year. Catcher Bill Dickey was in the middle of a seventeen-game streak when DiMaggio's started, and first baseman Johnny Sturm started one of his own around the same time, as did shortstop Frank Crosetti. Initially, some of the writers covering the team focused more on Sturm's streak than the others, because Sturm was playing first base, a position vacated by Lou Gehrig two years before when his illness prevented him from playing anymore. The Yankees had finished third in the American League in 1940 (but only two games out of first), and

1941 was shaping up to be worse. The writers doubted that Sturm would help much (they were right: in his only major-league season, he hit .239 with three home runs in 124 games) and for a time put the focus on him as an emblem of the Yankees' problems. One writer, Dan Daniel of the *New York World-Telegram,* sarcastically started tracking Sturm's streak when it reached four games, and continued through his eleventh straight on May 28. In the article in which Sturm's eleven-game streak is mentioned, Daniel also noted that Crosetti had a ten-game streak going and DiMaggio had hit in thirteen straight. Sturm's streak ended there, and writers soon turned their focus to DiMaggio's.

After that May 28 game, the Yankees were 22–18 (with one tie), 4.5 games behind the first-place Indians. Things started to turn around as DiMaggio's streak wore on. In mid-June, the Yankees ended a long road trip by sweeping three from the St. Louis Browns and two from the White Sox, at which point DiMaggio's streak was at twenty-six games and another streak was developing: the Yankees had hit home runs in nine straight games. In the course of winning the AL in 1940, the Tigers had set a record with a run of seventeen straight games with at least one home run. The Yankees broke that record on June 22, 1941, when DiMaggio hit safely in his thirty-fifth straight game and extended the homer streak in the same at bat. DiMaggio set the all-time record by hitting in his forty-fifth straight game and passing Wee Willie Keeler's record on July 2 against Williams and the Red Sox. The team home run streak had ended the day before at twenty-five games, but the Yankees were on a roll: in thirty-two games since May 28, they were 23–8–1 and in first place, two games ahead of the Indians. DiMaggio's run ended against the Indians on July 17, when he walked once and

3

grounded out three times, twice on hard grounders that Indians third-baseman Ken Keltner backhanded deep behind third base, narrowly throwing DiMaggio out each time.

The Yankees took all of the drama out of the pennant race, eventually winning the AL by seventeen games, but as the season wound down, fans had something else to watch: Ted Williams's drive to hit .400. At the time, Williams's feat did not garner widespread acclaim. No one has hit .400 since Williams, but it was not an unheard-of achievement in the early forties. In fact, DiMaggio had flirted with .400 two years before, sitting at .409 on September 9, but falling to .381 over the last few weeks of the season. Bill Terry of the Giants hit .401 in 1930 and it happened seven times in the 1920s, including three times in 1922 (George Sisler, .420; Rogers Hornsby, .401; Ty Cobb, .401). Hornsby (1922, 1924, and 1925) and Cobb (1911, 1912, and 1922) each accomplished the feat three times in their careers.

Even so, going back to 1876, the .400 mark had been reached only twenty-seven times, and as the 1941 season came to a close, people began to watch Williams to see if he could do it. And, as Robert Creamer notes, though other hitters had hit .400, the way Williams was hitting the ball was special:

> So Williams' .410 average in early September was splendid but not yet earthshaking. What was earthshaking—or fascinating, anyway—was the *way* he was hitting. He wasn't choking up on the bat and poking safe little singles. He was swinging hard, smashing out doubles, home runs, line drives, long fly balls. He had been well behind in the home-run race earlier in the year, but he hit so many late-season dingers that he moved past the Yankees' Charlie Keller into the league lead.

Williams was hitting, and he was hitting with power. Because he was a selective hitter and because other teams so often pitched around him, Williams also drew 145 walks.

Some of Williams's home runs during that 1941 season are the stuff of legend. He had started the season with an ankle injury and did not start playing every day until a couple of weeks into the season, at the end of April. In the next few weeks, he would set the tone for the season with some mammoth shots, including one in Chicago that landed on the grandstand roof in right-center field, estimated by some at six hundred feet. He'd had a homer earlier in the game, too, but that one only went five hundred feet. Later, though the All-Star game took place in the middle of DiMaggio's streak (he was at forty-eight games), with two outs and two runners on and the American League down 5–4 in the bottom of the ninth, Williams stole the show with a game-winning home run that hit the façade in front of the roof in right field in Detroit's Briggs Stadium.

Like DiMaggio, Williams started a hitting streak on May 15, though his run ended after twenty-three games. But during that run, he was amazing. As Leigh Moutville writes in *Ted Williams*:

> Six days after the start of his streak, he went 4-for-5 against the Yankees, then 3-for-7 in the next two days. He then went on a stretch of games in which he collected at least two hits per game. His average, which had been inching up in the first half of May, shot past the magic .400 mark on May 25 and went straight to .430. From May 17 to June 1, he hit .536. His average for the entire month of May was .436.

During only the dates that encompassed Williams's twenty-three-game streak, Williams hit .487 to DiMaggio's .368.

In the first after the All-Star game, Williams went 0–4 and his average dropped from .405 to .398. Another ankle injury kept him out of some games in July and limited him to pinch-hitting in others, and his average dropped a few more points. But as he returned, his average climbed again, and by the end of July he was back over .400. He stayed there through mid-September. The Red Sox played their last home games September 20 and 21 and Williams went three for seven, leaving his average at .405. He had six games left, three in Washington against the Senators and three in Philadelphia against the A's. The last two games against the Senators were a doubleheader, during which Williams went 1–7, dropping his average to .401. Joe Cronin, the Red Sox manager, and others thought that maybe Williams should just sit out that last, meaningless series, in order to protect the .401 average. But Williams would have none of it. In the first game against the A's, he went one for four, dropping his average to .39955, which, according to the rules, would be rounded off to .400. But less than .400 is less than .400. The last two games were, again, to be played in a doubleheader. (Two doubleheaders within a week? Those *were* the days!) Again, Williams insisted on playing. In the first game, he singled, hit a home run, singled twice more, and reached on an error. In the second game, he singled, doubled, and hit a fly out to left field. He'd gone six for eight to finish at .406 (or more precisely, .4057).

It is worth noting, too, that in 1941 the major-league scoring rules did not recognized the sacrifice fly, and counted them as outs in figuring batting averages. Give Williams a fairly conservative ten sacrifice flies and his average would have been .415, and there would have been much less drama on that last day of the season.

DiMaggio and Williams are among those who set the bar of excellence for major-league hitting. Few players put together the kinds of seasons they had in 1941 and, indeed, in many other years during their careers. Their accomplishments belie the extraordinary difficulty of hitting a baseball. Think about hitting a 95mph fastball. Depending on the pitcher and his delivery, the ball begins its flight roughly fifty-six to fifty-eight feet from the hitter. It is traveling about 139 feet per second, and so will cross the plate about four-tenths of a second after being released. To get an idea just how short a time this is, consider that it takes the average person a minimum of about two-tenths of a second to move his or her eyes from one point to another. If you fixate on the first letter on this line of text, and then as quickly as you are able move your eyes to read the last letter on the line and then immediately move back again to read the first letter of the next line, you will have taken more time than the 95mph fastball takes to travel from pitcher's hand to catcher's mitt. In that short interval, the hitter must discern what type of pitch it is, where it is going and when it will get there, decide whether or not to swing, and then guide the swing to the point of contact. Even a power pitcher's off-speed pitches, which might travel at 80mph, will cross the plate in under five-tenths of a second, about seven-hundredths of a second slower than the fastball.

It is astonishing that even a highly select group of athletes can hit major-league pitches. (As Ted Williams famously said, "Hitting a baseball—I've said it a thousand times—is the single most difficult thing to do in sport.") How astonishing? We know that as impossible as hitting a major-league fastball may seem, even weak-hitting pitchers do it once in a while. Whatever you think of interleague play, it gives us an interesting control group: because of the designated-hitter rule in the American League, those pitchers get little experience in the batter's box (and pitchers as a group spend much less time on their hitting anyway). When the American Leaguers play in National League parks, the AL pitchers do get the occasional hit. Based on their performance, we can estimate that an athlete who is not a hitter might be expected to bat about .100 with little power. Some of the difference between those AL pitchers and an everyday hitter are surely physical and are due to differences in such things as quickness, speed, and strength. But some of that difference between the AL pitchers and a regular hitter is also psychological, and due to the everday hitter's knowledge and experience.

Consider just one piece of information the hitter needs: where the ball will be when it crosses the plate. Narrow that down even more, to how high the pitch will be. (Given the shape of the bat and the path of the swing, there is more room for error in judging how far across the plate the pitch will be than there is in judging how high it will be—the sweet spot on the bat is much wider than it is high.) Depending on the pitcher's height and his delivery, the pitch will be released about six feet above the mound, which is raised ten inches above the plate. So the pitch will fall some distance from around seven feet above the hitter's feet to the height at which it will cross the plate. How much it drops will depend on the pitcher's aim (taking into account the effects of gravity), the pitch's speed, and what kind of and how much spin the pitcher applies to the ball. Using this and whatever other information he can muster, the hitter must predict how much the ball will have fallen by the time it crosses the plate.

And the timing of the swing requires that there be a prediction—a purely psychological process. Until a few years ago, a great deal of work had been done on the biomechanics of throwing, but much less was known about the biomechanics of hitting. These questions are of particular interest to those in the orthopedics community to whom players turn when injured or, increasingly, in an effort to improve their mechanics so as to prevent injuries and to maximize the force of their swing. Two research teams used high-speed photography to make a detailed analysis of the swings of professional baseball players. As shown in the figure on page 10, which was taken from one of the studies, from the point of initiation, when the player shifts his weight to his back leg and rotates his hips to "load" the swing, to the point of contact, when the hips have uncoiled and the arms have rotated to bring the bat into the hitting zone, the swing takes about .58 seconds (the follow-through takes another .4 seconds or so). That figure may sound overprecise, but the estimates from the two studies agreed to within a few one-hundredths of a second for both the total swing time and for various components of the swing. Even so, this only tells us what any hitter already knows: preparation for a swing has to start before the pitcher has even released the ball. What may be more surprising is that the hitter must know where to aim his swing before the swing itself begins; there is no time for any significant modification of the swing during the swing itself. In the figure, you can see that as the swing begins, the bat moves from a position roughly perpendicular to the ground to a position parallel to the ground, and then it rotates through to the point of contact with the ball. This entire movement takes about .18 seconds. There are at least two reasons to think that at, or perhaps even well before, this point in the swing, the path of the swing has already been determined.

One reason is that hitters work hard to develop a quick swing that will allow them to start the swing at the last possible moment. Well-worn, long-practiced actions become unitized so that they become what psychologists call ballistic—once begun,

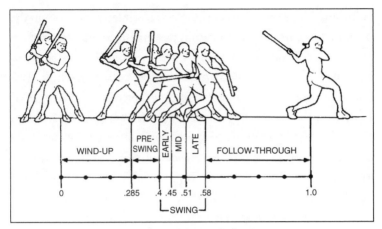

The timing of the baseball swing.

Reprinted with permission from Shaffer, B., Jobe, F. W., Pink, M., and Perry, J. (July 1993). "Baseball batting: An electromyographic study." Clinical Orthopedics and Related Research 292: 285–293.

they are difficult, if not impossible, to modify in real time; the individual elements of the action are molded together into one fluid unit. Think of tying your shoes or buttoning a button and imagine you were asked to change one small part of that action. To comply, you would have to slow everything down. The participants in the swing study depicted in the figure were professional players, hitters who had built their skills on thousands upon thousands of swings. Between work on a batting tee, in soft-toss and other hitting drills, and live batting practice, a player might take hundreds of swings a day. All that practice hones and then maintains the hitter's swing as a single unit. The complex chain of movements—rotations of the hips, trunk, and shoulders, flexion and extension of knees and elbows—all occur in exactly the right order and at exactly the right times. If the hitter and his coach determine that the swing needs to be modified, it may take a great deal of new work to make the change.

A study of cricket employing high-speed film of batsmen as they tried to hit a ball after a bounce provides the other reason to think that swings are essentially ballistic. In cricket, the bowler usually bounces the ball to the batsman, often with spin on the ball, hoping for an erratic bounce. The experiment was set up to maximize the chances for erratic bounces by having hitters hit from a mat under which several pieces of half-round dowel had been hidden; when the ball happened to hit one of those, it bounced in ways even more erratic than usual. The earliest that professional batsmen from the national team showed evidence of adjusting their swings after deviations in the ball's path was about .19 seconds after the deviation. This is probably the closest estimate we have of reaction time during actual batting. If we extend this finding to baseball, it appears that hitters must have made up their minds where to aim their swing by the time the ball is about halfway to the plate. And because the swing takes about .18 seconds, they must know where the swing will end before it begins. Any information the hitter gets in that last part of the pitch's flight arrives too late for him to use.

Keep Your Eye on the Ball?

There is even more reason to think that hitters must predict where the ball will be when it crosses the plate well before it gets there. The time-honored advice to hitters is "Keep your eye on the ball." But it turns out that this is impossible. The human eye simply cannot move fast enough to stay focused on the ball all the way from the mound to the plate. Although the ball's velocity is relatively constant from mound to plate, its *angular velocity* increases rapidly. When an observer watches an object move from one point to another, the rate at which the eyes must move to track the object depends on both the object's velocity and its distance from the observer, so we measure size and speed in visual angle and angular velocity. If you hold a quarter out at arm's length, it spans about two or three degrees of visual angle. Depending on where you are when you do this, that quarter might be just large enough to block from view a much larger object at some distance from you, maybe your favorite baseball stadium. Of course, the quarter and the stadium are not the same size in the way we normally think of size. But they are the same size in visual angle—they both span about two degrees. And both objects *are* the same size on the retina, the surface at the back of the eye that records light information. If you now move closer to the stadium, it will span more and more degrees of visual angle as its image on your retina expands.

Now imagine a car driving past the stadium, so that it gets from one end to the other in two seconds. When you are far enough away from the stadium that it spans two degrees of visual angle, the car's angular velocity is thus one degree per second. When you stand closer to the stadium, so that it is five-quarters (or ten degrees) wide, the car again takes two seconds to go from one end of the stadium to the other. The car's speed is the same in the way we normally think of speed, but its *angular* velocity is now five degrees per second, simply because your viewing position changed.

When you watch a pitch from the stands, the distance between the mound and home plate is shorter in terms of visual angle than it is when you stand in the batter's box. And when you are standing in the batter's box, the first ten feet of the path from the mound to the plate span a smaller angle than the last ten feet. So the angular velocity is greater as the ball gets closer, just as in the example with the car and the stadium. Thus, it is easier for the hitter to track a fastball right after the pitcher's release than it is just before it crosses the plate, because the ball is traveling fewer degrees of visual angle in the same amount of time. In fact, when a major-league pitch crosses the plate, its angular velocity can be more than five hundred degrees per second, so great that the eyes cannot track that part of the pitch's flight. Normally, humans can only track moving objects up to rates of about seventy degrees per second.

Of course, we know that major-league hitters are a select group—maybe an extraordinary ability to track fast-moving objects is one of the abilities that makes them special. Scientists have used various complex arrangements of instruments to measure where the hitter's eyes were pointed and how they moved while watching a pitch. In one study, hitters were asked to wear a pair of glasses fitted with a series of infrared light sources and detectors that were used to sense horizontal movements of the eyes. Additional sensors allowed researchers to compute the position of the head in all three movement planes—up-down, left-right, and tilt.

The ball itself was a plastic ball pulled along a string, rather than thrown, toward the hitter. It traveled at speeds up to the major-league limit of about 100mph toward the right-handed hitter, always on the trajectory of a high-and-outside fastball. This allowed for optimal viewing, both by the hitter and by the experimental apparatus. The results of the study are striking: hitters generally watch the pitch continuously from its release, but they lose it at some distance in front of the plate. The best any hitter did was to track the ball to around 5.5 feet in front of the plate. After that, the ball was moving too fast for him to follow it.

Sometimes the player watched the first few feet of the ball's flight and then moved his eyes quickly—in a manner similar to the way the eyes move during reading—to the anticipated point of contact and was thus able to see the ball cross the plate. Out of this come two strategies a hitter might follow for tracking a pitch. Under the "optimal hitting strategy," the hitter watches the pitch from release until its angular velocity is too great; this maximizes the information the hitter has for making and updating his prediction of the pitch's final location. Under the "optimal learning strategy," the hitter watches the pitcher's release and the initial flight of the ball, but then moves his eyes rapidly to the plate so that he can see the ball's arrival; this maximizes what the hitter can learn about the pitch's ultimate location, information that might be useful for the next pitch, later in the game, or in the next game against that pitcher. A young hitter or a hitter working on his ability to hit a specific pitch might use this strategy to learn how different kinds of pitches behave. (We do not see what happens during the time that our eyes make these rapid, saccadic jumps. If we did, we would only see a smear as our eyes passed rapidly over the world in front of us. Instead, we see only the scenes we fixated on before and after the eye movement.) Using either the optimal hitting or the optimal learning strategy, or any other strategy, the batter does not— cannot—see the entire flight of the ball.

The top performer in the experiment was a major-league hitter, catcher Brian Harper, then of the Pittsburgh Pirates. And Harper did achieve levels of tracking speed better than had ever before been recorded—he was able to track at about 120 degrees per second, nearly double the normal human capacity. So there is some support for the hypothesis that major-league hitters might simply be better at tracking fast-moving objects than the rest of us. But Harper was still nowhere near the 500 degrees per second needed to track a good fastball. Additionally, to achieve that high rate, Harper had to buck the conventional wisdom that tells the hitter to hold his head still. He got to 120 degrees per second by combining eye and head movements. And he still lost sight of the ball more than five feet in front of home plate. Other hitters might do better than Harper, but it is unlikely they could do better by a factor of four. The bottom line is that hitters cannot keep their eyes on the ball.

It is often said that Ted Williams claimed he could see the bat hit the ball. As he said in his book *The Science of History*: "I had 20–10 vision. A lot of guys can see that well. I sure couldn't read labels on revolving phonograph records as people wrote I did. I couldn't 'see' the bat hit the ball, another thing they wrote, but I knew by the feel of it." Williams seems to have understood how hard it is to see the ball the whole way to the plate. Even so, it is entirely possible to see the ball hit the bat, but only if the hitter takes his eyes off of the ball during the middle part of its flight in order to move them to the point of contact.

Predicting the Point of Contact

So, the limits of reaction time mean that the hitter must begin his swing at least .19 seconds or so before the moment of contact, and the limits of his tracking ability mean that the hitter cannot see the ball for some of its trip to the plate. Obviously, the hitter must make a prediction about where to make contact with the ball— what is interesting and important is how very *early* this prediction must be made. So how does the hitter make this prediction?

Return to the question of how far the pitch will fall by the time it gets to the plate. The hitter might ask himself (in a manner of speaking; none of this is thought to occur consciously), how much has the ball fallen when it reaches a particular point, say forty-five feet away? Given that piece of information, the hitter could extrapolate how far the pitch would fall the rest of the way. But this won't work either, at least not in this straightforward way. Although our two-eyed system of depth perception—called stereopsis—is remarkably good at perceiving relative depth, or which of two objects is closest, it is not very good for absolute judgments of depth. Seeing just one object, it is hard to tell if it is thirty-five feet away, or forty. So hitters cannot judge the rate that the ball is falling by simply relating how much it has fallen to the distance at which it stands at that moment, because they cannot judge that distance precisely. In fact, stereopsis may not be important at all, at least for some hitters. According to his optometrist, Babe Ruth had amblyopia, a condition which effectively would have made him a one-eyed hitter. (Although this has become part of the lore of optometry and is often cited in information offered to patients with amblyopia, a reconsideration of the record offers a different interpretation of Ruth's vision problems, attributing them instead to the later-developing cancer that ultimately killed him. If this account is correct, he would have had the benefit of both eyes during his playing days.)

So the hitter can see how far the ball has dropped, but cannot see precisely the distance over which it has dropped. This is crucial. If the pitch has dropped one foot when it reaches a point thirty-five feet from the hitter, it's one thing, but if the drop is one foot at forty feet away, it's quite another; all else being equal, when the second pitch crosses the plate, it will be lower than the first one would have been (see figure on page 17). As the figure shows, the angular drop for all three pitches is the same—each pitch would appear to have dropped an equal distance. Somehow, the hitter must "scale" the rate of drop, gauging it against something that will tell him the distance. Psychologists have proposed two ways this might be done. One is to scale by the size of the ball. As the ball approaches the hitter, its angular size increases—it "looms," as psychologists say, just as the stadium in the earlier example would grow in angular size as we approached it. The hitter knows from experience the angular size of the ball at the point of contact. By taking the known size of the ball into account along with the ball's rate of downward movement and its rate of looming, all of which are available in the scene in front of him, the hitter can in principle compute how far the ball will fall by the time it gets to the plate—again, unconsciously, very rapidly, and not necessarily in mathematical terms, but in terms that capture the mathematics of the situation.

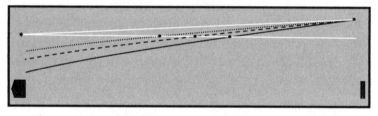

The trajectories of three pitches, from faster (dotted line) to slower (solid line). Because the angular drop of all three pitches, depicted by the white lines, is the same, all three would appear to have dropped the same distance, even though the slower ones have fallen more than the faster ones.

One advantage of the scaling-by-ball-size method is this directness; all of the information needed to make the calculation is available in what the hitter sees or already knows. In one study, researchers reasoned that if hitters use the size of the ball to scale the rate of drop, then changing the size of the ball surreptitiously should influence judgments about the ball's position in space. It would be as if Randy Johnson suddenly fired a slightly bigger or slightly smaller fastball through the strike zone. These pseudo-baseballs would loom differently from a real baseball, fooling any hitter who is counting on the size of the baseball remaining constant. Looming is a valuable signal from the environment—predators loom, for instance, as do objects we are about to collide with. The study also pointed to numerous other studies that show that animals and people are sensitive to looming. Frogs, chickens, and monkeys are all sensitive to it, as are ten-day-old babies. Maybe baseball batters use the same information—hitters would be able to predict the position of a ball if they (more or less) multiplied information about how fast the ball was dropping and how fast it was looming by the size of the ball.

To see if hitters might plausibly be using this information to judge how far a pitch would drop, observers in an experiment were asked to stand with their feet strapped to a narrow plank, wearing goggles that a computer could turn transparent or opaque. While in this position, they watched balls that were suspended from the ceiling swing in an arc from a position above and in front of them, past them on the right side, to a position above and behind them. At the time of the ball's release, the goggles were opaque; for a brief time just before the ball passed the observer, one lens was turned transparent. This allowed the researchers to control precisely how the observers viewed the passing ball. The observers were then asked to judge whether or not they could reach the swinging ball. Some of the balls were within reach, some were not. Critically, every now and then, unbeknownst to the observers, the researchers snuck in a ball that was slightly smaller or slightly larger than the rest of the balls. As they predicted, and as predicted by the scaling-by-ball-size hypothesis, bigger balls appeared to be farther away (less easily reached) than the standard-sized balls, and smaller balls appeared to be nearer (more easily reached) than the standards.

In another study, hitters viewed a pitch on a computer monitor several feet in front of them and swung a bat wired with sensors to "hit" it. The virtual pitches appeared on a black background, rather than in a virtual stadium, but the image of the ball grew in size on the screen as the pitch approached the hitter, creating what the researcher called "a compelling impression of motion in depth." The simulation also included details like shadows on the ball and different kinds of spin associated with different pitches. The sensors on the bat were able to record exactly when the swing was initiated, how long it lasted, and its exact path through the strike zone. By carefully coordinating this information with the computer's information about the pitch, the simulation was able to determine whether or not the bat would meet the ball and what the result would be, foul ball or fair.

In one of the experiments, pitch speed varied randomly over a range from about seventy to about eighty-seven miles per hour, with any speed in that range possible on any pitch. Under these conditions, the hitters failed miserably, achieving a batting average of only .030, and that was counting anything hit fair as a hit. With some virtual fielders on the virtual field, the average would no doubt have been lower still. The important observation is that all of the information needed to scale by ball size was available to hitters on every pitch—the size of the ball was not varied as it was in the other study—yet the hitters failed miserably. If they could use their knowledge about the size of the ball to get a sense of how far away the pitch was, then it should have made no difference how much the speed changed—on any given pitch, all the information the hitters needed in order to calculate where the pitch would cross the plate was available. So the hitters' failure under these conditions suggests that hitting is not based only on directly perceptible cues, and that hitters rely on other information.

Another way for the hitter to figure out where the ball is going is to scale the drop by the velocity of the pitch. If the player knows how fast the ball is moving, then, taking into account how long it has been traveling, he can figure out how far it has gone, and thus the distance of the ball from the plate. This is like those old algebra problems, put in baseball terms: "If a baseball leaves the pitcher's hand at 0:00.00 and is traveling 90mph, how far will the ball have gone at 0:00.15?" The problem here is that the hitter has no direct knowledge about how fast the ball is moving. This, again, would require him to know the distance to the pitch at that moment. So to scale by pitch speed, the hitter has to estimate the speed of the pitch. If this is what hitters do, the results of the above experiment make sense: the randomness of the pitch speed would make scaling by pitch speed very difficult; the more uncertainty there is about the speed of a given pitch, the less able the hitter would be to scale the rate of drop.

Further evidence for the scaling-by-pitch-speed theory comes from a second experiment, where each pitch was thrown at one of just two speeds, fast (around 85mph) or slow (around 70mph). This situation is more like real baseball, where pitchers typically throw just two or three different pitches. In this experiment, the hitters achieved a much better average of .120. (It is important to compare only across experimental conditions—with the average of .030 in the other experiment—and not with live baseball, where the perceptual and game information available to the hitter is much richer.) In this second condition, hitters faced much less uncertainty about the speed of the pitch, so estimation of pitch speed would have been much easier. More-over, a closer analysis of the results revealed that when hitters were late with their swing, as they would be if they mistook a fast pitch for a slow one, they almost invariably aimed their swing too low, in a location more consistent with a slower pitch (which has more time to drop). The reverse happened when they swung early: they almost always aimed their swing too high, as if they were expecting a fast pitch that would drop less by the time it reached the plate. The close relation between the timing of the swing and its location further supports the theory that pitch speed was playing a role in hitters' estimates of the height of the pitch. The same thing happened in another experiment. Batters swung at fastballs all pitched from a pitching machine at the same speed, except for a few randomly chosen pitches, when the pitching machine gassed up the ball to the plate at an extra 5mph. Consistent with the idea that hitters base their pro-jection of the pitch's path on an estimate of the pitch's speed, the hitters in this study misestimated the speed of these pitches at the regular speed, and consequently tended to swing under the pitch.

Another reason to favor the scaling-by-speed theory over the scaling-by-ball-size theory is that players' perceptions of ball size seem to change. It is common to hear players talk about "seeing the ball well" or not, or to hear them say when they are hitting well that the ball seems somehow bigger than a baseball, like a grapefruit or a melon or a basketball, or when they are not hitting well that it seems as small as something smaller than a baseball, like a pebble or a bullet or a golf ball. Pitchers who struggle are said to throw softballs; those who dominate are said to shoot peas. Researchers recently lent credence to hitters' perceptions by asking players in a recreational softball league to pick from among a range of black disks the one that appeared to be the diameter of a softball. And then they asked them how they had done on the diamond that day, and recorded each player's batting average. The result? Players who hit better chose a larger disk than players who didn't hit so well. When a player says the ball looks as big as a grapefruit, he's not just embellishing his story with a funny simile—the ball really does look bigger. Other researchers have found similar cases in which a person's level of performance in some task influences the way the task is perceived. Words that are more fluently recognized sound louder than words that are harder to recognize; targets in a dart-throwing game seem bigger when the thrower is more accurate; hills seem steeper when walkers face them while wearing a heavy backpack than when the walkers are burden free. This variation in the perceived size of the ball seems to reflect a general feature of perception, and is another strike against the scaling-by-ball-size theory.

Do Fastballs Rise?

Going into the 2003 World Series, after the Marlins had squeaked by the Cubs and the Yankees had beaten the Red Sox on Aaron Boone's home run in the bottom of the eleventh in Game 7 of the American League Championship, nearly everyone expected the Yankees to roll up another World Series win against the young and relatively inexperienced Marlins. But in Game 6 of the series, the Yankees found themselves down three games to two and facing Josh Beckett, who had pitched well against the Yankees in a Game 3 loss, striking out ten in seven-and-a-third innings while yielding just two runs. The twenty-three-year-old Beckett was pitching on just three days' rest, so perhaps the Yankees could force a Game 7. Beckett was still masterful, though, and shut out the Yankees in a complete-game five-hitter, clinching the series for the Marlins. How did Beckett pull it off? According to Thomas Boswell of *The Washington Post*, "he challenged the Yankees inning after inning in Game 6 with a mix of well-placed rising fastballs, a vicious curve and occasional changeups."

Many hitters, maybe even all hitters, will swear with resolute certainty that they have seen fastballs from hard-throwing pitchers like Josh Beckett or Roger Clemens or Nolan Ryan rise or hop just as the ball crossed the plate. This "fact" is so ingrained in the conventional wisdom that a popular book called *The Way Baseball Works* explains that "a 'four-seam' fastball gives the pitcher maximum velocity and can rise a few inches if thrown hard with a downward snap of the wrist and good backspin." Hitters see this with their own eyes—it must be true.

Except that it isn't. As physicist Robert Adair makes clear in *The Physics of Baseball*, the fact that the pitcher throws from a mound, along with the balance of physical forces like gravity and wind resistance, makes the rising fastball a physical impossibility, even for a side-arm pitcher like Chad Bradford of the Oakland A's. Adair concludes his discussion of the issue by saying that "overhand fast balls certainly do not rise."

As for the vicious curve, Boswell might have instead employed the time-honored description of vicious curveballs: he might have said that they "rolled off a table." Though hitters often claim to see curveballs with "late break," studies of the physics of the curveball, including a well-known stop-action photo study in *Life* magazine, show that curves follow a gradually arcing path; there is no sudden change of direction just as the ball gets to the hitter. Why, then, do players see the rising fastball and the sharp-breaking curve?

A final, intriguing reason to favor the scaling-by-pitch-speed theory is that it explains the rising fastball, or at least the illusion of the rising fastball. Remember that the hitter cannot see the last five or so feet of the ball's flight to the plate; he either tracks it from the pitcher's hand as far as he can and loses it for the last several feet, or he tracks the first part of the flight, rapidly moves his eyes to the plate, and catches just the very end of the pitch. Either way, part of the pitch is missing in the hitter's mental record. When the brain is missing information about some part of the world, it often fills in what is missing with its best guess about what should have been there, rather than seeing or hearing or feeling an incomplete perception.

Your brain is doing this right now: there is a blind spot in each eye where the optic nerve leaves the eyeball; there are no visual receptors in this spot, so the corresponding part of the image of the world is missing. The blind spots from the two eyes cover different parts of the visual field, so what one eye does not see, the other does. But notice that even when you close one eye, there is no "hole" in your picture of the world. Your brain is filling in that part of the picture. Take a look at the left panel of the next figure. Close your right eye and fixate on the black dot with your left, and then slowly move the page in and out from your eye. While maintaining fixation on the dot, pay attention to what happens to the ball. At some point, it will disappear, and then as you continue to move the book closer, it will reappear. The ball has at that point moved through your blind spot.

So where is the filling in? Now that you have had some practice finding your blind spot, try it with the middle panel. With right eye closed, focus on the middle panel's dot. When the baseball falls in the blind spot, it disappears, and most

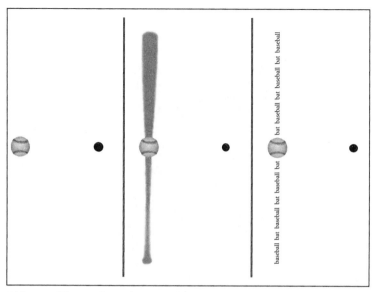

Pick one of the panels. With your right eye closed, hold the figure about a foot from your left eye, focusing on the black dot while noticing the baseball. Move the book slowly in and out—at some point the baseball should disappear.

people will see a complete bat. Try it. You know that the bat is not complete. But when the gray ball falls on the blind spot, the brain comes up with the most sensible "theory" of the scene, and concludes that this is a whole bat, so this is what you see. Try the right panel. There are limits to what the brain can do: it cannot fill in a pattern like a word, for example; most people will see empty space or a sort of smudge at that point.

Filling in is not a quirky anomaly of the visual system: it is a manifestation of a common, general-purpose process in perception and mental life. The brain must constantly generate theories and mental models of the world to make sense of the

Though the two baseballs are the same size, the higher one
appears to be larger than the lower.

objects and events it encounters. Illusions are often instances in
which this process goes a bit too far and produces a misinter-
pretation of reality. You see smooth motion at the movies, but
the movies are really just a rapidly shown series of still pictures;
nothing actually moves. Similiarly, one baseball in the figure
above appears to be larger than the other, but if you measure
you will find that they are the same size.

Tracking an object that will fly right by your head at 90mph
is an incredibly difficult feat. In fact, as we have seen, it is impossible. It is no surprise then that this process might be subject
to an illusion. Players are certain that they see fastballs rise. And
they do "see" fastballs rise, but probably only as a result of the
filling-in process. The theory works something like this: The

hitter is scaling by pitch speed. If he underestimates the speed, maybe thinking that a 97mph fastball is a 92mph fastball, then the ball will arrive sooner than expected and will not drop as far as expected. The hop or rise that the hitter sees the ball take in the last part of its flight is real, but only in the hitter's mind, in the same way that the smooth motion we see in a movie is real. The hitter's brain fills in with a "hop" that explains why the pitch ended up being higher than the hitter estimated.

Tim McCarver, catcher for the St. Louis Cardinals and Philadelphia Phillies in the sixties and seventies and now a television baseball analyst, has written about the rising fastball, but his impressions of that pitch seem to come more from his experience as a hitter than as a catcher. Because of their position, catchers can, of course, usually follow the pitch all the way from the pitcher's hand into their catcher's mitt. In his book *Baseball for Brain Surgeons and Other Fans*, McCarver wrote, "The fastballs of Tom Seaver and Nolan Ryan had hop at the end" and that when a pitcher throws a rising fastball, "batters swing under it." McCarver faced Seaver and Ryan as a hitter, but did not catch them (except Seaver, for one inning in the 1967 All-Star game). He caught Bob Gibson and Steve Carlton, two other famously hard-throwing pitchers who, it is likely, were seen by other players to throw rising fastballs. But McCarver does not mention his former teammates when he writes about pitchers who threw rising fastballs, even though he saw them throw many, many more pitches. Perhaps this is because of his experience catching them.

What about the sharp-breaking curve? Maybe you have guessed that these might result from misestimation in the other direction: if the hitter estimates the curve at, say, 80mph, when in fact it is moving at 75mph, that overestimate will lead him to think that the ball is closer than it really is, so the ball will have a longer distance over which to continue its fall, and will thus cross the plate at a point lower than the player's estimate would have predicted. How does the brain reconcile the projected path with the final location? With a vicious, Yankee-killing Josh Beckett curveball.

The Art of Guessing

The hitter's perceptual and motor limitations—however odd it may be to think of gifted players having such limitations—put them at a disadvantage, and subject them to the occasional illusory violation of the laws of physics, but their ability to think with the game saves them. Seeing the inventory of factors that restricts the hitter's ability to see the ball and react to it, we might be tempted to conclude that, Ted Williams and Tony Gwynn to the contrary, hitting is impossible. But of course, it's quite possible: even Bob Uecker could hit (sort of). Hitters use their vast experience and knowledge about the game to overcome the limitations imposed on the perceptual and motor systems. Some of the experiments cited earlier showed that if pitchers could vary their speed continuously, so that they could throw any speed in a 17mph range, hitting would be nearly impossible. But when the uncertainty about what pitch would be thrown is reduced, a hitter is able to narrow his focus and is better able to estimate correctly the pitch speed.

Uncertainty is the hitter's enemy. The best pitchers maximize that uncertainty. In 1999, Pedro Martinez had a masterful season and won the American League Cy Young Award, his second in three years after he won the National League award in 1997. In '99, Martinez's record was 23–4, leading the league in wins, his ERA was a scant 2.07, leading the league again, and he struck out 313 batters, leading the league once more. As *Sports Illustrated* writer Tom Verducci tells the story of that season, Martinez built that record on the strength of four pitches—fastball, cut fastball, changeup, and curveball—all of which he threw for strikes more than 60 percent of the time. Verducci illustrated Martinez's dominance by relating the story of an at bat in the 1999 League Championship Series, in which Martinez and the Red Sox faced the Cleveland Indians and their slugger, Jim Thome. In the fifth inning, Thome found himself ahead in the count, 3–0, "looking to hit the ball out of the stadium."

Everyone knows that 3–0 is a hitter's count; the pitcher needs a strike and is more likely to throw a fastball than some kind of off-speed pitch, the fastball being so much easier to control. But that wasn't so for the Pedro Martinez of 1999—he could throw any of his four pitches in any situation and count on throwing it for a strike most of the time. In this game, he was coming off an injury that limited the speed of his fastball but did not hamper his control. What happens next? Verducci tells it well:

> Martinez flips a 3-and-0 changeup into the strike zone. Stunned, Thome doesn't dare swing. "I can't go up there looking for a 3-and-0 change," Thome says. "That's not good hitting."
>
> Now Martinez spins a backdoor curveball that catches the outside corner. Thome does not—cannot—swing. A 3-and-1 hook? It's like seeing snow in August.
>
> O.K., Thome thinks, now just try to hit the ball. But what's coming? He can't be certain. This predicament is why Yankees manager Joe Torre will say one week later—after Martinez

has dealt New York its only loss of the postseason, a 12-strikeout, 13–1 laugher in Game 3 of the American League Championship Series—that trying to hit Martinez is "like trying to hit in a dark room." (It was the second time in five weeks that Torre had witnessed such frustration at the plate. On Sept. 10 Martinez had one-hit the Yankees, whiffing 12 of the final 15 batters to finish with 17 strikeouts.)

Martinez decides on a fastball. Of course, it is not just any fastball. It is a smart bomb laser-guided to skirt the inside corner of the plate. After the camouflage of a flirtatious changeup and a looping curveball, the fastball has the illusion of traveling faster than it actually does. "Put it this way," Thome says. "It had some hair on it."

Thome swings at it. He is too late. The pitch is past him.

In 2004, after several frustrating losses to the Yankees, Pedro declared that the Yankees were "his daddy." In 1999, though, he was their daddy. And Thome's. And everyone else's. His mastery that year shows how devastating uncertainty is for the hitter. Jim Thome is perfectly capable of hitting a fastball for a home run—he's shown that time and time again. But when Thome has no idea at all what pitch to expect, he is not the same hitter.

The conventional wisdom tells players not to think, to just see the ball and react. And there is some obvious truth in that idea: a corollary of the see-it-and-react approach is to look for a fastball, and adjust to any other kind of pitch. This makes sense on its face: being ready for the fastball still allows time to adjust to something slower, but if the hitter is set up for an off-speed pitch, by the time he could adjust to the fastball, it would be too late. In one of the virtual-reality hitting experiments, the hitters were players from either a recreation league or a college baseball team. One of the things that separated the two groups of players was how willing they were to change their expectation about an upcoming pitch based on the sequence of pitches to that point in the at bat. The pattern of successful and unsuccessful swings showed that although the more skilled college players shifted their expectations somewhat, it was not as much as the less skilled rec-league players. The college players tended to stay ready for the fastball; the rec-league players were more easily led to expect an off-speed pitch and then be surprised by a fastball.

Despite the time-honored advice about looking for the fastball and adjusting to the off-speed stuff, we frequently see hitters fail to swing at fastballs thrown for obvious strikes, even on two-strike counts. Incredulous, we think, "How could he have let that go!?" Sometimes we hear people say, "The hitter was thinking too much." But thinking is essential. It might sometimes lead to an embarrassing strikeout on a fastball right down the middle, but on balance, thinking is what makes hitting possible. Whether the player comes to expect a pitch by a process of conscious deliberation, or by intuition, the kind of thinking Malcolm Gladwell brought to the fore in his book *Blink,* those expectations are an important, if not essential, part of the hitter's skill. And of course, the idea is to think *before* the pitch, not during, when the focus should be on seeing and "reading" the pitch.

There's no better expert to go to than Ted Williams:

"PROPER THINKING" is 50 percent of effective hitting, and it is more than just doing your homework on a pitcher or studying the situation in a game. It is "anticipating," too, when you are at the plate, and a lot of hitters will say that is college talk for "guessing" and some will be heard to say in a loud voice, "don't do it!" They're wrong. Guessing, or anticipating, goes hand in hand with proper thinking. . . . You've got to guess, you've got to have an idea. All they ever write about the good hitters is what great reflexes they have, what great style, what strength, what quickness, but never how smart the guy is at the plate, and that's 50 percent of it. . . . At eighteen I might not have been quite as strong as I was when I was twenty-eight or thirty-eight, but I had better eyesight, better reflexes, could run faster, etc. But at seventeen or eighteen I wasn't thinking as clearly at the plate as I was later on. . . . Obviously, you don't just "guess" curve or "guess" fast ball. You work from a frame of reference, you learn what you might expect in certain instances, and you guess from there. Certainly you won't guess a pitch the pitcher can't get over; he might have a terrific curve, but if he can't get it over, forget it. Certainly the pitch you anticipate when the count is 0 and 2 (a curve ball, probably if the pitcher has one) is not the pitch you anticipate when the count is 2 and 0 (fast ball, almost without exception).

A little later he gives a hypothetical example of this kind of thinking, and then a real one:

Now if [the pitcher] throws a fast ball and misses, and throws a curve and misses, and I've got him 2–0, it's pretty academic to look for the fast ball on the third pitch. It's the easier pitch for him to get over. If he throws the curve and gets it over, I say to myself, "Well, he's got confidence in it, I'll look for another curve." He threw a curve at 2–0, why wouldn't he throw it again at 2–1? If he then comes back with a fast ball at 2–1, playing the game with me, then . . . I'm in trouble.

Most pitchers, of course, will have a high enough regard for their repertoire that if they get you out on a good pitch they'll invariably come back with it. The results of anticipating that pitch have been gratifying to me a thousand times, but I suppose the one I remember best was in the 1941 All-Star game. Two outs, two men on, and the American League trailing 5–4 in the ninth inning.

Claude Passeau of the Cubs was pitching for the National League. Passeau was a good pitcher. He had struck me out in the eighth inning on a fast tailing ball that acted like a slider. . . . He would jam a left-hander with it and get it past you if you weren't quick. I was late on that one, and as I came up in the ninth, I said to myself, "You've got to be quicker, you've got to get more in front." On a 2–1 pitch, he came in with that sliding fast ball I was anticipating, and I hit it off the facing of the third deck in right field.

As Williams's thinking illustrates, hitters can be clever and inventive when it comes to trying to figure out what pitch is coming. The game situation, the defensive alignment, or a given pitcher's tendencies can be used to help the hitter figure out what pitch is most likely. In his book *Men at Work*, George Will wrote case studies of a manager (Tony LaRussa), a pitcher (Orel Hershiser), a fielder (Cal Ripken), and a hitter (Tony Gwynn). The studies tell us something about the day-in, day-out work of the people in baseball, as well as something about their thinking. Will's portrayal of Gwynn reveals just how complex a hitter's understanding of the game can be. In looking for a hitter to study, Will could hardly have chosen better. In twenty seasons with the San Diego Padres, Gwynn put up a career batting average of .338, good for twenty-first best of all time. He finished in the top ten in batting average in the National League in fifteen of those twenty seasons, and led the league eight times. The only year his batting average was below .300 was his first; that was also the only year that he had more strikeouts (sixteen in 190 at bats) than walks (fourteen). His 162-game averages were fifty-two walks and only twenty-nine strikeouts. Tony Gwynn knew something about hitting.

In one interview with Will, Gwynn said, "If they play me up the middle they are planning to start me inside and get me out away. If they are playing me in the holes they will pitch me inside, thinking that if I pull it, it will go into the hole on the right side, and if I go inside-out I'll hit it in the hole on the other side." Other parts of Will's portrait of Gwynn show that he also took into account the ball-strike count, whether there was a runner on base, how many outs there were, who the pitcher was, and many other variables that could influence what pitch the pitcher might throw. And Gwynn describes looking for certain pitches, even off-speed pitches, in certain situations because his knowledge told him they were likely. He always tried to be ready to hit the fastball and react to anything else, but he also used his knowledge to get a sense of how likely "anything else" was.

Of course, it is one thing to make an educated guess about what pitch is coming, and quite another to *know* exactly what pitch is coming. In a hilarious scene in the movie *Bull Durham*, a journeyman catcher, Crash Davis (played by Kevin Costner), has an argument during a game about pitch selection with a hard-throwing raw pitching prospect, Nuke Laloosh (Tim Robbins). Crash trots to the mound to tell Nuke to stop shaking off his signs, and just throw a curveball like he was told. Nuke replies that he wants to throw the fastball, "to announce his authority." Crash relents, sort of, but on the way back to his position behind home plate, tells the hitter to expect the fastball. After the baseball clears the outfield fence (and then some), Crash walks to the mound, laughing about how far the ball went. Nuke says, "That sucker teed off on it just like he knew I was gonna throw a fastball."

Al Gettel was a pitcher for the New York Giants in their 1951 season, the year of Bobby Thomson's "shot heard round the world." Like Laloosh, Gettel knew how important it can be for a hitter to know what pitch is coming. Talking about the end of that season, in which the Giants made up a thirteen-and-a-half-game deficit in the last two months of the season, Gettel said to reporter Joshua Harris Prager, "Every hitter knew what was coming. Made a big difference." Prager's article in *The Wall Street Journal* on the fiftieth anniversary of the Giants' stunning season detailed how they stole the opposing catcher's signs during home games in the Polo Grounds. They hid a spy with a telescope in their clubhouse, which was located above the centerfield wall. From there, the catcher's signs were relayed by a bell and a buzzer to the Giants' bullpen, which was easily visible from the batter's box. And from there, one of the pitchers would relay the sign to the hitter by, for example, crossing his legs for a fastball. The Giants manager Leo Durocher (famous for saying "Nice guys finish last") held a meeting in late July and let the hitters know that they could have the signs relayed to them. Some hitters wanted them, some did not, but after that meeting, the Giants began their improbable comeback. Sign-stealing, of course, has a long history in baseball, and for good reason: it takes a hitter all the way from uncertainty to certainty.

Of course, because of sign-stealing and the advantage it confers on hitters, pitchers and catchers rightfully protect their coded communications—using more complex systems when there is a runner on second, for example. In his fascinating book, *Pure Baseball: Pitch by Pitch for the Advanced Fan*, Keith Hernandez of the Cardinals and Mets revealed his secret for peeking at the catcher's location, inside corner or outside. He would do this only occasionally, especially late in the game with runners on base, by moving his eyes back very briefly just as the pitcher looked over at a base runner. If he could see the catcher, Hernandez would know the pitch was to be over the outside corner; if not, over the inside. The story ends with Tim Mc-Carver, one of the catchers on whom Hernandez pulled this stunt, saying, "You know, you could get hurt that way"—that is, if the pitcher found out what the hitter was doing and threw a pitch inside after the catcher set up outside.

Pitchers also worry about "tipping" their pitches by doing something different for one pitch or another that the hitter can use to predict what pitch is coming. Milwaukee Brewers pitcher Ben Sheets learned from teammates in spring training before his rookie season in 2001 that before he threw a curveball, he raised the index finger of his glove hand—as good as letting the hitter see the catcher's sign for a curveball. The success of Sheets's season that year depended in part on his learning not to give away his off-speed pitch.

And of course, hitters can rely on the way the seams rotate, even very soon after the pitch has been thrown, to distinguish one pitch from another. In one of the virtual-reality experiments, rotation cues were added to the ball, which led to an improvement for most of the hitters. And in another experiment, hitters watched video clips of different pitches thrown with three different balls, one a standard baseball, another a baseball with the seams painted over, the third a baseball with the seams highlighted. When the seams were obscured, the hitters' ability to recognize the pitch decreased; when the seams were enhanced, their ability increased. Notably, it did not matter much whether they were allowed to see the whole pitch, or just the first half of it. By this time, under normal hitting conditions, they already would have had to have their minds made up about whether to swing.

A recent study suggests that the spins of different kinds of pitches create differing rates of flicker, which is another cue the hitter may be able to use to his advantage. With a four-seam fastball, the seams rotate so fast that the hitter may not see any flicker at all, at least until it gets very close. Some pitchers throw their curveballs so that four seams rotate through the field of view with each revolution, again eliminating flicker. Two-seam fastballs and curves thrown with only two seams probably create perceptible flicker, though. And, they create a perception of red stripes on the sides of the ball. For sliders, the reverse pattern may be true: a four-seam grip may create a pattern of rotation that leaves a telltale sign, which hitters perceive as a red dot around which the rest of the ball seems to spin, but a two-seam grip creates a pattern of rotation around a part of the ball that is plain white and is thus less noticeable. The authors of the study advise that "the pitcher should use a four-seam grip for fastballs and curveballs to remove the perceptual clue of the two red stripes and the flicker. Then, he should use the two-seam grip for the slider, to remove the clue of the red dot." Hitting may have just become even more difficult.

The hitter need not even be consciously aware of these cues. When George Will asked Tony Gwynn what it was about the pitcher, his delivery or his pitch, that tipped Gwynn off to the type of pitch that had been thrown, Gwynn answered, "The ball. Not his arm, not his motion, just the ball. You see it out there when he lets it go. You see something that tips you off." Noting that Gwynn "cannot say what it is or what he then does," Will reports that Gwynn said, "I see it and I react. You recognize what it is and your hands and body take over."

Will calls Gwynn's intuition "muscle memory," a term common among coaches and players. The term is an apt one, suggesting that the knowledge about the relation between whatever it is that Gwynn sees and the pitch that will likely follow is an integral part of the skill itself. There are forms of learning and memory that are implicit, that is, that are demonstrated only in the performance of some skill or task—such knowledge cannot be articulated easily, as Gwynn's description of his hitting shows. To study learning of this kind, other researchers and I have used a simple computerized reaction time experiment. A signal appeared in one of several locations, people pressed a key that corresponded to that location as quickly as they could, there was a brief delay, and then the next signal appeared. The people performing this simple task were not told that the signal followed a preset, relatively subtle, repeating pattern. With practice, of course, people responded to the signals more and more quickly; that happens even if the sequence of signals is completely random and unpredictable. But people get faster still when the sequence of signals follows a pattern. And if the pattern changed, their response time would suddenly increase, showing that some kind of knowledge about the pattern was influencing their responding, even though they typically could say little, if anything, about the repeating pattern. Indeed, people often think that the sequence that the signal follows is just random.

Numerous other studies have shown that people can be very sensitive to subtle, even subliminal, cues about predictable patterns of objects and events in their environments. In *Blink*,

Gladwell tells about several such phenomena, including the almost eerie tale of tennis pro Vic Braden discovering that he could tell before a player hit a second serve that it would be a double fault. One day at a tournament, Braden kept track and found that he correctly predicted sixteen of the seventeen double faults that occurred in the matches he watched. After he discovered this ability, Braden tried but could not figure out what it was that was cuing him to the impending double fault. This confirmed another of Braden's experiences: in his work as a tennis pro, he would often ask top players how they did what they did and was always disappointed with their answers. Just as he could not explain how he was calling the double faults, they could not explain how they succeeded at tennis. Tony Gwynn's inability to describe how he reads pitches reflects the same kind of intuitive knowledge.

Whether conscious or unconscious, these kinds of thinking can help the hitter reduce his uncertainty. To examine the role of cognition (expectancy) in hitting, another virtual-reality experiment was set up so that the virtual pitcher worked more like a real one—there were fastball counts and curveball counts. When the count on the hitter was two balls and no strikes, the simulation was more likely to throw a fastball; when the count was no strikes and two balls, the simulation was more likely to throw a curve. Hitters relied on these tendencies to improve their chances of hitting the pitch. Of course, like so many other situations in life, the advantages gained by these expectations come at a cost: as Keith Hernandez says, "If you set up mentally for the breaking ball or the change-up but the fastball comes instead, you're dead."

Sometimes the hitter *is* dead, frozen at the plate for a called third strike right down the middle. That is the price he pays for thinking, but it is a price well worth paying if he can guess right more often than he guesses wrong. Hitting depends on an estimate of pitch speed, so any information that can help in the making of that estimate improves the hitter's chances in the long run. As Boston and Milwaukee Brave great Warren Spahn famously said, "Hitting is timing. Pitching is upsetting timing."

CHAPTER TWO

Intercepting the Ballistic Baseball

OF ALL THE VIDEO HIGHLIGHTS WE SEE OF BASEBALL, THE most memorable may be footage of great defensive plays. Home runs and line drives are exciting, but what we remember about seeing them—Carlton Fisk waving his home run into fair territory in the twelfth inning of Game 6 in the 1975 World Series, Kirk Gibson pumping his fist after hobbling to the plate to smack a pinch-hit, game-winning home run in the 1988 World Series, or Mark McGwire hugging his son after crossing home with his sixty-second home run in 1998—is usually more the post-homer celebration than the swing itself. Pitchers are exciting to watch, too, but their accomplishments usually stretch out over several innings. Within a masterful performance, one Mariano Rivera cutter or Roger Clemens fastball looks much like another. But there are lots of ways to make a great catch.

In July 2002, on the occasion of Ozzie "The Wizard" Smith's induction into the Hall of Fame, *Baseball Weekly* ran a story on amazing defensive plays in baseball, and selected their top ten favorite plays of all time. Appropriately enough, The Wizard got top billing for a play he made early in his career, when he was still with the Padres. As he was diving for a grounder up the middle by Atlanta Brave Jeff Burroughs, the ball took a last-instant bad hop away from his glove—so Ozzie snared it with his bare hand. And then jumped up and threw Burroughs out at first. None other than Derek Jeter and Roberto Alomar, two middle infielders with their own stocks of great-play footage, rated that play the greatest they had ever seen. Alomar said, "That's got to be the most amazing play I've ever seen. . . . He's already diving, and the ball comes up, and he grabs it barehanded. . . . People don't realize how hard it is to catch the ball bare-handed," and Jeter added, "How do you react that quickly to a bad hop?"

Of course, greatness is a matter of opinion. Coming in second on the *Baseball Weekly* list was "*The* Catch," as it is usually called, Willie Mays's great over-the-shoulder grab in the 1954 World Series. The online encyclopedia Wikipedia even includes an entry entitled, simply, "The Catch." In the eighth inning of Game 1, with the score tied 2–2, runners at first and second and no one out, Vic Wertz hit a drive deep to center field. Mays was playing shallow in front of the 483-foot center-field fence at the Polo Grounds and turned to sprint away from home plate. Most fans thought the fly would hit the outfield wall well before Mays could get there, but Mays kept running and then suddenly reached up over his left shoulder and hauled it in. Mays finished the play with a strong throw back to the infield—the runner at second might have tagged and scored on such a long drive, but he (understandably) had not tagged up initially, and Mays's throw kept him at third.

The Catch's legend was born immediately. Writing in the next day's *New York Times,* Arthur Daley gushed that Mays's grab "had to be seen to be believed and even then you couldn't quite believe it" and that "catching the ball appeared a sheer impossibility." Both the *Times* and the next week's *Sports Illustrated* ran sequences of photos showing Mays sprinting back and finally making the catch.

Oddly, as remarkable as The Catch was, Mays and his teammates have frequently remarked that he made many others that were more spectacular, just not in the spotlight of the World Series. In fact, the very next day, a Giants scout named Tom Sheehan told *The New York Times* that Mays had made several catches that were more impressive. Don Mueller, whose ability to hit balls through the holes in the infield earned him the nickname "Mandrake the Magician," played right field beside Mays for several years. He once told me with conviction that Mays made many catches better than that one in the '54 World Series. Former player and ESPN commentator Joe Morgan has written that Mays himself has said the same thing.

Just a couple of innings after The Catch, another remarkable catch might have been made, but the fly ended up just out of the reach of Cleveland right fielder Dave Pope. As Roger Kahn wrote for *Sports Illustrated*, with one out and two Giants on base in the bottom of the tenth, "Jim Rhodes pinch-hit for Monte Irvin and lifted a fly into the breeze that blew toward right field. Bobby Avila, Cleveland's second baseman, started back for the ball. A customer in the right field stand muffed it. Three runs scored; the Giants had won." The right-field fence in the Polo Grounds measured a mere 270 feet down the line, which is about where Rhodes's pop-up cleared the fence. The next day's *New York Times* story on the game was accompanied by a shot of Pope leaping into the wall as he attempted to make the catch, with the ball just a few feet out of his grasp.

Jim Edmonds, center fielder for the Angels and then the Cardinals, has run into a few fences, too, and in so doing has contributed more than one great catch to the all-time highlight reel. Perhaps his greatest and most well known is one he made with the Angels in 1997 at Kauffman Stadium in Kansas City, which earned him third place on the *Baseball Weekly* list. With two on and two out in the fifth inning, David Howard hit a line drive deep to straightaway center. Like Mays, Edmonds turned and sprinted back toward the wall, finishing the play by laying out in a headlong dive that ended with him in the warning track and the ball in the tip of his outstretched glove. Angels second baseman Luis Alicea told the *Los Angeles Times,* "I don't know if Willie Mays would have had this one. Jim was playing so shallow, but he turned on the turbos and dove for it. You see guys dive to the side, to the left or right, but diving directly over your head is tough to do." Umpire Dave Phillips agreed, telling *The Kansas City Star,* "That makes Willie Mays's play look routine." Edmonds made his own play sound routine, telling *The Kansas City Star,* "I looked up and just saw the ball over the bill of my cap. I figured the game was on the line, so I figured I might as well lay out for this."

Smith, Mays, and Edmonds would be well known whether they had made these catches or not, but Al Gionfriddo owes his fame to one catch. Gionfriddo's career lasted just four seasons, ending in the 1947 season with the Brooklyn Dodgers. He appeared in 228 games, during which he achieved a career .266 average with two home runs and one immortal baseball memory. In the bottom of the sixth inning of Game 6 of the 1947 World Series at Yankee Stadium, with the Yankees leading the Dodgers in the Series three games to two, the Dodgers led 8–5, but the Yankees had runners at first and second with two outs and Joe DiMaggio at the plate. Gionfriddo had just been substituted into left field at the beginning of the inning. As told by Roscoe McGowen of *The New York Times,* "When DiMag' belted a towering drive that perhaps would have cleared the left field roof in Ebbets Field, Gionfriddo, who can run like a striped ape, raced back toward the low gate that leads to the visitors' bullpen. 'The ball hit my glove,' said Al, 'and a split second later I hit the gate. I knew I had it but I certainly couldn't have said I was going to get it—because how could any guy say he was on the ball all the way on one like that? It certainly would have gone into the bullpen alley for a home run if I hadn't got it.'" John Drebinger, also writing in the *Times*, captured DiMaggio's reaction, which is what many people remember about this catch—film clips show DiMaggio on his way around first and toward second, kicking the dirt in disgust in a rare show of emotion when he saw that the ball had been caught: "DiMaggio sent a tremendous smash in the direction of the left-field bullpen only to see Gionfriddo . . . rob Jolting Joe of his greatest moment. Dashing almost blindly to the spot where he thought the ball would land and turning around at the last moment, [Gionfriddo] leaned far over the bullpen railing and, with his gloved hand, collared the ball. It was a breathtaking catch for the third out of the inning. It stunned the proud Bombers and jarred even the usually imperturbable DiMaggio. Taking his position in center field with the start of the next inning, he was still walking inconsolably in circles, doubtless wondering whether he could believe his senses." It was the last catch Gionfriddo would make; there were no flies to left the rest of that day, and though he could "run like a striped ape," he never appeared in another major-league game. He haunted DiMaggio, though. Seven years later, when everyone was raving about The Catch, DiMaggio archly claimed that Gionfriddo's catch had been better.

Like Gionfriddo, Blue Jay Devon White had to contend with the outfield wall when he made the catch that put him on the

Baseball Weekly list. It was Game 3 of the 1992 World Series, with no score. Atlanta Braves Terry Pendleton and Deion Sanders were at first and second, respectively, in the top of the fourth inning with no one out. David Justice hit a line shot to the wall in center field. White turned and raced to the warning track and saw he and the ball would reach the wall at the same time. He made a backhanded catch just as he hit the wall. And again, people made comparisons to Mays's catch. "This one was better [than Mays's catch]," Roberto Alomar told *USA Today*. "Mays didn't hit the wall, but Devo did. He had to catch the ball and hit the wall almost immediately." The headline in the *Toronto Star* made it plain: "White's spectacular catch equal to Mays' grab in '54" and writer Dave Perkins marshaled his arguments: "Maybe Willie had to run 25 yards farther. Maybe White had a chance to half-turn and put up his glove. But Justice's shot had to have been hit more on a line than Wertz's. You can't hit it 470 feet without at least a little arc to it. Mays didn't have a wall to run into, either."

"There's no wind out there," White told Rosie DiManno of the *Toronto Star*. "I know where the ball is pretty much gonna go. I've practised that, so I'm pretty much confident that I can take my eye off the ball and still know where it's gonna go."

Baseball Weekly's list goes on, and of course there are hours upon hours of clips of great catches. We all have our favorites. I like the footage of a minor-league outfielder running through—not into, but through—a plywood outfield fence while attempting a catch (that clip is particularly wonderful because it is supplemented by clear audio of the collision—fortunately, the fielder was not seriously injured). Another old favorite is footage of San Francisco Giant Kevin Mitchell making a barehanded catch as he sprinted toward the left-field line.

And then there are the famous *non*-catches. Bill Buckner (enough said). Jose Canseco tracking down a fly ball near the fence only to have the ball bounce off his head and over the fence for a home run. And because I grew up a Reds fan, there's another Canseco clip I particularly like, from the 1990 World Series, in which Canseco gets turned around while trying to make a catch, with Jack Buck making the call, "and Canseco . . . cannot!" The blooper reels are filled with so many more.

Although fielders make plenty of errors in finishing a catch, they are usually in the right place, or headed there. Now and then, we see a fielder move one way for a ball and then change course. Almost always, though, the fielder seems to know from the crack of the bat, or maybe even before then, where the ball is going. The only question is whether or not he can get there in time. But though the judgment about where to go to catch the ball may appear intuitive, it would seem in fact to depend on calculations worthy of rocket science.

The Problem with Fly Balls

Our two eyes give us the ability to see in three dimensions. Shouldn't seeing where the ball is and where it is going be a relatively simple matter? Unfortunately, stereopsis, the creation of a three-dimensional view of the world from the two-dimensional views obtained by each eye, only becomes an effective cue for depth perception when the ball gets within twenty or thirty feet or so. And to prove the point that it plays relatively little role in helping an outfielder get to a fly ball, researchers had two fielders catch flies under normal conditions and while wearing an eye patch over one eye. One of the fielders had practiced for about an hour prior to the study proper; the other was previously inexperienced catching with just one eye. Balls were launched from a pitching machine on a direct line toward the fielder so that they would land within a range of eight to fifteen meters (or about twenty-five to fifty feet). Both fielders got their gloves on every ball; they had no difficulty getting to the right spot. The experienced fielder caught every ball. The inexperienced fielder had two bounce out of his glove, perhaps because stereopsis is more important when the ball gets closer. However, the researchers also noted that the inexperienced fielder "appeared somewhat 'ball shy' while wearing the eye patch" and that he preferred to catch the ball at arm's length.

Thus, all of the information for judging where a fly ball will land must be extracted from what is essentially a two-dimensional image. This is a much more complex problem. The fielder obviously need not know any formal mathematics, but his judgments can be described in those terms, and we need those formal principles to make sense of how he catches the ball using the information available to him. The formal theories can be complex: in a comment to the journal *Science,* physicist Robert Adair, author of *The Physics of Baseball,* confessed after reading one study that he "found the report difficult to understand." At the level of these theoretical models, this *is* rocket science, albeit at lower altitudes and slower speeds. The fielder is intercepting a ballistic object in more or less the same way that an antimissile defense system must intercept an incoming projectile. Even NASA has an interest in how these processes work; as we will see, one of their researchers has spent time working out how fielders catch fly balls. Happily for baseball fans, but sadly for the United States Defense Department, even a Little Leaguer can reliably do what some of the best engineers, armed with some of the most sophisticated technology available, cannot yet make an antimissile system do. (Of course, their ballpark is a bit more spacious.)

Scientists who study visual perception often talk about an *optical image* that roughly—but only roughly—corresponds to the image received by the eyes, which work somewhat like cameras. There is an aperture (the pupil) and some lenses (the cornea and a pliable crystalline lens behind the pupil) and a photosensitive surface (the retina). If we could look at the retina as a fielder catches a fly ball, we would see an image of the baseball tracing a path across the two-dimensional image of the baseball field. The optical image is not exactly that simple, however. The field of view is not constant, but moves as the fielder moves, and as he moves his head. It bounces as he runs, even if he is careful, as coaches advise, to run on his toes rather than on his heels so as to minimize jarring of the head. All this additional movement ultimately must also be taken into account, but for now, we can think of the optical image more or less as the fielder's view of the world, at the same time recognizing that this is an oversimplification of a very complex perceptual experience.

One analysis of this problem determined that the path traced by a fly ball across the fielder's view could correspond to an infinite number of flight paths in real three-dimensional space. How does the outfielder determine which of those paths is the right one? One possible solution is that he uses what he knows about gravity; the fielder could employ his knowledge about an object in free fall to infer the correct path. But in an experiment to check this idea, the same study found that people were basically unable to accurately estimate where a (computer-simulated) ball launched toward them would land. Later experiments confirm that people who merely stand in the outfield are quite poor at estimating where a fly ball will land.

There is other information in the field of view that can guide the fielder to the ball. One cue might be the way the size of the object in the image expands as it approaches. As the ball approaches the fielder, its image on his retina grows in size. Using knowledge about the actual size of the ball along with knowledge about how objects move when they are in free fall, both of which a fielder would have from his experience with fly balls, he could figure out where the ball would land. In one study, researchers reasoned that if fielders used this information, then changing the size of the ball and the effects of gravity at random should make catching impossible. Observers watched a computer screen on which a square object appeared to approach after being launched directly at them. Their task was simply to judge whether the object would reach their position or fall short. The square moved in the display just as it would move in the visual field in the real world, and it grew in size just as it would in the real world. The observers reported that the objects did indeed appear to move toward them. For some periods during the study, the initial size of the square and the simulated effect of gravity upon it remained constant from one launch to another. At other times, the size and the effect of gravity were changed randomly before each launch. If the judgment of landing position depended on these cues, then making that judgment should have been impossible in this second condition. However, although the observers were somewhat less accurate in their judgments when size and gravity varied randomly, in two different experiments they still performed quite well under those conditions. This again suggests that people use other cues in making these judgments.

Why Catching Is Not Impossible

To get a sense of the nature of these other cues, which depend more on geometric relations between the approaching object and the observer, consider first a simpler situation in which two observers, say a shortstop and a left fielder, or the drivers of two cars in a parking lot, have to judge whether they will collide. As the figure below shows, if, as the bodies continue on their courses, the distance between them decreases while the angle formed from the intersection of one course and the line of sight between the objects remains constant, the observer (the fielder or the driver) can determine that there will be a collision if speed or course or both are not changed. This algorithm offers a model of how judgments about collisions might be made. The next step, of course, is to obtain experimental evidence that tests whether this is what people actually are doing.

One early model of fly ball catching was developed by a Cornell physicist named Seville Chapman, who wrote that he was motivated in part by an essay by Vannevar Bush from his

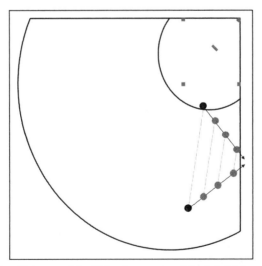

A simple collision model—if the shortstop and the left fielder maintain a constant angle between them, they will eventually collide.

Inspired by Pollack, H. N. (1985). "Letter." Science 268: 1681.

1967 book *Science Is Not Enough*. Bush was an influential engineer and inventor who had headed the Office of Scientific Research and Development during World War II and the Manhattan Project, and is also credited with foreseeing the creation of hypertext and the Internet. His essay "When Bat Meets Ball" shows that he was also interested in baseball; though, as Chapman points out in a footnote, Bush did not seem to understand it very well. In describing the game, Bush greatly over- or underestimated the speed of thrown or batted balls, the weights of baseball bats, and the distance that a "Texas Leaguer" would fly. Still, he made some astute observations. Among other things, he anticipated the much more recently accepted idea that on-base percentage, rather than batting average, is a better measure of a hitter's ability: "The batting average makes no allowance for a player's skill in judging pitches to get a base on balls. . . . A player comes to the plate ten times and gets one hit, terrible! But suppose he coaxed the pitcher into three passes in the process. He ought to be rated pretty well, but he isn't."

Bush also commented on fly ball catching, evoking The Catch: "Willie Mays, at the crack of the bat, will take a brief look at the flight of the ball, run without looking back, be at exactly the right spot at the right time, and take the ball over his shoulder with a basket catch. How he does it no one knows, certainly not Willie Mays. Nor could a whole team of physicists and psychologists tell him."

Taking up Bush's challenge, Chapman developed a model of how a fielder might compute, from the limited information in the fielder's view, where a fly ball would land. Chapman's model simplified the situation by considering only motion in the vertical direction, so the player only needed to move along one dimension, forward or backward. Anyone who has shagged a few fly balls or listened to a bit of commentary about the game knows that balls hit directly at an outfielder are the most difficult to judge. And of course, one of the amazing things about Willie Mays's catch in the '54 World Series was that the ball was hit more or less right at him. Still, this was a place to start. In the collision model illustrated on page 51, observers monitor the angle between their bearing and the line of sight between them and another object. In Chapman's early model of fly ball catching, he posited that the fielder monitors how fast the ball moves up through his field of view, with the additional complication that he moves in toward home plate or back away from it in order to control the movement of the ball within the field of view. If he moves in a certain way (assuming the ball will drop somewhere within his range), the ball will rise at a constant rate through his field of view, moving the same distance in the second second of the ball's flight as in the third, and so on. If he moves too slowly or too quickly, the ball will slow down or speed up in its movement through the field. Thus, this strategy is called "acceleration cancellation," because the fielder is thought to attempt to keep the image of the ball moving at a constant rate through his field of view: the model is thus called the Optical Acceleration Cancellation, or OAC, model.

The notion that the ball will rise constantly from the time that it is hit until the fielder catches it seems off in an obvious way: the ball has to come down, doesn't it? The key is to remember that the fielder is moving at the same time the ball is. Imagine the first few feet of the ball's flight—if you're standing in the outfield, the ball obviously begins to rise in your field of view. Now imagine the end point of the ball's flight—suppose that you are catching the ball with your glove positioned just above your forehead. In this position, you are looking almost straight up. If there were a camera mounted on your forehead, the ball would move constantly upward in the picture, which is what the OAC model assumes happens in the player's field of view. What the OAC model says (oversimplifying somewhat again) is that if the fielder moves so that the ball rises steadily in his field of view, he and the ball will arrive at the same spot at the same time. If the ball slows down or speeds up as the fielder moves, then an adjustment in running speed (and maybe direction) needs to be made.

By "controlling" the way the ball moves across the image, the player can guarantee he will arrive at the place where the ball will land at the same time as the ball. This strategy is called an "error nulling" strategy because the player's movement is determined by the ball's. If the ball strays from its trajectory (say, because of wind resistance), then the fielder will have to change his movement in sync with the changes in the ball's movement to keep it progressing in the same way in his field of view. So the system is assumed to employ a feedback loop: Monitor the optical acceleration. If it is increasing, slow down; if it decreasing, speed up. Repeat.

Some early evidence suggested that people do not use acceleration or deceleration as a cue in the way that Chapman's model predicts. However, a later study pointed out that people are relatively insensitive to changes in acceleration, and that the early studies may not have simulated changes large enough for observers to detect. The amount of acceleration needed to detect a change in velocity depends on the average velocity. A 10mph change from 10mph to 20mph would be easier to detect than a 10mph change from 100mph to 110mph. The later study showed that the difference in velocity from before to after acceleration has to be more than 20 percent of the average velocity for people to be able to detect the change. Perhaps if the objects in the early studies had accelerated more, observers would have used this cue. Indeed, the subsequent studies found exactly that: when the change in velocity was above the observers' threshold for detecting a change, the observers made correct landing judgments 86 percent of the time, whereas when it was below the threshold, they made correct judgments only 60 percent of the time, which is not much better than they would do if they were just guessing. This result suggests that people may use acceleration as a cue for catching after all.

The first application of Chapman's model to sports was not in baseball, but rather in cricket. Peter McLeod of Oxford was intrigued by the problem of fly ball catching because this ability, which appears so natural, also appears to be impossible: "Part of the attraction of [studying] catching is that it is straightforward to show that catching is impossible. If you assume that people work out from the speed at which the ball is hit, the angle of the trajectory and so on, where the ball is going to land, and run there to intercept it, it soon becomes clear that it's not possible for the fielder to pick up information with sufficient accuracy to calculate the trajectory." Rocket science will not work—human perceptual abilities are too limited for that. Chapman's model offered an alternative theory that showed why fly ball catching might be possible after all, and McLeod and some colleagues have found that the behavior of cricket fielders appears to comply with the model's predictions. For example, the model predicts that catches will be made on the run. If they use the OAC strategy, fielders will not run to the spot where a ball will land and stand and wait for it to arrive; they will get there at the same time the ball does.

McLeod launched cricket balls on a straight line from a bowling machine toward a fielder, and filmed the fielder as he made the catches. The launches were set to land unpredictably, several meters in front of the fielder, just a few meters in front of him, or a few meters behind him. In all three cases, the fielder began running within half a second or so, and kept running until he made the catch. For the catches several meters in front, the fielders steadily increased their speed, until they were running about 5 meters per second at the moment they caught the ball. For the catches just a few meters in front, they increased their speed at about the same rate for the first half of their run to make the catch, but then slowed and coasted at about 2 meters per second until they made the catch. Clearly, the fielders had the foot speed to get to the spot early and then wait for the ball on these shorter flies, but instead, they adjusted their pace so that they would get there at the same time the ball did. McLeod also estimated the angle of the fielder's gaze to the ball as he tracked it, computing from that the optical acceleration, which was found in all cases to hold steady around zero. The fielders appeared to be doing exactly what the OAC model said they should do.

While working as a postdoctoral fellow at the NASA Ames Research Center, with his interest in baseball already piqued by his work on hitting and the rising fastball illusion, Michael McBeath ran across Chapman's article and noted some potential problems with that model. One obvious issue is that the OAC model handles only those cases in which the ball is hit directly at the fielder, and thus covers only a tiny proportion of the balls the player must field. Any model that claims to explain how people catch fly balls has to say something about balls hit to the side.

And everyone knows that fly balls hit directly at the fielder are often the most difficult to judge—fielders often take a few steps in the wrong direction, moving in when they need to go back, back when they need to move in. It seemed to McBeath that if balls hit to the side were easier to catch, then a fielder might be using a cue that takes into account both the ball's movement from home plate into the field *and* its movement to his left or right. That might explain why balls hit right at a fielder can be more difficult to judge; only one of the usual two sources of information would be available.

McBeath and two colleagues, Dennis Shaffer, then a graduate student, and Mary Kaiser, a researcher at the NASA Ames Research Center, developed a new model. Kaiser's lab at NASA is devoted to understanding the role of visual perception in how pilots control vehicles. NASA supported the research on fly ball catching because the space agency has an interest in exploring the development of biologically inspired technologies. Understanding how people navigate three-dimensional space may help them develop ways for computers and machines to do it. Other researchers have applied similar error-nulling models to understanding how drivers brake their cars to avoid collisions.

McBeath's new model covered the whole range of balls that fielders catch and did not depend on the ability to detect small differences in acceleration. It depended instead on the ability to detect whether a line was straight or not, a task that studies of perceptual discrimination have shown is somewhat easier. In simple terms, the Linear Optical Trajectory, or LOT, model, holds that the fielder runs in such a way that the path the ball traces out across the fielder's view is a straight line. If the path deviates from a straight line, the fielder can adjust his path and speed to keep it straight. If he does this (assuming the fly ball is within his range), the LOT model guarantees that he will get to the place where the ball will land at the same time the ball does.

The LOT strategy works because it simultaneously controls two angles, one that captures how far to the fielder's side the ball will land and one that captures how far in front of or behind him it will land. Imagine the fielder's head turning as he follows the ball off the bat: his head will tilt up as the ball rises, and over as the ball flies to his left or right. The geometry works out so that as long as the relation between the up and over angles remains constant, the image of the ball will move on a straight line across the player's field of view. And if the player moves so that the ball stays on a straight line in his field of view, he and the ball will arrive at the same point at the same time. If the relation between these angles does not remain constant, the ball will curve up or down as it moves across the image, and the player will need to adjust his running path or speed (or both) in order to meet the ball.

This is an error-nulling strategy, too. Every fan knows that the paths of many fly balls are far from straight. How many potential home runs disappoint us by hooking foul? Some fly balls tail in one direction or another, some are pushed one way or another by the wind, some seem to "take off" when others "die." The home run that won the first game of the '54 World Series for the Giants appeared at first to be a pop-up to the second baseman, but the wind carried it over the right-field wall. Wind, temperature, and humidity all influence the ball's flight along with the physics of the collision between bat and ball. But the fielder need pay no attention to these factors if he can keep his eye on the ball (or if, like Devon White, he is making the catch in a dome and knows those factors do not matter). If he merely adjusts to changes in the ball's movement so that he keeps the ball moving in that straight line, he will arrive in the right place at the right time. The LOT strategy would allow Cleveland Indians right fielder Dave Pope to move with that pop-up to second base as it flew inexorably farther and farther, until the wall prevented him from finally settling under it.

One interesting thing about the LOT strategy is that it does not specify a particular path to the ball. The only constraint is that the path be linear in the fielder's view, and that only requires that those two angles stay in proportion to each other. An infinite number of paths to the ball would fit the bill. Of course, there are more and less efficient paths, and McBeath and his colleagues assumed that fielders would naturally opt for the efficient ones, those that keep the player moving in roughly the same direction throughout the catch, and minimize how fast he must run.

With those assumptions, the LOT model predicts that the outfielder's path to the ball will be curved slightly away from home plate, and that his speed will accelerate early in the path and then decelerate as he approaches the point where the ball will land. The McBeath group did two studies, reported in *Science* in 1995. In one, they filmed amateur outfielders (all college students) as they caught fly balls, and tracked their running paths and speed. Only a few of the balls were launched directly at the fielders; most were hit either to their left or their right. When the balls were launched directly at the fielders, the researchers observed more "backtracking and unsystematic sideways movement" in the running paths, which "may have been random anticipatory motion or possibly intentional attempts to induce lateral information." Those observations support McBeath's reasoning that "these cases are an 'accidental view' that may require an alternative strategy." When the balls were launched to the side in one direction or the other, the fielders' running paths curved as predicted by the LOT model, and their speed increased and then decreased as predicted by the model.

In the second study, a fielder actually fielded fly balls while carrying a video camera on his shoulder, keeping it aimed at the ball as he ran to make the catch. A few sample catches are shown in the figure below. Each line represents one catch, and each point

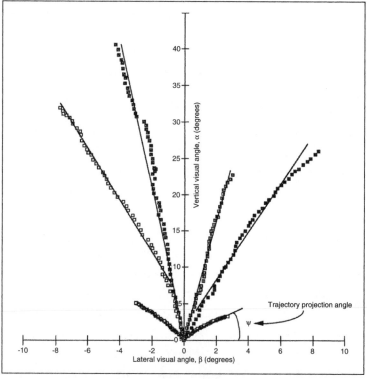

The optic trajectories of fly balls.

Reprinted with permission from McBeath, M. B., Shaffer, D., and Kaiser, M. (1995).
Science 268: 569–573. Copyright 1995 AAAS.

in those lines represents the ball's position in the fielder's view at intervals of one-thirtieth of a second. Mostly, as you can see, the lines trace out linear paths in the fielder's view, again confirming the LOT model. There are some exceptions, but as McBeath and his colleagues noted in their report, those often occurred when the fielder abandoned one linear path for another, as you can see in the case of the third line from the left side of the figure.

McBeath and his colleagues have looked for evidence relating to the LOT theory off the baseball field as well, going so far afield as to explore catching by nonhumans. He and some colleagues have developed a working robot that implements the LOT strategy. The robot is not yet ready to be fitted for a baseball glove, but it is programmed to use the LOT strategy to get to the right place to catch a balloon. Though this demonstration does not prove that humans use LOT, the success of the robot provides a demonstration that LOT works in principle.

In another study away from the ballpark, this one led by Dennis Shaffer, the LOT group strapped small video cameras to the heads of a springer spaniel named Romeo and a border collie named Lilly, both of whom were proficient Frisbee catchers. The dogs obligingly wore backpacks containing transmitters that sent the signal from the cameras to a VCR. The investigators were thus able to track the trajectory of a Frisbee as the dogs chased and caught it. The result: dogs seem to know the LOT strategy, too. A figure of the videotaped trajectories of the Frisbees thrown to Romeo and Lilly looks just like the one from the study with humans (see the previous page). Once again, the trajectories are close to straight lines, as predicted by the LOT strategy. And once again, the rate of increase in the vertical direction is roughly constant, as predicted by the OAC model. As McBeath and his group interpret these results, people, robots, and

Frisbee-catching dogs use the LOT strategy, supplemented by the OAC strategy. This may reflect a general tracking strategy used by many species. The LOT group cited numerous examples of other organisms, including various insects, bats, and birds, that appear to follow similar strategies.

Despite the seeming universal usefulness of the LOT strategy, there has not been universal agreement about whether outfielders actually use it. When McBeath et al.'s paper appeared in *Science,* there was a flurry of critical responses, and questions have been raised about the theory ever since. The main critic of the LOT theory has been Peter McLeod, whose study had demonstrated the viability of the OAC model. (A colleague once cracked, "Theories are like toothbrushes: everyone has one and no one wants to use someone else's.") In one study, McLeod and some colleagues observed systematic deviations from the predictions of the LOT model, such that for many catches, the optical trajectories were curved, rather than linear. This occurred, they argued, because fielders only sometimes, but not always, controlled the lateral angle to the ball as the LOT theory predicted, although they *did* control the vertical angle as the OAC theory predicted. McLeod and his colleagues concluded that the "predictions of the LOT theory have not been supported by our data. Therefore OAC remains the best account yet of catching behavior."

Shortly after that paper appeared, Shaffer and McBeath published a new study in which they aimed to compare the LOT and OAC theories by pushing the theories beyond their limits— they measured the optical trajectory when outfielders attempted to catch flies beyond their reach. Again they acknowledged that in previous studies, all of which examined successful catches, fielders maintained OAC at the same time that they followed the LOT. By seeing which strategy controlled the fielder's running path longer when the ball was uncatchable, they hoped to determine which strategy was primary. Imagine Vic Wertz's drive landing ten feet beyond Willie Mays's outstretched glove. As in the original study, they both filmed the running paths of the fielders in one experiment and had the fielders aim a video camera at the fly ball in another. Even for uncatchable balls, in the first experiment, the fielders appeared to take the less direct and curved paths to the landing location predicted by the LOT, rather than the straight and more direct paths specified by OAC. In the second experiment, the video recordings revealed that the fielders maintained a linear optical trajectory longer than they maintained cancellation of optical acceleration. For balls that landed in front of the fielder, 85 percent of the time the ball's path in the fielder's view followed a straight line longer than acceleration remained constant. For balls that landed behind the fielder, the LOT was maintained longer than OAC 100 percent of the time.

Still, McLeod was not convinced, and he stated his view plainly in the title of a comment on Shaffer and McBeath's study of uncatchable fly balls, "The Optic Trajectory Is Not a Lot of Use if You Want to Catch the Ball." He concluded the paper by noting that in an earlier study, he had found "a range of conditions under which the predictions of LOT theory did not hold. Shaffer and McBeath have now added to these." Other papers and additions and modifications to the two models have ensued. McLeod has added to the basic OAC model to create GOAC (Generalized Optical Acceleration Cancellation) and McBeath told me that his group is extending their work to the fielding of ground balls. Other researchers have found both strategies wanting in various ways. Of course, this is the way science works: ideas compete until one of them (or some other idea altogether) best explains the phenomenon in question.

Although they disagree about which model is the best description of a fielder's behavior, McLeod and McBeath agree that the more important point is that fielders are using a method that involves the interplay between what the fielder sees and what the fielder does. As McLeod put it: "We are in complete agreement that fielders follow a control strategy rather than, for example, calculating where the ball will fall and running there, or recognising that this is a similar trajectory to one caught before and running to the same place. The control strategy comes from watching the ball, and then moving at a speed and in a direction which brings about a [response] in the fielder."

Catching with Your Eyes Closed

As researchers sort out the differences between the OAC and LOT strategies, there are other questions to be answered. What is the nature of the optic image? One study shows just how much complex information must be taken into account. Players were filmed as they made catches, and the degree to which they moved their heads and eyes was recorded. The measurements revealed that both eyes and heads track the ball through much of its flight. The amount the image of the ball moves across the retina, therefore, cannot account for how much the ball actually moves. In principle, for instance, the fielder could keep the ball's position fixated at a particular point on the retina by moving his eyes and head to compensate for movement of the ball. Even if that were the case, the information about movement might still be obtained from the retinal image if movement of the background is taken into account. That is, if the fielder kept the ball's position fixated at a point on the retina by moving the eyes and head, the image of the background would move across the retina instead. To test that idea, fielders were required to catch glowing fly balls in the dark—if perception of the ball's trajectory depends on movement of the background on the retinal image, then catching should be impossible under such conditions. But it turned out to be quite possible, though somewhat more difficult than in lighted conditions. So it cannot be the motion of the ball on the retina, or the motion of the background, that fielders rely on. The information on which the OAC and LOT strategies operate must therefore be at some higher level of the nervous system, and must presumably integrate information from the eyes with information from the muscle systems that move the eyes and head along with the vestibular system, which senses how the body is oriented and moving in the environment.

The research on fly ball catching is interesting and fun because it involves baseball, but it may also help psychologists decide between two alternative approaches to understanding how perception works in general. Both the OAC and LOT theories subscribe to a view of the mind that links our perception of the world directly with the actions that we take in it, so that the brain's perceptual and action-control systems are linked in some way. The founder of the *ecological psychology* movement, James J. Gibson, promoted this idea, saying "we must perceive in order to move, but we must also move in order to perceive." Gibson was reacting against the more traditional *information processing* metaphor for perception, in which the perception and action systems may communicate, but are functionally independent. In this tradition, the mind is likened to a digital computer, with input processes (perception), central processing (symbolic thought), and output processes (action). The information processing model holds that the raw perceptual information is not enough to guide perception; the signal is ambiguous, and so other processes, like memory and inference, must be used in order to decode the input. But as we have seen, in the OAC and LOT models, all the information necessary to make a catch is directly available to the fielder—he relies on the acceleration of the ball through his field of view or on whether the ball traces out a straight line in the field of view. There need be no inference, that is, no information processing. The success of the OAC and LOT models in accounting for outfielder behavior offers support for Gibson's argument that perception and action are inextricably linked—this is the point on which McLeod and McBeath were in agreement.

The continuous interplay of the outfielder's monitoring of the ball's trajectory and his making adjustments to keep that path straight might explain why outfielders sometimes run into walls—they do not really know where they are going until they get there. After objecting to some aspects of McBeath's theory, physicist Robert Adair offered an alternative idea, one essentially consistent with the information processing viewpoint: "The player picks [a path] that leads to the falling ball, using the judgment of up-down ball flight patterns gained from practice." That rough idea (not that Adair offered it as a complete theory) suggests that once the player sees enough of the early flight of the ball, he knows where it will land. Adair is arguing, in line with the information processing model, that perception occurs first, then processing of that perception (like comparison to memories of other catches), then action.

But players tend not to know where the ball will land when standing in a stationary point in the outfield. As Al Gionfriddo said about his catch, he knew he had it, but could not have said he would get it. In fact, fielders standing still in the outfield are poor judges of whether or not a ball is catchable. In one study, fielders wore special LCD glasses that could be closed precisely one second after a ball had been launched for them to catch. Rather than try to catch the ball blindfolded, the fielders were simply asked to judge whether or not the ball was catchable, and then their judgments were compared with performance under conditions where they actually attempted to catch the ball. Fielders in both conditions, stationary and running, had the same amount of time to watch the ball's flight, but in the running condition they were allowed information about the perception-action coupling. According to the OAC and LOT models, this would give the fielders at least some sense of whether or not they were able to control optical acceleration and the linearity of the optical trajectory. If Adair's memory model (and the information processing model in general) is correct, it should not matter whether they are running or not—they see the same ball trajectory in both conditions. The fielders were clearly better able to judge the fly ball if they were allowed to run, supporting the theories that link perception with action. This explains why fielders run after balls that land several rows back in the stands—they do not know initially that is where those balls will land. If they did, would they bother running after them? And this may explain why fielders sometimes run into (or through) outfield walls—they do not know the ball will land on the other side until they get there.

No one suggests that the OAC or LOT or any similar strategy is conscious, or even that outfielders know that the ball follows a straight line in their field of view. It is not that the outfielder solves some complicated equation while he is running to figure out where the ball will land. The geometry merely describes what the outfielder may be doing. We need only assume that young outfielders learn that the linear optical trajectory, or some other cue, is a useful indicator of where the ball will land. Some ballplayers have told McBeath, after hearing his theory, that they then can see that the ball does follow a straight line, but it is not something they normally think about as they make a catch. They just go where the ball is going. McLeod and some of his colleagues have found that people who seem to follow the OAC model say, when asked to describe their strategy, that they do something completely different.

Nor do researchers necessarily think that these are the only cues that outfielders use. The OAC and LOT strategies may be the natural starting point, techniques that children learn to use to catch. But players may also learn to use other information, and may even deliberately try to override their natural inclination to make a catch using OAC or LOT. McBeath, for instance, is quite willing to agree that outfielders, especially skilled ones at the college and professional level, likely use many different cues and strategies in their fielding. One thing that the reports about the catches on *USA Today*'s list of amazing catches make clear is that outfielders often take their eyes off the ball. Both Mays and Edmonds turned their backs on the ball and sprinted toward the outfield fence. And Devon White flatly stated that he could take his eye off the ball if he needed to.

In an August 2005 game between the Giants and the Cardinals, J. T. Snow hit a fly ball to deep, straightaway center field, over the head of center fielder Jim Edmonds. Although he did not repeat the catch that put him on the *USA Today* Top Catches List, he did make a very nice catch that likely violated OAC and LOT models. After sprinting back toward the wall, Edmonds had to turn and take a couple of steps back in toward the infield to make a low, basket catch of Snow's fly ball. Afterward, the television cameras caught him pointing to his eyes as he apparently explained to teammates that he couldn't see the ball. The control models of catching obviously depend on the fielder seeing the ball—Edmonds evidently used something other than optical acceleration or the optical trajectory to get near the point where the ball would land.

In line with Adair's comment, one cue may well be experience. Remember Devon White talking about how he knew how fly balls behaved in the Sky Dome in Toronto. One study compared how quickly novice and expert fielders got a jump on fly balls. The novices had no baseball experience; the experts were professional players in the Netherlands and one major-league outfielder from the United States. In further support of the importance of action in the perception of catchableness, the researchers found no difference between the experts and the novices when they made judgments standing still. It was only in moving that the difference between the two groups became apparent. The novices made many false starts, moving in the wrong direction, particularly on balls that would land behind them. On average, the novices actually started to move before the experts, but it was because they were fooled by many balls that landed behind them. The expert fielders did not make those missteps. The researchers wrote that the "experts succeeded more often in initially setting up the correct relation between perceptual information and running actions" and that they were "better attuned to [ball flight] information."

McBeath has even looked at how the movement of other players on the field can act as a cue. If you stand on a field and watch not the ball, but how other people watch the ball, you can still get a good sense of where the ball is, just as if you come upon a crowd of people who are staring at something in the distance and your own gaze is drawn in the same direction. If you are an outfielder and everyone else on the field is looking in your direction, you know the ball is headed your way. But if a fly is hit and the infielders are all looking in the direction of home plate, you know the ball will not even reach the outfield.

McBeath had people watch video of a fly ball shot by a camera positioned at the vantage point of the left fielder. He edited the tape so that the ball followed its normal flight to its apex and then froze there, in midair. Then he asked people to judge where the fly ball would land. Baseline measurements were taken from videos that included both the other players' and the ball's position. Surprisingly, when McBeath edited the ball from the video, leaving just the other players on the field as cues to where the ball would land, people were still able to perform almost as well as they had when the ball was in the video. But when he left the ball in and edited the other players from the scene, judgments about where the ball would land were dramatically impaired. When he crossed two videos, so that the ball's flight and the movement of the players on the field conflicted, judgments were still worse. McBeath is quick to admit that "we don't have any evidence that they use this to help them catch a ball" but that "I think people don't realize that it's not just the ball that they're using to put together the 3D scene."

Even the sounds of the game may influence the fielder's judgment of where the ball will go. McBeath went on to speculate about how, with two initial ball trajectories that looked similar, one of a home run and one of a soft pop-up to the outfield, the roar of the crowd, or lack of it, might be a cue the fielder could use. And Adair suggests that the "crack" or "thud" of the bat on the ball, along with the appearance of the hitter's swing (Was it a fluid swing he was able to stay back on, or was he fooled and only managed to get the bat on the ball with his weight out on his front foot?), may also help the fielder judge where a just-batted ball is going.

The OAC and LOT models also may only apply to typical, basic fielding skills. Professional players, with all their experience and training, may use other strategies to make their catches. Obviously, only players as skilled as Willie Mays or Jim Edmonds can turn their backs on home plate and catch a fly ball they cannot see for most of its flight. And professional players also practice positioning themselves to make a throw after the catch—if they *can* get to the point where the ball will land, or better still just a bit behind it, they can catch the ball in a position to make a strong throw back to the infield. One of the replies to McBeath's original article on LOT was signed by Lewis A. Chodosh, #9 of the Jansport HBs Baseball Club (and the Department of Molecular and Cellular Engineering at the University of Pennsylvania Medical Center), Lawrence Lifson, #14 of the Lombadi Baseball Club (and J. Crew, Inc.), and Cliff Tabin, #7 of the Jansport HBs Baseball Club (and the Department of Genetics at Harvard Medical School). In their letter, Chodosh and his fellow player-scientists reported, contrary to the catch-the-fly-on-the-run prediction of the OAC and LOT models, that of 179 fly balls caught in twelve sample games, 83 percent were caught while the fielder was standing still. Note that, in an effort to factor out the influence of the need to make a throw, Chodosh and his colleagues excluded from their analyses any balls caught with runners on base and fewer than two outs. Of course, it may be that once a player learns to set up to make the catch as if he will need to follow it with a throw, that he catches all flies that way. In any case, McBeath readily concedes that professional outfielders, by virtue of their expertise and the high level of performance required of them, may do things differently than the models allow.

Another factor that complicates matters is what McBeath calls phase two of the catch. In his studies of fly ball catching, a play counted as a catch if the fielder simply got to the right place at the right time. McBeath was not interested in whether the ball hit the glove and fell out or even if it hit the glove at all (he would not care that Kevin Mitchell used his bare hand rather than his glove to make a catch), just in whether the player was in the right position—for McBeath's purposes, the ball that hit Jose Canseco in the head and bounced over the fence counts as a catch. Canseco got phase one right—he got to the right place. It was in phase two that he had the problem. Great catches may depend more on the part of the catch that McBeath calls phase two, less on phase one. Diving, pulling the ball into an outstretched glove, playing an outfield fence—those all come into play at the end of the catch. Indeed, flies that some outfielders might have to dive for might be routine catches for other, speedier fielders. But great and routine catches alike depend on a remarkable ability to judge where the ball will land in the first place.

In phase two of the catch, the fielder has to position himself so that his glove hand can reach the ball. Right- and left-handed fielders running to catch a ball hit to their right may approach it differently in order to get the glove hand to the right place. On a ball hit behind him, the fielder may have to turn in order to make the catch; again, this may cause a deviation from the path predicted by the LOT strategy at the very end of the catch. Indeed, McBeath and his colleagues stopped measuring the running path about half a second before catches were made in order to eliminate these deviations from their analyses—the LOT model was never meant to account for them.

In addition to the player's efforts to position his glove for the catch, the visual information available to him at the end of the catch changes. Early in the flight of the ball, many of the cues we can use to judge depth are not available to the fielder because the ball is so far away. Binocular vision will not help, nor will the rate at which the size of the ball expands in the optic image as it approaches. But as the ball gets closer, these cues can be helpful. For instance, the visual cue called *convergence* relies on the way our eyes point inward toward each other when an object they are focused on comes near. Hold your index finger at arm's length and focus on your finger as you draw it in toward your nose; your eyes will cross. The closer the finger gets, the more they cross. We can use the degree of convergence as a cue about how far away an object is out to distances of about twenty feet; at distances greater than that, our eyes point out in parallel.

Another important variable for the final part of the catch is probably what psychologists call time-to-contact (which they designate with the Greek letter tau, τ). Time-to-contact is probably judged in large part as a function of the way the ball's image grows or looms, in the fielder's view, as it gets nearer, and is an especially effective cue when objects get close. People are generally very good at judging τ, and it probably provides the basis for judging exactly when to open and close a hand or glove to make a catch. Studies have even shown that there are specialized nerve cells in the brain that respond selectively to time-to-contact information. We have not said anything yet about the catching of ground balls, largely because little work has been done on that problem. Time-to-contact may play a more central role in fielding a ground ball, at least for infielders, because of the shorter distances. But it may not be the only cue. McBeath has recently begun work to see if the LOT model can be extended to ground ball catching. Maybe he'll soon have as much to say about Ozzie Smith's great stop on that grounder as he does about the great fly ball catches that have been made.

CHAPTER THREE

The Mind on the Mound

BASEBALL WOULD NOT BE LOVED AS IT IS IF NOT FOR THE drama inherent in pitching. Announcements about upcoming games are almost always adorned by the names of the starting pitchers. ("In an interleague contest between the Yankees and the Mets, it will be Mike Mussina taking on Pedro Martinez . . ."). It is almost impossible to imagine how different baseball was when the pitcher's job was akin to what many coaches do today in "coach-pitch" youth baseball: just throw it up there so the batter can hit it.

On May 20, 2006, Mussina matched up with Martinez in an early season interleague contest that featured both stellar and atrocious pitching. Mussina and Martinez did their parts—much of the stellar came from them, as one would expect from the records each of them had compiled. Mussina was a bit older, entering professional baseball after being drafted by Baltimore out of Stanford in 1990, and making his major-league debut in 1991 when he started twelve games and posted a 2.87 ERA in eighty-seven-and-two-thirds innings. Martinez was signed by the Dodgers out of the Dominican Republic in 1988 and debuted briefly in 1992 with eight innings of work, and then worked primarily as a reliever for Los Angeles in 1993, pitching 107 innings with a 2.61 ERA.

Each of them steadily added to those impressive beginnings. Mussina was selected as an All-Star his first full season, in 1992, and four more times by 2006, had won six Gold Gloves, and had been in the top ten in the American League in ERA in nine of his fourteen full major-league seasons and in the top five in wins and strikeouts six times each. He had never won a Cy Young Award, though he had finished high in the voting several times, coming in second once to Martinez. Mussina had consistently ranked among the league leaders in other stats such as complete games, shutouts, and innings pitched.

Martinez's record was even more impressive. He had been an All-Star seven times in his fourteen full major-league seasons, and had won the Cy Young Award three times and finished second or third another three times. He had led his league in ERA five times and been in the top five in wins six times, as well as leading his league in strikeouts three times and finishing in the top five another eight times. And he, too, had consistently ranked among the league leaders in other statistics, like complete games and shutouts.

Come May 20, 2006, Mussina (3.61) and Martinez (2.73) were ranked fourteenth and first, respectively, in ERA for active pitchers with more than 1000 IP. In career walks per nine innings, they ranked sixth (2.04) and fourteenth (2.37) among active pitchers; in strikeouts per nine innings, they ranked fifty-second (7.17) and third (10.25) all-time; in strikeout-to-walk ratio, they ranked ninth (3.51) and second (4.32) all-time. Based on measures Bill James developed in his book *The Politics of Glory,* which is about qualifying for the Hall of Fame, Martinez is a lock for entry; Mussina's case for admission was more marginal at that point, though another Bill James–invented metric showed that several Hall of Famers have had statistics similar to Mussina's through 2005 when they were also thirty-six years old.

There are other differences between the two hurlers besides their Hall of Fame prospects. Martinez had been brash and out-spoken. During an incident with the Yankees when he was with the Red Sox, he famously appeared to threaten to throw at their heads, and in a bench-clearing brawl he was charged by Yankee coach Don Zimmer, whom Martinez sidestepped and pushed to the ground. In 2004, after a frustrating Red Sox loss to the Yan-kees, Pedro said he would call the Yankees "my daddy." Mussina has kept a lower profile, even in New York, preferring small-town Montoursville, Pennsylvania, to Manhattan, and is often described as quiet and cerebral, having finished a degree in economics at Stanford in three-and-half years.

Despite the differences in performance and personality, there are similarities in these pitchers and the way they ap-proach the game of baseball. Most importantly, Mussina and Martinez are each often described as power pitchers with excel-lent control of multiple pitches, any one of which they can throw on any ball-strike count. However, neither man has the typical frame of a power pitcher, which we associate with the sturdy builds of Roger Clemens and Curt Schilling or the lanky limbs of Randy Johnson. Questions about the five-foot-eleven, 180-pound Martinez's durability come regularly; he has faced them all through his career. Mussina, a bit bigger at six-two and 190 pounds, has still been described as "unimposing" and "slight" on the mound. Early in 2006, when Mussina and Martinez ranked fourth and fifth in season-to-date strikeout-to-walk ratio, the other eight players in the top ten averaged six-four and 226 pounds. But Mussina and Martinez had adjusted well to the changes brought on by the wear and tear of years of pitching. The game on May 20 looked to be a pitcher's duel.

Pedro had a smooth first inning. After Johnny Damon grounded out to first, Derek Jeter hit a routine ground ball single into left, but it rolled inexplicably through Cliff Floyd's legs, leaving Jeter standing on second. No matter. Jason Giambi flew out to center, and then Martinez got Alex Rodriguez looking for a called strike three on a pitch at the knees and on the outside corner. Thirteen pitches, inning over.

The first inning was rockier for Mussina, who would have some bad luck that day. Jose Reyes hit a weak grounder toward third, and in rushing to pick up the ball and make a throw, Rodriguez pulled Giambi off the bag at first. In the next at bat, Reyes took off to steal second and catcher Kelly Stinnett's throw went into center field, putting Reyes on third with no one out. Mussina struck out Kaz Matsui, but then Carlos Beltran hit a belt-high pitch over the outside corner deep to left. The fly could have been caught, but Miguel Cairo, a second baseman playing the outfield because of Yankee injuries, got a slow jump on the ball—it dropped for a double, scoring Reyes. Carlos Delgado then grounded out weakly to second before David Wright drove a ball that appeared to be knee-high and off the outside corner of the plate—a pitcher's pitch—to straightaway center, just beyond Johnny Damon's reach, scoring Beltran. Cliff Floyd grounded out to end the inning. Mussina might easily have given up no runs with that kind of pitching, but instead the Mets scored two, both unearned.

That first inning more or less set the tone—both pitchers pitched the way they usually do. Over seven innings, Mussina allowed five hits and zero walks, and struck out seven. Martinez allowed four hits and one walk, and struck out eight. Both pitched around several errors (there was a total of seven in the game, four by the Yankees). Martinez threw 102 pitches, 67 for strikes; Mussina threw 68 of his 98 pitches for strikes. But where Martinez gave up zero runs, Mussina gave up four. In addition to the two unearned runs in the first, he gave up solo home runs in the fourth and seventh. In the fourth, Delgado hit a belt-high pitch that appeared to be off the plate outside, and in the seventh Floyd hit a breaking ball that was up and over the plate, maybe the only real mistake of his own that cost Mussina a run.

The eighth was uneventful, and then the Mets turned the ninth over to their new closer, Billy Wagner, whose fastball blazes in the upper nineties. In the five previous years, Wagner had converted 266 of 284 save opportunities, and to that point in 2006 was 3–0 with a 1.80 ERA and twenty-eight strikeouts in twenty innings pitched, having converted eight of eleven save opportunities. He had picked up one of those wins the night before, when he struck out Jason Giambi, Alex Rodriguez, and Kelly Stinnett in order on twelve pitches in the top of the ninth with the tie scored. The Mets then scored the winning run off Mariano Rivera in the bottom of the frame.

Saturday would be Wagner's turn for trouble. Giambi singled to center on a 2–0 count. Alex Rodriguez walked after Wagner had him 2–2; the 2–2 pitch was close, low and away, but the 3–2 pitch was low and not so close. Wagner started Robinson Cano out with a fastball over the outside corner for a strike, but then Cano singled on the next pitch, a slider about belt high. That scored Giambi and moved A-Rod to second. Miguel Cairo flew out to center on a 2–1 fastball, and then came what seemed to be the turning point. Rookie outfielder Melky Cabrera started in a 0–2 hole with two called strikes and a slider inside at the knees followed by a fastball over the outside corner. Then he fouled off two fastballs and a slider, which were followed by two high fastballs to make the count 2–2. He fouled off another slider, then took a fastball inside for ball three, and then fouled off a fastball over the outside corner. On the eleventh pitch of the at bat, catcher Ramon Castro set up inside for another fastball, but Wagner missed wildly, outside and so high that Castro had to jump up to catch it. That loaded the bases with just one out.

Yankees catcher Kelly Stinnett batted next, and walked on four straight pitches: ball one up and away, ball two *way* up and away, almost wild, ball three high, and ball four off the outside corner. That scored Rodriguez, making it a 4–2 game. Then Wagner promptly hit pinch hitter Bernie Williams in the thigh with a slider, scoring Cano and making it 4–3. Wagner was pulled for Pedro Feliciano, who got Johnny Damon to hit a ground ball, but the Mets missed turning the double play by half a step and Cabrera scored to tie the game at four. The Mets escaped the ninth without further damage, but the Yankees eventually won it in the eleventh, 5–4. Wagner's line was ⅓ IP, 2H, 4ER, 3BB, 0K.

You can imagine that a performance like that from a pitcher as reliable as Wagner in a nationally televised Yankees-Mets game makes news, a lot of news. Wagner, to his credit, and just like Rivera had done the night before, stepped right up and took responsibility for the failure. "I let them back in. I just stunk." Martinez, who did not get the win he should have had, was sympathetic: "I've been there many times, done it to myself many times. I can understand how the person out there is feeling. I can feel bad for Billy. You can't say anything bad." Oh yes, they could. "No Excuses for the Inexcusable" (*Newsday*); "Wag

the Dog" (*New York Post*); "Wagner Goes from Torrid to Hor-
rid" (the Newark *Star Ledger*).

The New York *Daily News* ran a story with the headline
"Wagner Case Not Closed: Hints at a Willie Mistake," which in-
timated that Wagner was displeased at being used in a non-save
situation. According to the article, he did little more than admit
to being surprised at being called into the game, which is no
more than most everyone else watching felt, including Mike
Mussina, who said, "I was surprised when Wagner came back
with a four-run lead, and he just pitched last night." Another
judgment also seemed a bit harsh: "Wagner did not simply fail
to throw strikes. He failed to tempt Yankees hitters." Although
Wagner started off the first two hitters with 2–0 counts, he otherwise made most of his pitches, especially during Cabrera's at
bat. Sometimes you do have to credit the hitter, after all. To say
he didn't tempt Yankee hitters forgets that he gave up two hits,
had a 2–2 count on Rodriguez before walking him, and threw
two strikes and five more pitches for two-strike fouls to Cabrera
before walking him. It was only the eleventh pitch of that at
bat that seemed wildly off target.

After the walk to Cabrera, Wagner clearly seemed rattled.
He walked Stinnett on four straight and then hit Williams with
the fifth. With those last six pitches, something clearly seemed
to change—Wagner had been throwing his fastballs and sliders
more or less where he wanted them, maybe a little less accurately than usual, but more or less where he wanted them, for
twenty-five pitches. Throwing accurately at that velocity is extraordinary, and that ability, when examined closely, reveals
some extraordinary human psychology, as does what happens
when that ability breaks down.

Throwing in baseball may be harder than the throwing

required in any other sport. In football, the target is moving, but the target can also adjust to the throw. Dart throwing is an oft-used but poor metaphor for throwing a baseball. Throwing a baseball with the force and the accuracy that the game requires, especially in pitching, is much more difficult than throwing darts. Better that darts players aspire to be pitchers. Bruce Lowitt of the *St. Petersburg Times* had it right when he wrote that darts player Peter Mills "is as deadly with a dart at 7 feet, 9 ¼ inches as Greg Maddux is with a baseball at 60 feet, 6 inches." Throwing a baseball over the inner or outer half of the plate (a window eight-and-a-half inches wide through which the almost three-inch-diameter baseball must pass) from the distance of fifty-six feet (about where a pitcher releases a pitch) requires an accuracy of about half a degree, but hitting the one-and-a-quarter-inch inch bull's-eye (single or double) from the regulation distance of seven feet, nine-and-a-quarter inches requires accuracy of only three-quarters of a degree. To "paint the black" and throw the ball only over the outer edge of the plate, the pitcher has about one-quarter degree (about three inches) room for error; hitting the double bull's-eye, the half-inch red dot in the center of the dartboard, leaves slightly less than one-third degree margin for error. I will grant that the baseball player has more room for error in the vertical direction to hit the strike zone, but if he is too "wild in the strike zone" the hitter will punish him. Plus, it must also be granted that the baseball player has to throw *hard.*

Champion darts player Leighton Rees (in a contest in 1976, Rees hit the bull's-eye in 86 of 141 tries) described the ideal throwing position for a darts player as one with the feet "positioned level with the oche, approximately eighteen inches apart, firmly anchored but relaxed" and "firm enough to prevent your

Throwing a pitch over the corner of the plate and at the knees requires more accuracy than hitting the bull's-eye on a dartboard.

body from moving after you have thrown." (Oche—which rhymes with hockey—is the word for the mark behind which darts players stand when they throw.) "Once the legs and lower body are stabilized, your upper torso must be adjusted to suit the position of the chest, neck and head.... Technically, the deltoid muscle then holds and stabilizes the arm at the shoulder, assisted by the neck, shoulder and back muscles. Your non-throwing arm should be totally relaxed, loosely holding your remaining darts." And finally, "the elbow is the crucial pivot of the backswing. It must be totally relaxed from the start to the finish of every throw and must not waver from its initial position, either vertically or horizontally."

Contrast Rees's description of dart throwing with the results of a biomechanical study of pitching, which measured precisely the forces generated by a professional-level pitcher's delivery. The description is peppered with specific measurements of torque and compressive forces applied to various pieces of the anatomy of the shoulder and arm, along with a list of the different kinds of injuries that those forces might produce. Suffice it to say, as another study did, that "spontaneous fracture of the humeral shaft in throwers is a rare but well-known phenomenon. . . . The torque acting about the long axis of the humerus was calculated in 25 professional baseball pitchers throwing in game situations. . . . The magnitude of the peak humeral torque averaged 48% of the theoretical torsional strength of the humerus, suggesting that repetitive stress plays a role in humeral shaft fractures." These are no exaggerations—many baseball fans will remember that Tom Browning broke his arm throwing a pitch for the Cincinnati Reds in 1994, as did Dave Dravecky of the San Francisco Giants in 1989 (though Dravecky had cancer surgery on that arm in 1988, which likely contributed to his injury; the cancer would later return, and he eventually had to have the arm amputated).

So not only does throwing a baseball require more accuracy than throwing a dart, it must be done violently. Roger Kahn, in *The Head Game*, his case study of pitching, writes about watching Tom Glavine work in the bullpen the day after a start. Glavine, recovering from the previous day's outing, would throw lightly that day, at about 80 percent of his normal exertion. He began at around the usual distance between pitcher and catcher, and gradually stretched the distance to 90 feet, then 120. Kahn stepped into the batter's position to get a look at Glavine's stuff. From 60 feet, then from 90 and 120, Glavine pounded the catcher's mitt (Kahn noted that Glavine was throwing hard enough that the catcher still wore a mask), keeping the ball "low and away" first at the regular distance, and then still at the longer distances. Hitting the roughly twelve-inch-diameter catcher's mitt from 120 feet is approximately equivalent to hitting the double bull's-eye.

Baseball doesn't require this kind of throwing just from pitchers. Fielders throwing to a base face a somewhat easier challenge in terms of accuracy, as the other fielder who catches the throw can reach for it. The exact distances of throws made by fielders vary widely, of course, but a throw directly to a base requires roughly the same accuracy as that required for the pitcher to hit the catcher's mitt (for, say, a throw from the catcher to second base or from third base to first) or for the pitcher to throw the ball over one side of the plate or the other (for an outfielder throwing home from middle-deep center field). And though fielders' throws may not reach the velocities of a Nolan Ryan's or Randy Johnson's, anyone who has seen a catcher throw out a base stealer, a shortstop cut a ground ball off in the hole and peg a throw that just beats the runner to first, or a right fielder gun down a runner at third or home, knows that the fielders throw some serious fastballs.

In the movie *Bull Durham*, the raw pitching prospect Nuke Laloosh says, "Baseball is a simple game. You throw the ball, you hit the ball. Simple." But throwing was anything but simple for Nuke (at times, he was as likely to hit the team mascot standing near the dugout as he was to throw a strike). Throwing a baseball is never simple.

Throwing depends on the coordination of two complex abilities. Throwing an object to hit a distant target requires a keen sense of spatial relations, including the abilities to judge distance and to calculate the appropriate trajectory from our hand to the target. In baseball, more often than not, the target is stationary, though the player making the throw may be moving.

In other sports, like football, both the thrower and the target may be moving. We are equipped with an impressive ability to figure how to get a ball from here to there, even when here and there are both in motion. To hit that smaller-than-a-bull's-eye target, and hit it with a fastball, a slider, a curveball, or a changeup, requires a keen sense of space.

Throwing also depends on the rapid and flexible programming of a complex series of actions. The throwing motion seems so natural that it is easy to forget that it involves a well-coordinated, precisely timed series of actions of not only the shoulder, elbow, wrist, and fingers, but the legs, hips, and torso as well. Throwing is, unlike many actions, ballistic. When we reach to pick up a baseball from the infield, we can monitor and modify our movements as they take place—the movement is a "closed loop" action because visual and kinesthetic (our sense of our own movements) feedback can be used continuously to adjust and correct the movement as it occurs. When we throw that baseball, however, the action is an "open loop" action. It occurs too rapidly to be guided by continuous feedback; our nervous system is simply not fast enough to achieve this kind of control. The throwing motion must be programmed in advance. That elegant and complex series of movements of the legs, hips, torso, etc., must all be set up somewhere in the nervous system before the throw is made. Even Leighton Rees's precisely controlled flick of the elbow depends on this ability.

Each of these abilities, the sense of spatial relations and the programming of a series of movements, plays a significant role in current theories about the evolution of the brain. Throwing itself figures prominently in some ideas about how unique features of our brain, such as the ability to use language, developed during our evolutionary history.

One of the critical observations about throwing is that boys are, on average, better at it than girls, even from a very young age. Of course, some girls are better at throwing than some boys, but on average, boys are better. And of course, some of this difference may be in the way boys and girls are socialized, with boys being encouraged to throw more than girls. However, these differences emerge very early, even in preschool, and are on average very large. It is unlikely that they are entirely driven by experience; it is more likely that throwing ability is a sex-linked trait, or that abilities that contribute to throwing ability are genetically linked to sex.

Spatial abilities, in particular, appear to be strongly linked by sex. Evidence for sex differences in cognitive abilities is sometimes regarded as controversial, but there is a lot of evidence to show that they exist. Females, on average, have greater abilities than males in some areas, and males, on average, have greater abilities in others. And many of these abilities are influenced by sex hormones. For instance, females exposed in utero to greater-than-normal levels of male sex hormones have stronger-than-average spatial abilities; males with lower-than-normal levels of those same hormones have lower-than-average spatial abilities.

Spatial ability is correlated with throwing ability. An often-cited study had sixty-seven fourteen- to sixteen-year-old boys make twenty throws each at a canvas on which was drawn a series of five concentric circles from one to five feet in diameter. Their throws were to be both as fast and as accurate as possible, and the researchers recorded how far from the center of the circle each throw was, in both the vertical and the horizontal directions.

Each of the boys also completed a paper-and-pencil test of spatial ability called the Primary Mental Abilities Test, an intelligence test no longer in wide use. More modern testing of spatial abilities typically uses items like those shown in the next figure.

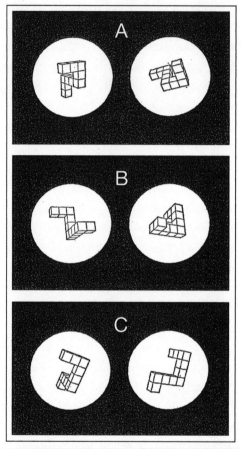

A test of visuospatial abilities. People are asked to judge whether the figure
on the right can be rotated such that it would be congruent with the
figure on the left. For the top two examples, the correct answer is "yes";
for the remaining example, the correct answer is "no."

*Reprinted with permission from Shepard, R. N., and Metzler, J. (1971). "Mental rotation of
three-dimensional objects." Science 171: 701–703. Copyright 1971 AAAS.*

If you have good spatial abilities, you can easily see that in panels A and B, the right-hand figure is a rotated version of the figure on the left, but that in panel C, the two figures are different—there is no way to rotate the right-hand figure so that it is congruent with the left-hand figure.

The study found that these kinds of spatial abilities were related to throwing ability. The better a boy was at these kinds of spatial tasks, the more accurate his throws were in the vertical direction. There was no relation between spatial ability and accuracy in the horizontal direction. This may make sense, when we remember that it is three-dimensional spatial processing that seems to be linked by sex. Left-right accuracy is essentially a one-dimensional judgment. Accuracy in the vertical dimension, which corresponds to distance, requires more of a judgment about movement in three-dimensional space. Indeed, a later study repeated the experiment and found the same result in the vertical direction, but also showed that spatial ability was associated with accuracy in the horizontal direction, but only with the target down on the ground, thus turning the throwing test into more of a three-dimensional task.

Were we to give a test like the one on page 88 to Mike Mussina, Pedro Martinez, and all the other pitchers who have made it to the major-league level, we would likely find that they outscore the average male by a substantial margin.

This finding also supports the conventional wisdom in baseball that it is easier to teach a pitcher to move his pitches around laterally (from the inside part of the plate to the outside part of the plate) than it is to teach him to move his pitches around vertically, up and down, in the strike zone. That is, if the ability to aim in the vertical direction is biologically determined, it will be more difficult to train. The ability to aim in the horizontal direction, not being so determined, may be more susceptible to the control of a teacher and less dependent on innate ability.

The researchers related their findings to notions about evolution this way:

> The existence of an X-linked behavioural trait in the present would constitute independent evidence for a sexual division of labour during the 99% of human history that men have been hunters. Certainly, directional orientation and memory for visual landmarks must have been required for a man to find his way back to the group. If, in addition, spatial ability were positively related with judgment of distance and throwing accuracy in males (for example, as regards such weapons as stones and spears), this could presumably have allowed them to hit game at greater distances, thereby making hunting less hazardous and resulting in longer-lived hunters as well as more meat.

Athletes' salaries show that strong throwing abilities put more meat on the table in modern times, too—in 2006 Mussina was taking home $19 million and Martinez nearly $15 million. Indeed, it may be no accident that sports involve so much throwing. Evolutionary theorists have supposed that evolution even endowed us with a predisposition to find throwing enjoyable, so that it was an activity in which young males would be likely to engage, thus practicing the ability for later hunting. Consistent with that observation, young males in modern preliterate societies have been observed to do much more throwing during play than young females.

Many evolutionary theorists have argued that around the same time that spatial abilities were developing in the nascent human brain, other features of the behavior of modern Homo sapiens were also emerging, including, for example, tool use, early language, and the ability to plan ahead over longer time periods. One theorist, for instance, suggests that throwing and these other behaviors all require preplanning of sequences of actions before they are carried out. Modern-day observations show that chimpanzees—our closest living relative in the evolutionary tree—also throw, but only relatively inaccurately and only to short distances. Our early ancestors may have moved from provoking herds to stampede by relatively short, imprecise throws of branches, to more precise throwing of stones to stun or injure, or maybe even occasionally kill, their prey. Over time, hunters with more accurate throwing skills would have selective advantages, maybe because they could provide for themselves better and more safely (throwing at dangerous animals from a longer distance) or maybe because hunting prowess was a way to win favor with females.

Better control of the arm for throwing could have then led to greater capabilities in the fashioning and use of tools, and the ability to precisely control the mechanisms of the arm and torso might have transferred to the ability to precisely control the jaws and lips, aiding in the development of language, and so on. To achieve a throw of a particular velocity and distance, each component of the overall movement must be coordinated at some higher level—how the wrist should move depends on what the elbow will do, which depends on the shoulder, and so on. Such coordination could in turn improve the neural machinery available for other tasks.

Baseball players throw from a pitching delivery, from a standard infielder's position, from their knees, across their bodies—in every one of these, the components of the movement will be different, but all the components will be coordinated. Such control must be hierarchical, in that some overriding planning process must guide all of the component elements—they cannot operate independently. Similarly, language use is hierarchical. The way you say the "sh" sound in "she" is different from the way you say it in "shoe" because control of vocal production coordinates the production of nearby sounds in a phenomenon known as *coarticulation*. Language is also hierarchical in the way that sentences are constructed; words in a sentence are not chained together, one after another, but are ordered based on a treelike (that is, hierarchical) structure of phrases and their constituents. Similarly, throwing requires top-down organization of the component movements. The way the shortstop's wrist moves depends on whether he is throwing across his body to second base after stopping a grounder up the middle, or from his knees to third base after he has made a diving stop in the hole. So throwing and language both have somewhat similar underlying requirements for sequencing ability, and may have a common evolutionary origin.

Evolutionary theory can help us understand how the ability to sequence an action like a strong throw at an animal, or at home plate, may have developed in our species over time, but it does not tell us much about how that sequencing actually takes place. Think of the range of motion in your shoulder, in your elbow, in your wrist, and in your fingers. Now, multiply all of those possibilities at each joint to get the conceivable range of the entire throwing motion. Standing in close to a target, standing a bit farther away, standing to the side—how, from all of those possibilities, is one particular motion, one particular sequence of actions in those joints, selected and planned? When throws miss the intended target, what went wrong in the sequence?

Using elaborate apparatus to monitor the movements of the shoulder, arm, wrist, and hand, some researchers set out to tackle this question, beginning with the issue of constraints—how, from the many possible positions that the arm and hand could take in making a throw, is one selected? What they found, by having a group of "accurate throwers" make several throws at each of nine targets arrayed in a three-by-three-foot square grid in front of them, was that the hand (and the rest of the arm) adopts a position close to what is likely the optimal position for throwing at a given target, and adopts that same position consistently each time it throws at that target. This suggests that the throwing control system might adopt this position in order to keep the wrist joint and the row of knuckles across the back of the hand, oriented in the same way with respect to gravity, perhaps because this maximizes the efficiency of the throw and the transfer of energy between hand and ball.

Whatever the reason these constraints were adopted, this consistency of hand orientation need not be the case, in principle. The hand could take on different positions relative to the rest of the arm at the time of ball release, as illustrated by Tom Seaver's advice to young pitchers to "try many different wrist positions in throwing the fastball. A slight turning of the wrist inward or outward will cause a different movement on the ball. Analyze and cultivate the feeling of that movement." In fact, when throwers were asked to turn their hands clockwise or counterclockwise at the time of the throw, they were readily able to do so, and thus added another degree of complexity to the throwing motion. As the report points out, this is exactly what pitchers do when they throw breaking pitches. And anyone learning to aim a curveball or slider will tell you that releasing the ball from the hand that way is far from the optimal way to throw, requires a great deal of practice to learn, and is fraught with error even after lots of practice by the very best pitchers—hence Billy Wagner hits Bernie Williams with a slider sometimes.

And watch Mike Mussina's smooth, classically compact delivery, and then compare that with Chad Bradford's insane-looking sidearm delivery. (Bradford came in to finally get the last out for the Mets in that horrible bottom of the ninth.) The system tends to choose a simple, well-constrained delivery, but it is not limited to that, and may instead adopt a position that conforms to other demands (hiding the ball, comfort, protection from injury, or just conformity to a well-developed habit).

Another difficult aspect of throwing is the timing of the release. Another early study shows that even for recreational players the timing of ball release must be fairly precisely controlled. Two different measures, the onset of opening the fingers and the release of the ball from the middle finger, showed that 95 percent of on-target throws left the hand within a window of time just ten one-thousandths of a second wide. Later studies would show that for more highly skilled throwers, that window is closer to seven one-thousandths of a second wide. Extrapolations from data like these show that to achieve the accuracy of a major-league pitcher, control is required to within one or two one-thousandths of a second. Again, this is consistent with what we know about pitching: pitchers and pitching coaches will tell you that release point is everything in controlling a pitch.

Another study ruled out two other potential causes of throwing errors. It could be that the fingers release the ball at the wrong time, it could be that one (or more) of the joints begins its movement at the wrong time, or it could be that one (or more) of the joints moves too slowly or too quickly once it does begin moving. Throwers were asked to throw tennis balls at a target one-and-a-half or three meters away. The researchers then related the degree of inaccuracy (in the vertical direction) of the throws to the pattern of joint and finger movements they measured, and found that inaccurate throws were related to the timing of ball release. Variations in the position and velocity of the other parts of the arm occurred but were not associated with errors. Instead, the time of release, as related to the time when the fingers began to rotate relative to the movement of other parts of the arm, predicted the magnitude of the error.

When Billy Wagner lost control of his pitches, it is likely that he lost control of his release point, rather than that part of his arm was moving the wrong way or at the wrong time. Even when Mussina and Martinez, who pitched brilliantly, missed the exact spot they were aiming for, they were likely just a bit off in their release point.

Again, it does not have to be this way. In dart throwing, for instance, accuracy seems to depend more on the speed and direction of the hand during the throw than on the precise time of release. Leighton Rees's instructions about throwing a dart bring this home: "It is vital, once you have found a comfortable grip, to duplicate it with every throw. . . . Keep your release simple, keep it smooth, keep it consistent. That is the secret. Make sure each release takes the same time." But darts are thrown at a much lower speed, so perhaps it makes sense that the mechanisms would be different. Because of the lower speed, darts have a longer time to drop due to gravity. This is just another reason not to compare pitching with dart throwing.

Because the timing of the opening of the fingers determines where the throw will go, it is possible that throwers hit targets at different heights or distances by changing the timing of the opening and closing of the fingers. A more recent study tested this idea by having throwers throw to targets at varying heights and distances. But it turns out that it is the angle of the fingers at ball release, rather than the timing of ball release, that changes in order to change the direction of the throw, for example when a shortstop throws to second as opposed to first base. Again, this helps the system solve the problem of having many ways to achieve the same ends. Even though a variety of combinations of movements and release times would all get the ball to the intended target, this result suggests that only the one variable, the direction of the fingers, is changed, thus simplifying the problem for whatever part of the brain controls throwing.

And though much is still not known about exactly how that control is achieved, one idea is that the timing is triggered by feedback from other parts of the throwing motion. The fingers might open a certain amount of time after the elbow or wrist has moved. To test this in another study, the throwing motion was "perturbed" in different ways. Sometimes, a rope attached to the subjects' arms unexpectedly was caught in a mechanism fixed behind them, so that their elbow was either prevented from extending altogether, and flexed instead, or so that the extension of the elbow was slowed. In neither case, however, was finger opening affected; it occurred anyway, and at its normal time. So finger opening would not appear to depend on the time of elbow extension.

The throwing motion was on other occasions perturbed by having subjects make several throws with a light, plastic ball, and then switch to a tennis ball that had been filled with concrete. Though people are fairly good at adjusting to the difference in weight, they don't adjust quite enough on the first throw with the heavy ball, and the wrist does not flex as quickly as it should, so the ball goes high. Even so, timing of finger opening was again unchanged, and thus would not appear to depend on the time that the wrist flexes, either.

The timing of all of these motions seems to rule out the use of this kind of feedback as well. The delays are too short—the report on this study reviews a range of evidence on estimates of the time it would take for a signal to travel up to the central nervous system from the arm and another signal to get back down to initiate a muscle movement. Depending on the type of measurement taken, the estimates ranged from about forty to two hundred milliseconds for feedback to arrive. In this experiment, finger opening was initiated about twenty milliseconds after elbow extension and about five milliseconds after the wrist began to flex, times that are far too short for finger movement to have been initiated by feedback. So although this study does not tell us how movement is controlled, it tells us one way that it is not controlled.

Another possibility that can be ruled out is the idea that some kind of central neural timer, a sort of mental metronome, is used to time the opening of the fingers such that at a given time during the throw, they spring open like a starting gate. In a couple of studies, the timing of relations between different parts of the throwing motion was investigated by having people throw at slow, medium, and fast speeds (which averaged about 20, 40, and 50mph, respectively). One idea about how people might control the speed of a throw is that they simply speed up or slow down the throwing motion—a fast throw is simply a slow one sped up, with all the same relative movements of the different parts of the arm during the sequence of the throw. The elbow, for instance, would move in the same direction and to the same degree, but do it faster in the faster throw. The research showed that this is true to an extent, but only for certain aspects of unskilled throwing (for throws made by the left arm in right-handed skilled throwers). For skilled throwing, it is hardly true at all. There were many differences in the angles and degree of movement of various parts of the arm in fast throws as compared with slow ones. The starting and finishing positions of the shoulder, as well as some rotations of the shoulder during forward movement, for instance, were quite different.

When the Yankee and Met pitchers warm up before entering the game, or before beginning an inning, by making softer, more casual tosses, they are not simply changing the speed of their delivery, they are changing the whole delivery. When a pitching coach like Leo Mazzone advises, "When I talk about throwing off the mound between starts, I'm referring to a 70 percent of max effort for 10-15 minutes," he may well be encouraging an effective technique, but it is not because the pitcher is using the same delivery he would use in a game, just slowed down a little. The delivery is different from the one performed at "max effort." Still, that may well be an effective practice regime, just as hitters taking batting practice with slower pitches is effective.

One exception to this finding was turned up in another similar study, which showed that the velocity of the fingers opening to release the ball did vary with the speed of the throw. In this limited part of the throwing motion, "a fast throw was the same as a slow throw sped-up." The degree of movement of the finger was the same from the time it started until the ball was released, but the time that movement took was longer for slower throws. So, no, the fingers do not spring open like a starting gate. Rather, they seem to open in synchrony with the changes in the spatial position of the hand as it moves through the throw. This suggests that control of finger opening is governed not by some kind of timer, but rather by a mental model of the spatial structure of the throwing motion. Finger opening may not be a matter so much of when, as of where.

So coaches are right about release point—it's crucial. One thing they may not be right about, at least in a literal sense, is the notion of wrist snap. One instructional book says, "When throwing the ball, the pitcher's wrist pulls back and then snaps forward to a bent position." No less an authority than Tom Seaver writes, "Snap your wrist like a whip." But the wrist does not really snap like this during a fast throw. If you think of the position where your hand sticks straight out from your forearm as zero degrees, about twenty-five milliseconds before ball release, the wrist moves from around minus fifty degrees (bent back about as far as it will go) to around minus twenty, still bent backward a little bit, at the time the ball is released. Another twenty milliseconds or so after ball release, the hand nears zero degrees, then recoils back to minus twenty again (remember, the throwing motion is violent), and then returns again to near zero. The wrist never really flexes.

Some other studies may hold the clue as to why. Incredible "back forces" are put on the wrist as the rest of the arm drives it forward. The throwing motion itself is pushing the wrist into the extension position. Partly this is due to the ball. One study showed that the amount of force depended on the weight of the ball, and the degree of force with which the fingers pressed on the ball changed accordingly. Even so, control of finger opening remained precise (except for that very first throw when a heavier ball is introduced, but even there, it was close). Grip force also increases steadily during the backswing and beginning of forward motion of the arm.

All of this may be due to the exploitation by skilled throwers of what are called "interaction forces," which are forces produced passively at one site in the arm by the actions of other parts of the arm. Some of the forces generated at the wrist, for instance, are the consequence of rotation of the elbow. Unskilled throwers do not appear to take advantage of the interaction forces in ways that would allow them to throw faster. But skilled throwers do. The actions reflected in increased finger and grip pressures may be part of the way that these interaction forces are controlled.

Interaction forces also must be "damped" as the throw is completed so as to prevent injury. Faster throws do not lead to more violent snapping (or any snapping, really) of the wrist. This suggests that this braking might be controlled, again, by some kind of internal model of the throw that programs the actions of the various parts of the arm according to the distance, speed, weight of the ball, and so on.

Many other parts of the brain are at work, too, and are likely the causes of problems like the ones Billy Wagner had against the Yankees that day. We will consider this kind of problem in more detail in the chapter on streaks and slumps, but we cannot overlook a question here as obvious as "What happens to a guy like Rick Ankiel or Chuck Knoblauch or Mackey Sasser who suddenly loses the ability to throw accurately?" Of course, we can talk only in generalities—one case may be very different from another. For instance, Ankiel was quite young and inexperienced when his problems emerged; Knoblauch and Sasser were veterans. And many other differences in experience and personality may have contributed to the problem. But there are some well-known psychological pitfalls that might cause or contribute to cases like theirs.

The general trap is thinking too much, but there are different ways that thinking can hurt. One is thinking "don't," as in "don't throw a wild pitch" or "don't throw it over the first baseman's head and into the stands." Cognitive psychologists have done study after study that demonstrates that when we think about a concept or a perception or an action, sometimes called a representation, or a *schema,* a corresponding part of the mind is activated, and that this activity can influence later thought and behavior. For example, if you do a simple task like reading words flashed on a computer screen one at a time, and at one point read the word "DOCTOR," and then a short time later the word "NURSE" appears, you will respond to "NURSE" faster than you would have if the earlier word had been "TRUCK" or something else unrelated to "NURSE." This *priming effect,* as it is known, helps show how activating a schema can influence how we think and respond later. More recently, brain imaging studies have shown that having people imagine a visual scene activates many of the same areas in the brain that are active when people actually see such a scene. So we can suppose that thinking "don't throw a wild pitch" activates the wild pitch schema, which then may take control of the throwing motion.

Another way thinking too much can hurt is by interrupting the smooth control of the throwing motion. If a player begins to question his ability to throw, he may try to make sure that he does everything right, that at each step in the delivery, his hips, shoulders, elbows, and so on are in the right place and moving in the right direction at the right speed. But recall how quickly the throwing motion must be completed. Attempting to monitor it as it runs off might be possible only if it is interrupted midway through execution, or broken down into a chain of separate movements rather than run off as a single, fluid motion.

The next time you tie your shoes or button a button, try to monitor each component of the overall movement, as if you have to write an instruction book on how to get dressed. A movement you have completed without fail thousands of times will suddenly become cumbersome and error prone. One of the oft-repeated claims about Knoblauch's problems was that if the play was going to be a close one, so that he had to field the ball and throw quickly, he would likely not make a throwing error, but if he had time to think, an error was more likely. The bad news for pitchers, of course, is that there is *always* time to think.

What the thrower wants is for that motor program to take over and run off as it has been practiced those thousands upon thousands of times. As we have seen, even minor errors in that program, say releasing the ball one-thousandth of a second too early or too late, can lead to an inaccurate throw for a major-league pitcher. But those errors are a routine function of a motor system that, if left alone, will on average perform well. When that system is interfered with, by an inappropriate prime or by overmonitoring, it will likely misfire, and Bernie Williams will take one in the thigh. Most times, these problems can be corrected. Wagner was able to go out the very next day, the Sunday rubber game with the Yankees, and successfully complete the save. But sometimes, likely for very idiosyncratic reasons, the player may simply not be able to stop thinking too much.

CHAPTER FOUR

Choosing Up Sides

THE ANNUAL DRAFTS FOR PROFESSIONAL BASKETBALL AND football are held in front of live crowds in New York City and are televised with coverage by a team of analysts who, along with dozens of other journalists, talk and write about the event for weeks. Baseball's drafts, by contrast, are held by conference call.

There are lots of differences between the baseball draft and the others that account for the difference in media attention. Baseball teams select from a much larger pool of players that includes high school students, junior college students, and juniors and seniors at four-year colleges, most of whom are unknown to the national baseball audience. Basketball and football select primarily from the pool of college players, and of those, mainly players from big-time Division I programs. The baseball draft is fifty rounds long (with some additional "supplemental" rounds during which teams that lose players to free agency are given additional picks), as opposed to two rounds for the NBA draft and seven for the NFL. In baseball, draft picks cannot be traded as they can in other sports, further taking some of the drama out of the proceedings.

In baseball, a player seldom makes it to the major leagues

the year he is drafted. In fact, that has happened only nineteen times, most recently when Xavier Nady joined the Padres right after being drafted out of college. Even top draft picks often take a few years to reach the show. And baseball seems to be more of a hit-or-miss proposition than the other sports. There is definitely no certainty in the football and basketball drafts, either; some of the picks pan out, and some do not. But the uncertainty may be greater in baseball because many players, especially the ones drafted out of high school, will need several years more to develop. Even without considering the possibility of injury, it is obviously more difficult to make projections that far into the future than it is to determine whether a player can be of more immediate help to a team.

It should be no surprise, then, that baseball organizations have a difficult time deciding on their selections, particularly in early rounds. High draft picks command large signing bonuses and an investment of time and resources in the minor leagues while they are developing. A look at the history of first-round draft picks quickly reveals a number of decisions that, in hindsight, appear ludicrous. In 1980, as the Mets were trying to decide whom to select with the first pick of the draft, they were trying to guard against a mistake previous management had made in 1966, when they drafted a catcher named Steve Chilcott one pick before the Kansas City A's took Reggie Jackson with the second pick. Chilcott never made it to the major leagues, and is the only number one pick since the draft started in 1965 who did not make it (through 1998—some of the number one picks since then have already arrived in the majors; at this writing the rest are still in the minor leagues). The Mets were trying to decide between Darryl Strawberry and Billy Beane. Some in the organization wanted to draft Beane, but Frank Cashen, who had been hired as general manager only a few months before, decided they would go with Strawberry. As it turned out, they got Beane, too. The Mets had the twenty-third pick of the first round, as well—compensation for a free agent they had lost—and used that pick on Beane.

Strawberry would later have all kinds of well-publicized problems, but in 1980, no one could fault Cashen for drafting him. He was eighteen, six feet four inches tall, a standout in basketball and baseball while at Crenshaw High School in Los Angeles, and, as reported by George Vecsey in *The New York Times*, had wowed scouts, one of whom told Vecsey that Strawberry was "the best prospect I've seen in the last 30 years." Later that summer, Strawberry received the Tanqueray Award, which recognized the top amateur athlete in the nation. And before off-field problems sidetracked his career, Strawberry was for several years one of the top hitters in the game, an All-Star from 1984 to 1991, and one of the key players in the Mets' World Series win in 1986.

Whereas Strawberry succeeded on the field, Beane failed. Strawberry joined the Mets in 1983, and though Beane enjoyed some success in the minor leagues, he never made it in the majors. His career ended after six seasons in which he accumulated 315 plate appearances and a .219 average with just three home runs. But Beane enjoyed success of another kind. In 2003, Michael Lewis's best seller *Moneyball* made Beane famous in some quarters, infamous in others. The book tells the story of how Beane, after failing to find the success predicted for him as a player, went on to work in the Oakland A's front office, eventually rising to the position of general manager. There he continued developing a philosophy adopted by his predecessor, Sandy Alderson, of using statistical analyses to guide both off-field and on-field decisions. Among other things, this approach focuses more on on-base percentage than batting average in evaluating the quality of hitters, and bucks the conventional wisdom on situational bunting and base stealing. *Moneyball* instantly made Beane one of the chief advocates of this philosophy, and the most well-recognized target of its opponents.

Lewis says that he wrote *Moneyball* because he wondered how it was that the A's were achieving the success they were with a payroll that was so small by comparison to those of other teams. The answer to his question was Beane, the A's general manager, and his embrace of statistical analyses of player value, which helped him find value in the market for players where other teams were missing it. Lewis's is a compelling narrative that traces the development of baseball analysis from the early work of statistics guru Bill James through the embodiment of that analysis in a comprehensive philosophy that dictated everything from how often the A's would use the sacrifice bunt and the steal to how much they would pay for different kinds of talent, and it makes Beane look like the genius he probably is. His record speaks for itself. From 2001 to 2006 (Beane took over in 1998, so we can assume that by 2001 the team was clearly shaped by his thinking), the A's had more regular season wins (573) than anyone but the Yankees (592), and had spent only $300 million on payroll, to the Yankees' $977 million. (If I'm paying the bills, that half-a-billion dollars and change that he saves me makes Beane a genius.) The Yankees won nineteen games more than Oakland, but at a cost of about $35 million per win. In fact, during that period, the A's outspent only seven teams, and only outspent the lowest-spending team, the Tampa Bay Devil Rays, by $95 million. Thus, twenty-one teams outspent the A's but won fewer games, often many fewer: the Mets, for instance, spent more than twice as much on payroll during those six years, but won ninety-nine fewer games. The criticism of Beane has been that the A's have not won in the post-season (until they won a Division Series in 2006) and did not win their division in 2004 and 2005. Although the Yankees have fared better in those terms, winning their division in each of those six years and some Division and American League Championship Series (but not the World Series), they have not had the success that one might expect of a team that outspends its nearest competitor by more than three to one.

Not everyone was so impressed; a lot of the attention garnered by *Moneyball* was negative, from various general managers, scouts, and commentators who preferred a more traditional approach to the game. One of the disputes raised by *Moneyball* was its claim that the A's system of player evaluation was superior to that of most other teams, which is what made it possible for the Oakland management team to find all that undervalued talent. Again, as Beane's career itself demonstrates, it has historically been very difficult to project whether a young baseball player will develop into a major league–caliber talent. Plenty of very high draft picks never make it to the majors, and there are many well-known cases of players selected near the end of the draft who turn into stars at the major-league level (Mike Piazza was selected in the sixty-second round of the 1988 amateur draft). When looking at the range of talent available, teams have to decide on what basis they will judge which players to draft (or make a trade for, or sign as a free agent) and which players to avoid.

Obviously, there is a range of potential ability in the pool of available players. Some players will go on to be stars, some will be steady everyday players, some will have fine careers as journeyman role players, some will get close, but not quite make it, and many—most—will not pan out at all. To the extent that they can account for this *variability* in player production, teams can make better projections about how good a prospect might eventually be. Accounting for the variability in one aspect, like batting average, means identifying other aspects that can sort batting averages along some meaningful dimension. For statisticians, the variable to be predicted is the *criterion*; the variable being used to make the prediction is, naturally enough, the *predictor*. For instance, we know that right-handed batters generally hit better against left-handed pitchers than right-handed pitchers. Sure, for some right-handed hitters, the opposite is true, and the pitcher's throwing hand makes more of a difference for some hitters (who are thus more likely to be platooned at a position with another hitter) than it does for others. But on average, righties bat better against lefties. The throwing hand of the pitcher is thus a reliable predictor of some of the variability in the criterion variable batting average. In general, the more such predictors we can identify, the more variability we can explain. Branch Rickey famously said that "luck is the residue of design." Rickey's definition matches the statistician's: in statistics, design is how much of the variability in the outcome variable we can account for with a model constructed from predictor variables; luck is that variability that is left over, everything that we cannot explain. In statistics, the difference between the actual observed value of the criterion variable and the value predicted is called the *residual*. Luck is the residue of design.

In baseball, we are interested in variability between players—why was Darryl Strawberry better than Billy Beane—and we are interested in variability within players (or teams of players)—why are there streaks and slumps, why does it matter whether the game is at home or away, is a player's performance affected by things like trades and free agency? This chapter focuses on the first of these sources of variability; the next chapter will take on the second.

What teams are trying to do—whether they think of it in these terms or not—when they decide what players to draft is to identify predictor variables that account for variability in certain criterion variables. *Moneyball* made the claim that the A's were succeeding on both sides of the equation: they had done a better job of identifying the criterion and predictor variables. On-base percentage and slugging percentage are only two of many possible offensive statistics on which the A's could have focused. Once they selected those criterion variables, they had to find good predictors, and finally settled on college hitting statistics as among the best of the ones available. Just as there are many potential criterion variables, there are many possible predictors. Some teams rely heavily on ratings made by scouts, especially when scouting high school players, for whom statistics are necessarily less meaningful because the level of competition can be so different from one high school game to the next.

Some teams also rely on psychological variables to try to project how productive a player will be. Part of the *Moneyball* story is the resistance of many people who have been around the game a long time to rely on anything other than the judgment of scouts and other "baseball men." According to Dave Ritterspusch of the Baltimore Orioles, there is a "tendency by people in baseball to not want to go beyond the physical. They don't want to hear about, can't see beyond, physical ability. The same people believe the earth is flat."

Psychologists have long been involved in the assessment of talent, the quantification of the ways in which people differ, and the recruitment and assignment of personnel: a subfield of psychology known collectively as *psychometrics* is devoted to the development of ways to measure psychological variables that are relevant to various judgments that we make about people. Intelligence and other aptitude tests were developed to help account for variability in, among other things, academic performance; colleges and universities have students take the SAT or the ACT because those tests account for some of the variability in the student's academic performance in college. Measures of various kinds have been developed to assess for symptoms of psychological disorders; clinicians use these tests to help in the understanding and treatment of their clients' problems. Personality tests have been developed to measure everything from extraversion to the need for cognition, a trait that leads people to seek out intellectual challenges; companies use these tests to help select people for roles in their workforces. Not surprisingly, tests have also been developed to identify traits that are associated with success in sports.

Quickness of Eye and Hand

Some of the early attempts at using psychological measures to identify the traits of successful players could not have seen the differences between Darryl Strawberry and Billy Beane because they focused on perceptual and motor abilities that both men seem to have in common. Such attempts to put psychological science to use in player selection date back at least to 1921, when an article about one such study appeared in *Popular Science Monthly*. The cover of the issue features a photo of Babe Ruth adorned in the garb of the psychological laboratory of the period. The Babe is wearing a pneumatic tube around his chest and swinging a bat outfitted with electrodes that measure the beginning and ending of a swing. The headline reads, "Why Babe Ruth Is Greatest Home Run Hitter" and the article presents the results of tests on Ruth conducted at the Columbia University Laboratory of Psychology.

Babe Ruth in the Columbia University psychology laboratory.

As *Popular Science Monthly*'s story demonstrates, from the early days of baseball on, the public has had a keen desire to get inside the minds of the best players. We want the nature of the magical powers that the rest of us can only dream of possessing. As it turns out, Babe Ruth, not surprisingly, did have some mental abilities that put him in a "league of his own." For example, the time it took him to react to a visual signal was much faster than normal (160 one-thousandths of a second to the normal 180). He also reacted much faster to sound than the average person (150 one-thousandths of a second to the normal 160), and measurements of his eye-hand coordination ranked

111

him at a level better than 98.8 percent of the population. His ability to perceive information in a glance was much better than normal, too: when cards with different numbers of dots scattered on them were flashed rapidly, Ruth could accurately count up to twelve dots—the average person peaks at around eight. When the cards had letters on them, he could identify six of eight when the average person could get only about four. As Hugh Fullerton, the author of the article, noted, "The secret of Babe Ruth's ability to hit is clearly revealed in these tests. His eye, his ear, his brain, his nerves all function more rapidly than do those of the average person. Further, the coordination between eye, ear, brain and muscle is much nearer perfection than that of the normal healthy man." Fullerton then dreams breathlessly of a day when scientific "ivory hunters" would "organize a clinic, submit candidates to the comprehensive tests undergone by Ruth, and discover whether or not other Ruths exist." (In 2006, *GQ* persuaded St. Louis Cardinals slugger Albert Pujols to visit some laboratories at Washington University, where he matched the Babe as an outlier in basic perceptual and motor skills.)

It has been over eighty years since those first tests were done on Ruth, and while psychologists still may be some way from creating Fullerton's clinic, they are coming gradually closer to an understanding of who becomes a superstar and why. The differences that the *Popular Science Monthly* article first reported have continued to be observed in studies over the years. One difficulty with many of these studies, however, is that they have not been designed to tease apart the causal link between fast reaction times or other keen perceptual abilities and success in baseball. It could be, as we naturally assume, that having a fast reaction time is a prerequisite for baseball success. But it could also be that experience and practice in baseball lead to baseball success, and reaction time improves along the way.

For instance, another study, this one of baseball players in western Australia, found that the more advanced players were much faster and much more accurate, on average, than less advanced players at making reaction-timed judgments about videotaped pitches. But the more advanced players also had an average of more than thirteen years of experience playing ball, whereas the less advanced players had less than eight years' experience on average. It could be that had the two groups of players been tested before they ever started playing baseball, we would have found the same kind of reaction time difference, that difference being a prerequisite for success. Or it could be that at that early stage, there would have been little difference between the groups, and the difference emerged over the years of additional practice by the better players. In that case, the difference would be one of expertise, rather than one of native psychological quickness. Indeed, another study found that reaction time differences between players and nonplayers disappeared when both groups were given a lot of practice with the reaction time task.

Even so, among a sample of players in the AA Southern League, reaction time did predict about 7 percent of the variability in batting average. Corner infielders and outfielders had the fastest reaction times, which is what we would expect since those positions are typically associated with better hitting ability. Middle infielders were next fastest, then pitchers, and then catchers. Now, of course, there would also be some variability in reaction time within these groups, just was we see variability in batting average within those groups. These are just averages. But the general trend is for players with faster reaction times to have better batting averages. Considering what we know about hitting (see Chapter 1), this makes sense—the faster a player can react, the longer he can wait to begin his swing, giving him a longer look at the pitch.

Baseball players' eyes are better, too. A study of several visual abilities showed that players are superior to the normal population. Instead of 20/20 vision, more than 75 percent have 20/15 or better, and 42 percent have 20/12.5 or better (at twenty feet, they can discriminate, say, the difference between an *o* and a *c* that the rest of us would have to stand at 12.5 feet away to see). Fifty-eight percent of players, as opposed to 18 percent of the rest of the population, rate "superior" in stereoacuity, which is the ability to perceive fine gradations of depth in stereoscopes, like the popular View-Master toys. The very large majority of baseball players are also better than average in perceiving contrast between a figure and the background.

Baseball players also appear to be less susceptible to the Pulfrich Phenomenon, which is named after the German physicist who first explained it in 1922 (despite the fact that he could not himself see the illusion because he had sight in only one eye). The illusion was originally demonstrated with a pendulum that was swinging along a line perpendicular to the viewer's line of sight. When it was viewed under normal conditions, the viewer simply saw a pendulum swinging back and forth. But when it was viewed with one eye behind a filter (like a sunglass lens), the pendulum appeared to swing around on an elliptical path, rather than simply oscillate back and forth. A related illusion that might be easier to try yourself can be seen when looking at a television that is tuned to an open channel (so that you see what is usually called "snow"), again with one eye behind a filter (a lens from a pair of sunglasses will do). People see two sheets of flickering dots, one moving to the left, the other moving to the right. Ballplayers are less susceptible to the Pulfrich illusion than the rest of us, suggesting that their depth perception abilities are greater than normal. Also, the threshold for seeing the illusion is higher for major-league than minor-league players, and an index of the threshold for seeing the illusion is a good predictor of a major-league player's batting average (accounting for nearly 50 percent of the variability in a sample of eighteen players).

Perhaps the most important form of acuity for baseball, or even for vision in general, is dynamic acuity, the ability to see detail in an object that moves in relation to the viewer, like a fastball. Elite athletes in general, and especially elite baseball players, have especially good dynamic visual acuity relative to other athletes, who in turn have better dynamic acuity than nonathletes. Ted Williams, for instance, is often said to have been able to read the label on a rotating 78rpm record. Though he denied that rumor, his dynamic acuity is certain to have been better than most. Techniques for measuring dynamic acuity vary, and there are no agreed-upon standard methods or standards of comparison. As technology improves, so likely will measurement of this potentially all-important ability. It is known that dynamic acuity is not necessarily correlated with static acuity (the kind measured with the usual eye chart).

Which of the player's eyes is dominant may also be related to hitting ability. Because each eye gives a slightly different view of the world, when we sight an object, one eye's view is dominant. You can determine which of your eyes is dominant by, with both eyes open, holding up a thumb and lining it up between your eyes and a point in the distance (you may notice the two different views of the thumb, but line it up quickly and without thinking about the two different views). Then, holding your thumb steady, close one eye at a time. For most people, the thumb will stay lined up with the chosen point for one eye or the other. If it is lined up for your right eye, you are right-eye dominant. If the thumb is just to the left of the point with the right eye, and just to the right with the left eye, then you have central dominance, in which the contributions of the eyes are balanced. If it is lined up for your left eye, you are left-eye dominant.

Although an early study turned up no relation between hitting and eye dominance, a more recent one found that eye dominance may influence hitting ability after all. In a sample of nonplayers, the dominant eye was on the same side of the body as the preferred hand for 65 percent of the people—this is called uncrossed dominance. People with crossed-eye dominance— that is, the dominant eye was on the opposite side of the body from the dominant hand—made up 18 percent of the sample, and the remaining 17 percent had central dominance. In a sample of college hitters, only 40 percent had uncrossed dominance, but 35 percent had crossed dominance, and 26 percent were central dominant. Looking at performance on the field, crossed-eye hitters outperformed uncrossed, and central dominant hitters were best of all.

The authors of the study warn that trying to change the pattern of eye dominance is dangerous, and can lead to permanent double vision and other problems. But young hitters might consider changing the side of the plate they hit from, so that people with dominant right eyes bat left-handed and vice versa.

There are other considerations when it comes to which side of the plate to hit from, however. Which of the player's hands is dominant will also influence his hitting ability. Using the player's throwing hand as indication of left- or right-handedness, a recent study found that, of the 3,355 hitters (pitchers excluded) with more than 502 at bats, 269 were switch-hitters, 2,027 batted right-handed, and 1,059 batted left-handed. It has long been known that left-handed hitters have an advantage in baseball. They stand closer to first base than right-handed hitters, and at least historically, many right-field fences were closer than left-field fences. (For example, the Brooklyn Dodgers' Ebbets Field was 297 feet down the right-field line and 348 feet down the left; the Pittsburgh Pirates' Forbes Field was 300 feet down the right-field line, and 365 feet down the left.) And left-handed hitters face right-handed pitchers more often than right-handed hitters face left-handed pitchers. The study confirms the advantage gained by all of these factors: left-handed hitters as a group outperform right-handers in batting average, slugging percentage, and home runs. They also walked more than right-handers, but the result for strikeouts was more complex, and perhaps suggestive of how hand preference relates to the coordination of action between a preferred and a nonpreferred hand.

An interesting result of this study was what it showed about the choices players make in which side of the plate to hit from. There was an enormous difference between players who threw left and those who threw right. Left-handed throwers also hit left-handed, almost universally. Only about 4 percent of the left-handed throwers chose to hit from the right side of the plate, and another 4 percent to switch-hit. For right-handed throwers, however, 22 percent chose to hit left-handed, and 9 percent chose to switch-hit. Again, this makes sense given the advantages that left-handed hitters have in baseball.

But within the group of left-handed hitters, there were two

groups of players, those hitting with their preferred hand on top (left-handed throwers) and those with their preferred hand on the bottom (right-handed throwers). Because of the predominance of right-handers in the population, there have actually been more right-handed left-handed hitters (about 60 percent of the total) than there have been left-handed. This provided a very interesting comparison of how handedness relates to motor control (the opposite comparison, of right- and left-handed hitters batting from the right side, was untenable, given the very small number of players who threw left but batted right). The left-handed throwers outperformed the right-handed throwers in batting average, slugging percentage, and home runs. But the right-handed throwers outperformed the left-handed throwers in walks and strikeouts.

The authors liken this to the backhand and forehand strokes in tennis. The backhand is more "closed," with the player tending to face away from the net; the forehand is "open," with the player facing to the net. Closed swings have a more limited range of motion (and are thus somewhat more controlled). The trade-off is that open swings, with their wider range of motion, generate more power. The hitter has a choice of stance, of course, and we see both relatively open and relatively closed stances. For a right-hander hitting from the left side, the open, forehand type of swing would rely more on his nonpreferred left hand, but the closed, backhand type of swing would rely more on his preferred right hand. So because the right-hander tends to adopt the more controlled backhand stroke, where the left-hander tends to adopt the more powerful forehand stroke, we see find that right-handers have a bit more control (more walks, fewer strikeouts) and the left-handers have a bit more power.

The Psychology of Baseball

Personality Differences

All the studies of reaction time and visual perception tell us how Darryl Strawberry and Billy Beane differ from the rest of us. As Dave Ritterspusch of the Baltimore Orioles said to me, "These guys are freaks. It's roughly one male in every two million who is capable of playing baseball at the major-league level." Aside from the obvious physical differences—Strawberry and Beane are faster and stronger and quicker than the rest of us—elements of athleticism encompass psychological differences. Strawberry and Beane perceive the world more rapidly, they make decisions more rapidly, and they organize and guide their movements more rapidly.

But another question then emerges: how are Strawberry and Beane different from each other? As the debate in the Mets front office about who to draft makes clear, at the beginnings of their respective careers, they were valued roughly equally by those who judge young baseball talent. Both were judged to be "five tool" (hitting for average, hitting for power, speed, fielding ability, and throwing arm) prospects, and both likely had many of the psychological traits required, too, such as the fast reactions and keen perceptual abilities that allow quick responses to different kinds of pitches. Both were expected to become stars. But Beane and Strawberry differed in important ways. Personality differences, for example, may have played a critical role in the ultimate destinations of the two Mets prospects.

Strawberry's major-league debut was on May 7, 1983, and he faced Cincinnati Reds ace Mario Soto. Strawberry struck out three times and fouled out once, but even so, he said afterward that he was "not nervous, just hypered-up." His difficulties at the plate continued through July—on July 11, he stepped to the plate in the eighth inning with the score tied 5–5, none out and a runner on first, having already struck out twice and with his batting average at .198. He told reporters he looked to the third base coach expecting the bunt sign, but didn't get it. "My reaction was, 'Good.' Then I thought about hitting one out of the park and winning the game." And he did. When asked if the homer boosted his confidence at all, Strawberry answered, "I'd say encouragement rather than confidence. I've always got the confidence. I know I'm going to hit plenty more in situations like that." And he did. He finished the season with a .257 average and twenty-six home runs in 420 at bats and won Rookie of the Year. When he faced Soto again on Opening Day in 1984, Strawberry went to the plate wanting to prove to himself that "I can hit anybody," and he did, homering on Soto's third pitch.

In its description of a rare home run hit by Beane when he played for Detroit, *Moneyball* suggests an answer to the question about how Strawberry and Beane differ. Beane was acting as a "foil" in a simulated game set up for a starting pitcher about to return to the lineup from an injury. All eyes were on the pitcher, and all minds were on his rehabilitation, when to everyone's astonishment, Beane parked a home run in the upper deck of Tiger Stadium. As Lewis figures it, in this no-pressure situation, Beane's raw athletic talent could show through. But when the pressure was on in a real game, that talent disappeared. Lewis wrote, "Inside a batter's box he experienced a kind of claustrophobia. The batter's box was a cage designed to crush his spirit." Beane eventually realized that whatever physical talents he possessed, he lacked something—something mental— that he needed to be a major-league hitter.

Why was Beane crushed by the pressure of the batting box, whereas for Strawberry, the batter's box was no problem? Based on the Mets' difficulties in deciding whom to draft, we can reasonably say that Beane and Strawberry had roughly similar physical talents. How do two players so nearly equal in ability fare so differently?

The comparison between Beane and Strawberry is no fluke—players judged (by their position in the amateur draft) to be of roughly similar ability quite often fare very differently. Ritterspusch, director of baseball information systems for the Orioles, notes that major-league baseball teams spend a lot of money scouting amateur players, then combine to spend about $50 million a year on the signing bonuses paid to first-round draft choices, and then spend another small fortune on the minor-league systems in which they will see whether those players will become major league–level talents.

Ritterspusch was one of the first in baseball management to capitalize on the importance of psychological differences among players. He started as scouting director for the Orioles in 1973, the same year that a psychologist named William Winslow began testing players for Major League Baseball. The potential value of the test made an impression on Ritterspusch that year, because it was one of the reasons that he chose Eddie Murray in the third round of the '73 draft. Success like that, even if it were only accidental, will naturally make an impression. But, over the succeeding years, as he monitored the relation between a player's score on Winslow's test and that player's ultimate success in professional baseball, Ritterspusch accumulated enough evidence to convince himself that Eddie Murray's Hall of Fame career was no lucky accident, just as the divergent baseball trajectories of Billy Beane and Darryl Strawberry were no accident. Ritterspusch believes that Murray's success was completely predictable from his psychological profile.

Murray was drafted young; as a high school senior he was

a year younger than many of the other players available in the draft. Perhaps this is why there was little interest in him from most other teams. When he later had a chance to look at other teams' draft lists from that year, Ritterspusch found that Murray was not high on any of them. But Murray's profile on Winslow's test made him attractive to the Orioles: he was reserved, a quality that Ritterspusch hypothesizes other teams incorrectly interpreted as a lack of drive, but Murray was also composed, and perhaps "just a little hostile." When Ritterspusch went to negotiate with Murray in East L.A., he got some confirmation of his judgment of Murray's psychological makeup when he found that Murray's mother, in particular, seemed to embody the same traits. He saw that she ran a taut ship, and found that she proved to be a tough negotiator.

Though the Orioles replaced him as scouting director in 1976 when the team's management changed hands, Ritterspusch stayed in touch with Winslow and collected the profiles of players like Barry Larkin, Scott Rolen, and Matt Williams, and pitchers like Roger Clemens and John Smoltz. One of the other players Ritterspusch selected in 1973 was Mike Flanagan, who also had a strong psychological profile and would also go on to a productive career, which included a Cy Young Award in 1979. After serving as pitching coach and broadcaster for the Orioles since his retirement as a player in 1992, Flanagan was named in 2003 to be the Orioles vice president for baseball operations. He rehired Ritterspusch, who in the meantime had entered the military and risen to the rank of colonel and also spent some time with the Department of Labor, and who brought back to the Orioles his respect for psychological testing, which had continued to grow while he was away from the game. All that time, Ritterspusch was maintaining in his basement that collection of profiles he was getting from William Winslow, following players as they rose through the ranks of professional baseball, or failed to do so. By the time he got back to the Orioles, he was more convinced than ever of the value of Winslow's Athletic Motivation Inventory (AMI).

Winslow was not the original author of the test, but had recognized its potential value to organized sports and purchased the rights to it from the psychologists who developed it. It was a moneymaker until regulations deriving from the federal law known as Title IX began to be enforced in the late 1970s; the law required equal opportunity for male and female athletes in colleges and high schools. Programs that had once been able to afford Winslow's test were suddenly scrambling for money to fund new programs for female athletes and thus no longer able to afford the AMI. Since the market for it collapsed, the AMI has been sold only by word of mouth, but all the major professional sports organizations use it to some degree. Frank Marcos of the Major League Scouting Bureau describes the test as "a crucial element of an evaluation" of a prospect. In 2005, twenty of the thirty major-league teams agreed enough to lead them to subscribe to Winslow's report.

The AMI was originally written in the 1960s by two professors, Bruce Ogilvie and Thomas Tutko, and a graduate student, Leland Lyon, at San Jose State College (now University). Ogilvie and Tutko were building reputations as leading sports psychologists—Ogilvie, for instance, is called by some "the father of applied sports psychology." The trio's interest in athletes and sports was more than academic. According to Winslow, Tutko and Lyon had played baseball and Ogilvie had been a wrestler, and all three were eager to apply the scientific method to their love of sports. Ogilvie and Tutko started the Institute for the Study of Athletic Motivation in 1963, and began by studying "problem athletes," work that culminated in 1966 with their book *Problem Athletes and How to Handle Them.*

Part of the motivation for the development of the AMI was the pattern of results that Ogilvie and Tutko obtained with those athletes who "displayed such severe emotional reactions to stress that we had serious doubts about the basic value of athletic competition." The early picture they had was one in which competitive sports is debilitating, leaving the athlete depressed, anxious, deceptive, uncooperative, or compromised in some other way. To get a better view of the whole picture, they decided to expand their work to include a wide range of athletes, and by the early 1970s they had tested about fifteen thousand athletes at a range of levels and in a variety of sports. The picture was entirely different after they had generated a more representative sample. They concluded that "the higher the achievement, the greater the probability the athlete would have emotional maturity or control. Sport is like most other activities—those who survive tend to have stronger personalities." Sports, according to Ogilvie and Tutko, is an intense selection mechanism, in which athletes must quickly evolve and cope, lest failure on the playing field winnow them from the population. "A young athlete often must face in hours or days the kind of pressure that occurs in the life of the achievement-oriented man over several years. The potential for laying bare the personality structure of the individual is considerable. When the athlete's ego is deeply invested in sports achievement, very few of the [psychological] protective mechanisms provide adequate or sustaining cover. . . . Under such intense pressure, with threats from so many different directions, personality flaws manifest themselves quickly."

Lyon's master's thesis, completed in 1972, was devoted to development of the AMI and built on the work discussed in Ogilvie and Tutko's book on problem athletes. At that stage, about two thousand athletes into their testing, they had identified a range of 150 personality features that might be relevant for success in sports, but noted that their research was showing that there was a small set of traits that appeared with some consistency in successful athletes. With testing and development, they ultimately arrived at a list of 11 personality traits that were relevant to athletic performance.

Further refinement led to the Athletic Success Inventory, a 190-item personality test, and the somewhat shorter, 130-item Athletic Success Profile. The tests included a random mix of questions designed to measure each of the eleven traits, along with questions that assessed accuracy and objectivity. The accuracy questions were designed to ensure that the athlete understood the test items and how to respond to the test. If there were any problems, for example if the athlete did not read English well, the test should yield a low accuracy score. The objectivity questions were designed to assess for any self-serving bias. Of course, athletes asked by a scouting agency to take one of these tests want to present themselves in the best possible light. The tests include questions designed to measure that kind of bias, which is reflected in the objectivity score.

There are two broad categories of traits, according to Winslow. Attitudinal traits are those that tap into factors that may change over time, whereas emotional traits are those that represent relatively enduring qualities of the athlete's personality. *Drive*, for example, is an attitudinal trait that corresponds to what we normally think of as ambition, the player's desire to be successful. The ASI measures drive with questions like

"I frequently practice on my own in addition to required practice sessions" (a. true; b. somewhat true; c. false). A player's drive might change: an unattached freshman in college might have a drive score near the top of the scale, but then lose that drive when he falls in love and wants to start a family with his girlfriend. Ritterspusch offered his own example of the different kinds of traits, with a slightly different terminology. He called traits that might change over time, like *coachability,* "maintenance skills," as opposed to critical skills, which he did not believe changed over time.

Other purely attitudinal traits include *leadership,* which is the extent to which the athlete wants to be responsible for or control others (e.g., "I don't speak out in team or strategy meetings, because I do not think I can add to the discussion." a. true; b. in between; c. false). This trait would be more relevant in, say, a basketball point guard than in a center, and perhaps more relevant in team sports than in individual sports. Coachability measures the player's respect for coaches, team captains, and other authority figures (e.g., "When my coach criticizes me, I become upset rather than feel I have been helped." a. sometimes; b. seldom; c. rarely). *Trust* is a bit like self-confidence, applied to the team (e.g., "I believe there are things happening among my fellow athletes that I don't know about." a. sometimes; b. seldom; c. rarely, if ever). It measures the extent to which the athlete believes he can rely upon his teammates. In basketball or hockey, for instance, does he take the shot himself, or pass to a teammate?

Aggression, responsibility, emotional control, mental toughness, and *self-confidence,* in contrast, are emotional traits. Aggression is related to the athlete's tendency to try to "force the action" and "make things happen" (e.g., "I always try to make

things happen rather than react to the actions of my opponents."
a. true; b. somewhat true; c. false). Responsibility is the athlete's
willingness to accept responsibility for the outcomes on the field
(e.g., "When a team loses, it is usually more the team's fault than
it is the coach's fault." a. very true; b. true; c. somewhat true).
Emotional control measures how well the athlete controls his or
her emotions in a stressful situation (e.g., "I lose my temper
during competition." a. sometimes; b. seldom; c. rarely). Baseball
players who frequently throw their batting helmets or smash wa-
ter coolers with baseball bats don't have a lot of this. Mental
toughness measures how well a player can rebound after a significant failure or a tough loss, or function well under a harsh
coach (e.g., "I feel miserable after losing in competition." a. always; b. usually; c. sometimes). Frank Marcos of the Major
League Scouting Bureau put it this way: the test can tell you "Is
he the kind of kid who needs a kick in the ass or the kind of kid
who needs a pat on the back?" Self-confidence is what it sounds
like: the extent to which the athlete believes he or she has what it
takes to succeed (e.g., "I don't think I am as good as most of the
athletes in my league or class." a. true; b. somewhat true; c. false).

Determination and *conscientiousness* have both attitudinal
and emotional components. Determination is the athlete's willingness to put forward physical effort and make sacrifices, such
as playing through pain (e.g., "When I start working on a new
skill or when exercising, I usually work until I'm exhausted."
a. very true; b. true; c. somewhat true). Conscientiousness measures whether the player is thinking primarily of himself or the
team first (e.g., "My personal desires sometimes tempt me to
bend or break certain rules and regulations." a. true; b. in between; c. false).

Ritterspusch emphasizes that some traits are much more

important than others, an assessment with which Winslow concurs. Each of them plugs the raw information from the AMI into an equation that gives different weight to different traits. Understandably, neither wanted to share his secret formula— Ritterspusch and the Orioles used theirs to make decisions about what players to draft, and Winslow had a commercial interest in his. However, Winslow conceded that self-confidence was the best discriminator of successful from unsuccessful athletes. Ritterspusch was similarly guarded, but his description of Eddie Murray as "reserved, composed, a little hostile" sounds like a reference to someone high in emotional control, self-confidence, and mental toughness, with a dash of aggression.

There have been numerous studies of the AMI and its successor tests, which have supported their reliability and validity. For instance, test-retest reliability is high. If the test is given to the same player on two different occasions, he will tend to get roughly the same score. Or, if the questions related to each of the eleven traits are randomly split into two separate sets, the scores from each set will be closely comparable. And the test appears to measure something of value for success in athletics. According to both Ritterspusch and Winslow, the average score on the tests increases at each level of baseball success, from high school to different levels of college play, through the different levels of the minor leagues and into the major leagues. And within the major leagues, players who go on to be stars (which Ritterspusch defined as the top 10 percent) scored higher on average than the next 20 percent, who in turn scored higher on average than the regulars, who scored higher than the bench players. According to Ritterspusch, the elite players might score as much as 50 percent higher on certain traits than the regulars. The test thus has predictive validity: players who score high when they are scouted are more likely to be successful as their careers develop.

There are a few studies in the public domain that have examined the issue that is of more interest here: the relation between scores on the AMI and performance in baseball. William Winslow and the Institute for Athletic Motivation encouraged continued evaluation of the reliability and validity of the AMI by sharing data with various researchers interested in personality and sports. One study explored how well each of the eleven traits measured by the AMI predicted success in baseball. It used the AMI scores of 2101 players who took the test between 1975 and 1985 and simply looked at their success in professional baseball: some were not drafted at all, some were drafted but did not make it to the major leagues, and some made it. The results support the inferences we have already drawn about the test: self-confidence and determination were the two most consistently useful predictors, and emotional control and mental toughness were also important. There were some interesting results with some of the other traits, as well. The average coachability score for a player who was drafted was *lower* than the score for a player who was not; similarly, drafted players on average scored lower on leadership than the nondrafted players. In talking about the relative values of the different traits in predicting success, Ritterspusch mentioned that there are "some traits where we don't want a guy to score high." Perhaps coachability and leadership are traits like that.

In another study, the AMI scores of recreational and college baseball players were compared. A similar pattern of differences emerged: self-confidence, emotional control, and mental toughness (along with drive and aggression) were again the traits that distinguished the less- and more-advanced players.

We can also get some insight into the validity of the approach that underlies the AMI from research that employed a similar test, this one developed primarily by Ronald Smith, a psychologist at the University of Washington who has worked with the Houston Astros. The Athletic Coping Skills Inventory-28, or ACSI-28, consists of seven scales, each derived from an athlete's responses to four questions. The scales are similar (though not an exact match) to the AMI: the *Peaking Under Pressure* scale identifies whether an athlete feels more challenged or more daunted by pressure situations; *Coping with Adversity* identifies how well the player handles failure and loss, and so on.

Smith tested 104 players, 57 pitchers and 47 position players, at the A and AA levels in the Houston Astros minor-league system in 1991, all of whom had played at least some of the 1990 season with an Astros farm team. Smith also had access to ratings that the managers and coaches made of each player's physical skills, like bat speed and power for hitters, and velocity and movement of the fastball and quality of off-speed pitches for pitchers, which were averaged into an *Overall Average Evaluation,* or OAE. Smith used the OAEs from the first half of the '91 season as an index of the player's physical ability. The study used two criterion variables—statistics from the 1991 season (batting average for the position players and ERA for the pitchers) and survival, which was simply whether the player was still in professional baseball two and then three years later.

Given two players of equal physical ability, as assessed by the OAE, the ACSI-28 could account for a meaningful proportion of the remaining variability in performance. For hitters, 21 percent of the variability in batting average could be predicted by the OAE; another 20 percent could be accounted for by the

ACSI-28. The test did even better with the pitchers. The OAE accounted for only 3 percent of the differences among ERAs, but the ACSI-28 accounted for 38 percent of the remaining variability. The lack of a relation between the OAE and ERA raises some questions, of course. The OAE may not be a good measure of physical ability. Or, ERA might not be the best way to measure the effectiveness of a pitcher. Or, raw physical ability may not be a strong determinant of pitching skill. Whatever the case, it is impressive that a simple twenty-eight-item personality test can account for that much variability in performance on the field.

Is 20 percent, or even 38 percent, of the variability a meaningful amount? The SAT is widely used in making college admissions decisions because people believe it has value in predicting a student's success in college. Whether it is, in fact, of value or not is beside the point here. The point is that a study by the University of California found that the SAT could predict about 13 percent of the variance in first-year GPA. Using that figure as a benchmark, Smith's test did a remarkable job, especially with the pitchers.

Smith also found that his test could predict with some accuracy who would survive in professional baseball two and three years later. He first reasoned that the ACSI-28 had to do better at predicting survival than the base rate. That is, about 75 percent of the players were still in professional baseball two years later; at three years, that figure dropped to about 25 percent. So if he simply predicted that everyone would survive after two years and no one would survive after three years, he would be right 75 percent of the time. To be valuable, the ACSI had to do better than the base rate, and it did, by an additional 10 to 20 percent. However, the ACSI did no better than the OAE; that measure added about 20 percent to the base rate prediction. Still, the results are encouraging. A simple twenty-eight-item personality test was just as good at picking successful prospects as experienced coaches who had worked with those players for at least a year or so. Smith's research suggests we might actually be getting closer to that "ivory hunter's clinic" that Hugh Fullerton dreamed of in his 1921 *Popular Science Monthly* article.

Moreover, when we look closely at the components of Smith's ACSI and how well it predicted success, we can make some reasonable guesses about what it is on Winslow's ASI that Ritterspusch and other decision makers in Major League Baseball find so useful. Although Smith was using all seven traits to predict performance and survival, as with the ASI, some traits were better predictors than others, particularly in the player's ratings of themselves. (As measured by the manager's or coach's ratings, the seven traits were more broadly predictive. But since the ASI is completed by the player, let's focus on the player's own ratings with the ACSI.) For hitters, confidence and achievement motivation and coping with adversity were the most important traits. For pitchers, it was confidence and achievement motivation again, along with peaking under pressure.

The profile of success that emerges from the various studies of the AMI and from Smith's study emphasizes personality traits like self-confidence, mental toughness, emotional control, and aggression. Although the key traits are the same, there are slight differences in the profiles of successful pitchers and those of successful position players. Ritterspusch believes that pitchers score higher on some of the secondary traits, and that pitchers are more driven, and a little more aggressive. Of the position players, infielders as a group were more like the pitchers than the outfielders, but that difference is relatively slight.

As *Moneyball* makes clear, confidence and emotional control were precisely the elements of the psychological game with which Billy Beane seemed to struggle. This is, of course, easy to see after the fact. Interestingly, although Beane apparently took one of Winslow's tests and scored well, he still failed to excel as predicted, largely, according to *Moneyball,* because of his psychological makeup. Of course, the test is not a perfect predictor: some people who score well, like Beane, will still fail, and some who score poorly might succeed. Or perhaps Beane scored very well on the traits that did not matter as much, like trust, and not so well on the ones that mattered a lot, like self-confidence, emotional control, and mental toughness.

In a review of several of the studies that had been done with the AMI, it emerged that the constellation of traits that seem to be important for baseball are more similar to those important for individual sports like tennis (where mental toughness and determination were most important) and wrestling (where self-confidence and emotional control were among the most important) than to those important for team sports, in which some of the same traits are important, but so are conscientiousness and leadership, two traits that never seem to emerge in studies of baseball. We often hear talk of a baseball player's leadership in the clubhouse, but these tests suggest that this is a relatively unimportant trait for success. On one hand, this makes sense: at its core, baseball centers on the one-on-one matchup of hitter against pitcher. There is no one for the player to lead in that situation but himself.

On the other hand, there are, to my knowledge, no studies that look at the importance of these traits at the team level. Do teams that succeed have a mix of leaders and followers? Are successful teams made up of largely conscientious and responsible players? ESPN columnist Rob Neyer has written several times about team chemistry, arguing that it is most likely effect rather than cause. Winning produces good chemistry, rather than good chemistry producing winning. I tend to agree, but to be fair, to know for sure we would need a study that asks, "All other things being equal, do teams with certain mixes of personality traits fare better than others?"

Why did Billy Beane abruptly give up as a player? Why did he not seek the services of a psychologist and try to change his makeup? Lewis wrote in *Moneyball* that Beane "thought it was just bullshit to say that his character—or more exactly, his emotional predisposition—might be changed. 'You know what?' he said. 'If it doesn't happen, it never was going to happen. If you never did it, it wasn't there to begin with.' All these attempts to manipulate his psyche he regarded as so much crap." How much crap is it? Can these factors, in fact, be changed?

Remember that the AMI is composed of the traits that Winslow called attitudinal traits and emotional traits, and that he explained that attitudinal traits like coachability are perhaps more likely to change over time than emotional traits like self-confidence. Here again, we lack a thorough study that provides data on this point. But Dave Ritterspusch had Rafael Palmeiro retake the test in 2004, nineteen years after he first took it, and found that Palmeiro's scores had hardly changed. Like Beane, Ritterspusch also emphasized that it is possession of these traits that leads to success, rather than the other way around, saying about great closers, for instance, that "key traits made them what they are. It wasn't success that produced those traits." Ogilvie and Tutko took this view, too: "Athletic competition has no more beneficial effects than intense endeavor in any other field. Horatio Alger success—in sport or elsewhere—

comes only to those who already are mentally fit, resilient and strong."

Recent reviews of research on personality paint a picture like this: to a point, these views are correct; personality dispositions, as measured by personality tests, do show a remarkable consistency over the life span. Few psychological variables, other than measures of IQ and other cognitive abilities, show as much consistency from one point in life to another. And though we often sense that our personalities change with time, they are actually more stable than we believe. One study had people fill out a personality profile at one point in time and then, ten years later, asked them to fill out that same profile again, answering the questions as they applied at that time, and then a second time, answering the questions as they remembered answering them in the original session ten years ago. The results showed that the person's actual personality profile at the later time better matched the original profile than their memory of the original profile. People thought they had changed more than they actually had.

However, there are also some identifiable patterns of change over the life span, suggesting that personality is not absolutely fixed. People really do mature as they get older, becoming more emotionally stable and conscientious, for example. There is thus evidence for relative stability in personality from one point to another, with some room for change. Psychologists who study personality have advanced various theories to try to account for these patterns of similarity and change over time.

One idea that seems particularly apt for sports is the set-point theory, which is the idea that our genetic endowment sets a range within which various attributes, like intelligence and personality traits, may vary. A person with a high set-point for intelligence may have the genetic endowment for an IQ in the range of 115–135, but environmental variables like nutrition, a stable family environment, and appropriate mental stimulation will determine where in that range the IQ will settle. Physical attributes like strength and speed are probably similar. No amount of training can change the upper limits of a person's speed or strength; those are determined by his genetic endowment. I could have trained full-time for ten years and my hands would never have been as quick as Darryl Strawberry's or Billy Beane's. And mental training probably could not give Billy Beane Darryl Strawberry's confidence at the plate; again, the upper limit of Beane's confidence as a player was probably set by his genes. Coaches and scouts often say, "You can't teach speed." Speed was one of the five tools that Billy Beane was supposed to have. You probably can't teach personality either; though, like speed, it can be refined and developed.

Another thing Billy Beane knew is how limited his "deficiency" (if it can even be called that) was. He told Michael Lewis that "it's not a character flaw; it's just a character flaw when it comes to baseball." You have to be one in 2 million to have the total package of physical and psychological abilities required to succeed in baseball at its highest levels of competition. Still, from Major League Baseball's perspective, it is a deficiency not to have certain personality traits. As much as Dave Ritterspusch is looking for players with all of Eddie Murray's positive attributes, he is also trying to "avoid bad investments" by looking for "failure patterns" in the ASI as a "prophylactic way to not select players likely to fail."

Even the label "self-confidence" that Ogilvie, Tutko, and Lyon used to describe the trait that they were measuring is narrowly defined to apply to competitive sports. Billy Beane surely has plenty of confidence; few could be as successful as he has without the confidence to make the judgments and decisions that he has made, especially in the face of a torrent of public questioning and criticism. John Mozeliak, assistant general manager of the St. Louis Cardinals, says that now, in dealing with other baseball executives, "Beane exudes confidence." It's just not the kind of confidence a hitter needs in the batter's box.

CHAPTER FIVE

Streaks and Slumps

Baseball is obsessed with the recent past—how many games has a player hit in safely, how many straight starts has a pitcher lost, how many of the last several one-run leads has a bullpen saved, how many wins did the team have on the road trip that just ended? Every radio and television broadcast of a game is peppered with references to streaks and slumps. Perhaps this is ironic, given that baseball is often celebrated for having such a long season, a gauntlet sufficiently challenging that only the truly best team will prevail. Moreover, players only qualify for batting or pitching titles if they have played a requisite amount, and the eligibility rules for the Hall of Fame require that a player compete in at least ten seasons. Baseball is in many ways a game of the long run. Even so, we baseball fans routinely scrutinize much smaller batches of performance: after the All-Star break, against left-handed pitchers, in September, in one-run games, in the rookie year, during the last ten games.

Before each game, each team's media relations department releases "game notes" to the press. Many of the statistical tidbits we hear during a broadcast come from these notes. In addition to providing a snapshot of the team's and its players' performance at that point in the season, the game notes implicitly raise all kinds of psychological questions about how and why performance fluctuates over time.

Do Players Run Hot and Cold?

*A's **OFFENSIVELY**: Batting .248 on the year, which is the second lowest mark in the AL (Cleveland .246) and fourth lowest in the Majors . . . have scored just 251 runs on the year, which is the second lowest total in the AL (Cleveland 247) . . . have hit 10 home runs in the last 11 games but have just 38 homers for the season, which is the fewest in the Majors (Seattle 41) . . . the A's also rank last in the Majors with 146 extra base hits and a .358 slugging percentage . . . have fanned just 308 times this season, the second fewest times in the Majors (San Francisco 295).*

Eric Chavez is batting .312 (29–93) with six home runs and 22 RBI over his last 24 games (since May 16) after hitting .190 with two home runs and 11 RBI over his first 37 games.

Mark Ellis was 0–3 yesterday and is hitless in his last eight at bats . . . however, is 15–52 (.288) over his last 15 games after going 2–19 (.105) over his previous seven games.

Scott Hatteberg was 0–4 yesterday and is 10–45 (.222) with 10 strikeouts over his last 14 games.

Jason Kendall was 1–4 last night and has hit safely in all four games on this trip (5–15, .333) . . . is now 6–26 (.231) over his last seven games after hitting safely in an A's season high tying nine consecutive games (14–38, .368).

Mark Kotsay went 1–2 yesterday and is now 4–19 (.210) on the trip.

Nick Swisher was 1–4 yesterday and is now 2–15 over his last four games following a career best eight game hitting streak (12–30, .400).

—Oakland Athletics Game Notes, Sunday, June 12, 2005
[ellipses and bold text in original]

These game notes clearly bemoan the A's hitting woes midway through the 2005 season. But by the end of the season: Oakland was batting .262, putting them in the middle of the pack at seventeenth of the thirty major-league teams (the Indians had moved all the way up to .271, good for sixth place in the major leagues). The A's were in ninth place with 772 runs in 2005; the Indians were seventh with 790. Oakland ended the season with 155 home runs, in eighteenth place, and Oakland's slugging percentage of .407 put them in twenty-second place. The only statistic that seemed to stay about the same was the A's hitters' tendency to avoid the strikeout: they ended the season with the lowest total in the major leagues, with 819.

It may not surprise you that Oakland finished the year much better than they started it. Recent A's teams have been famously streaky. From 2000 through 2005, a period which they began with four straight seasons in the playoffs (then just missing in 2004 with a 91–71 record, one game behind the Angels, and finishing 2005 at 88–74, seven games back of the Angels), the A's had an overall winning percentage of .588, but were only 75–75 in April and 79–83 in May. Overall, June (102–59, or .634) and July (98–63, or .609) showed dramatic improvement, with continued or even better performance in August (114–55, or .675) and September/October (103–65, or .613). Each of those years except 2003 also included at least one month with a losing record, 12–13 in April 2000, 8–17 in April and 12–15 in June 2001, 10–17 in May 2002, 11–12 in April 2004, and 7–20 in May 2005. Each of those years *also* featured at least one stellar month in the second half of the season, 22–7 in September/October 2000, 22–7 in August and 23–4 in September 2001, 24–4 in August 2002, 20–9 in August 2003, 20–8 in August 2004, and 20–6 in July 2005. The A's came up short in both 2004 and 2005, but even in those years, they were much better in the second half than in the first.

What is the psychologist to make of all of this? These are differences *within* a player's or team's performance over time, rather than differences *between* one player or team and another, but the same basic principles that we discussed in the last chapter apply here, too: we want to account for as much of the variability in performance over time as we can. The variability we cannot account for, the residual, is left to random error.

We all know that chance plays a role in baseball, but we want to keep what we must relegate to chance to a minimum. To see if changes in a player's performance from one at bat or one game or one week to another are caused by some psychological factor, we need to be able to compare the degree of change that we observe over time with what we would expect from unsystematic random variation. Increases or decreases in performance could be rooted in something psychological ("he's in a slump because he's pressing") or they could simply be due to a run of luck or some combination of the two.

Take a hypothetical player, nicknamed "Cube," who some fans call a streaky hitter. Cube has a batting average of .333. Like every hitter over the course of a season, he will have some games where he gets no hits and some where he gets more than one hit. He will have some hitting streaks during which he gets at least one hit in each of some number of consecutive games. And he will have some slumps, series of consecutive games in which he gets no hits. To decide if Cube is really streaky or not, we need to know how many streaks and slumps we would expect to occur if chance were the only factor, as if Cube were a die we threw, counting any throw showing a one or a two as a hit and anything else as an out (and ignoring walks, sacrifices, and everything else). So we throw the die a lot, assuming three at bats per game for 162 games per season. If we do this for one hypothetical player, we get results like the ones in the figure, which shows a tick up if Cube got at least one hit, and a tick down if he got none. His longest hitting streak was nine games (highlighted); his worst slump was four games.

A record of whether the hypothetical player Cube got at least one hit (upticks) or went hitless (downticks) over the course of a season.

We can tally how many streaks and slumps Cube had of each length; the table on page 144 shows that he had fifteen one-game streaks (if we can call them that), five two-game streaks, and so on, as well as the totals for nine other similarly simulated clones of Cube, all .333 hitters. One lucky hitter, Clone5, managed an eighteen-game hitting streak. And Clone5 looks like a streaky hitter—he also had hitting streaks of ten and twelve games, both longer than Cube's longest. But we know it

Games in Hitting Streak:	Cube	Cube Clone 1	Cube Clone 2	Cube Clone 3	Cube Clone 4	Cube Clone 5	Cube Clone 6	Cube Clone 7	Cube Clone 8	Cube Clone 9
no hits	54	49	62	36	59	43	57	51	55	51
1	15	6	16	8	12	15	12	10	22	11
2	5	9	6	4	14	2	8	10	7	6
3	6	4	6	3	5	4	3	7	5	8
4	1	4	3	4			3	2	4	2
5	5	2	3	1	4	4	1	3	2	4
6	2	1		3	1	2	2		1	1
7	1	1		2	2		1	1	1	1
8	1	1	1	1	1	2	1	1	1	
9	1	2	1					1	1	
10			1			1				1
11										
12		1		2		1	2			
13								1		1
14										
15										
16				1						
17										
18						1				

The number of hitting streaks of a given length for Cube and nine clones.

was only luck, since we were throwing a die to determine whether he got a hit or not. Using computer simulations and probability theory in this way, we can generate a standard of comparison for any baseball statistic.

Was the early 2005 performance of the Oakland A's due to some psychological issue, or was it just a bad run of luck? Without the comparison, we do not know if we even need to consider psychological causes for Oakland's relatively poor batting average in the first couple of months of 2005 (it was much lower than their average for 2004, which was .270), or their run of ten home runs in eleven games. Should we regard these merely as random fluctuations, or as the result of some "funk" the A's seem to be in at the beginning of every year? If baseball players are really "streaky," then their behavior has to differ in some systematic way from what we expect by chance. Are the A's more or less a coin that comes up heads 27 percent of the time, or was their batting average to that point in the 2005 season a consequence of their not "seeing the ball well"?

Stephen Jay Gould, the Yankee fan and author of the collection of baseball essays *Triumph and Tragedy in Mudville* (he also dabbled in paleontology), described in another of his essays some analyses on this question that were done by his friend physicist Ed Purcell, also of Harvard.

Purcell reportedly calculated the expected numbers of various baseball streaks and feats, and determined that, with one exception, the observed numbers all fell within the range of what would be expected by chance. Using analyses like the one presented in the table on the facing page, if our favorite player had a hitting streak of thirteen games one year, we would not make much of it: the simulations show that a streak of thirteen games is well within the bounds of what we would expect by chance. Purcell's analyses showed that this same conclusion held in general for the variety of streaks that baseball fans like to follow.

The one exception, to Gould's delight, was Joe DiMaggio's fifty-six-game hitting streak. According to Gould, Purcell's calculations showed that

> to make it likely (probability greater than 50 percent) that a run of even fifty games will occur once in the history of baseball up to now (and fifty-six is a lot more than fifty in this kind of league), baseball's rosters would have to include

either four lifetime .400 batters or fifty-two lifetime .350 batters over careers of one thousand games. In actuality, only three men have lifetime batting averages in excess of .350, and no one is anywhere near .400 (Ty Cobb at .367, Rogers Hornsby at .358, and Shoeless Joe Jackson at .356). DiMaggio's streak is the most extraordinary thing that ever happened in American sports. He sits on the shoulders of two bearers—mythology and science. For Joe DiMaggio accomplished what no other ballplayer has done. He beat the hardest taskmaster of all, a woman who makes Nolan Ryan's fastball look like a cantaloupe in slow motion—Lady Luck.

And remember that after going hitless in the fifty-seventh game, DiMaggio started another streak, that one lasting sixteen games. And that he had a sixty-one-game hitting streak at age eighteen, when he was playing for the San Francisco Seals in the minor leagues. Purcell's calculations have been backed up by others. One estimate calculated that the odds of DiMaggio starting a fifty-six-game hitting streak on a given day were about two in a million; starting with different assumptions but using the same basic method, another arrived at a figure of slightly less than one in a million. Of course, DiMaggio had multiple opportunities to start such streaks; for instance, the first study figured there was about a one in twenty-five thousand chance that DiMaggio would have at least one streak that long sometime in 1941. Long odds, no doubt. But they also noted that there were thirty-two players with lifetime batting averages at or above DiMaggio's lifetime average of .325, and that over the careers of that entire group of players, the odds of at least one streak of fifty-six games would be about one in sixty-four. Those are still long odds, but perhaps no longer unimaginable. Either way, it was Purcell's judgment that, except for DiMaggio's streak, the variability we see in baseball is about what we would expect to see if it was all due to nothing more than luck.

Not just sports statisticians, but psychologists have also been interested in how much of the variability in performance is random and how much due to a player actually being "hot" or "cold," though psychologists have investigated this question more in the basketball arena than in the baseball stadium. In 1985, Thomas Gilovich, Robert Vallone, and Amos Tversky did a now-famous study of streaks in basketball. Their conclusion, that basketball players do not get hot and cold at different points in a game, and that instead, their sequences of made and missed shots are just what would be expected from random variations in performance, launched a vigorous field of inquiry about the streakiness (or not) of performance in sports.

The Gilovich study's conclusions caused a sensation when they were picked up by the media. The late Red Auerbach scoffed, "Who is this guy? So he makes a study. I couldn't care less." Bobby Knight said, "There are so many variables involved in shooting a basketball that a paper like this really doesn't mean anything." Sports fans see streaks with their own eyes, and they hear about them on virtually every broadcast. (The study also offered an account of why people believe there are streaks, even when the statistics seem to show otherwise, but the fan's perception of statistical phenomena in baseball is the subject of another chapter.) For the discussion in this chapter, it is enough to say that people are driven to find pattern and predictability in the world, which usually serves us well. But when there is no pattern, we often see one anyway, because we detect such things by using various mental shortcuts and rules of thumb, rather than computing them objectively the way we could with the principles of statistical theory. In the same way that our visual system is susceptible to illusions like the rising fastball, our cognitive system is susceptible to illusions of cause and effect.

Or, says the dean of baseball statisticians, Bill James, maybe the fans believe it because there's something to it after all. James recently pointed out a logical flaw in much of the research being used to make the argument that there are no hot hitters (or pitchers, shooters, or goalies). In an essay titled "Underestimating the Fog," he reminds us that just because you cannot see something does not mean that it is not there; the fog might be thicker than you think. Maybe the sequence of hits and outs looks like the sequence we would get from rolling dice because the outcomes of at bats are essentially random. Or, maybe the sequence of hits and outs looks random because we have not found a way to see through the fog. It might be that our measures are not sensitive enough to pick up streaky hitting, or it might be that we are looking for streaks and slumps in the wrong way. James's opinion is that the question of whether hitters get hot and cold is still open.

One potential problem with the way we look at streaks and slumps is that simply looking at whether or not an at bat resulted in a hit is to look past how well the ball was hit. A lazy infield pop-up and a line drive that knocks down the third baseman and breaks three bones in his glove hand both go into the scorebook as outs. A sizzling line drive up the middle and a bloop over the second baseman's head both go into the scorebook as hits. So when a ball is put in play, the result depends to some extent on the quality of the contact the hitter makes, and to some extent on luck.

Another issue is that every at bat occurs in a different situation: day game or night game, home game or away game, against a middle reliever or flame-throwing closer. All of those factors affect the hitter's chances, as does the fact that a sequence even as short as ten at bats extends over many days. Suppose streaks really do occur, and a player was in the middle of one when he had to face Nolan Ryan at his best. Maybe that hitter even had some good at bats against Ryan, but his hot streak was, nonetheless, put on hold for one day, at least in box scores. In statistical terms, the probability of a success in an at bat cannot be constant as is usually assumed. The analyses of DiMaggio's hitting streak used his lifetime batting average (.325) to determine the probability of his streak, but his batting average was .357 in 1941, the year of the streak, and because his seasonal average declined more or less steadily with age, to around .300 when he retired, that .357 probably wasn't a fluke. DiMaggio was probably *really* a better hitter in 1941 than in other years, and not just better because of a bit of luck. If that is true, then DiMaggio's streak was even *more* likely than the calculations above would lead us to believe. In general, a hitter's probability of a hit in a given at bat is certainly not his lifetime batting average, as many of the statistical analyses assume. Instead, the probability of success changes with every at bat, depending on an exceptionally large array of situational factors. There is a lot of room here for Bill James's fog.

It is no wonder, then, that hitters often ignore the box score result of an at bat and focus instead on the quality of the contact they made. George Will described Tony Gwynn's feelings about two at bats in a game in early 1989:

> The previous night he had hit two balls hard. One pleased him, the other distressed him. The pleasing one was an out, the distressing one was a home run. When he hit the ball hard

for an out, as he started his stride forward his hands moved in the opposite direction. They came back so he could keep the bat back long enough to "inside out" the ball to left field, lashing a line drive that was caught by the left fielder. . . . On the home-run swing, his hands came forward too soon. That is what he means by being "out in front." He drove the ball to right field. Sure, it went over the fence, but he knows that over the course of the long season, hitting the ball that way is a recipe for the sort of frustration he experienced in 1988.

Given the number of variables in game situations and the role that luck can play, some psychologists interested in streaky performance have designed studies that minimize those factors so that true streaks, if they occur, are easier to see. One study looked for streaks in the golf putting and dart throwing of samples of volunteers who attempted three hundred putts or throws in short sessions. The researchers chose these relatively staid conditions for their studies because "any game that is sufficiently interesting to draw spectators may be too complex for a rigorous streak analysis." Their choice was an apt one. Their analysis revealed hot and cold streaks—the test subjects were not behaving as dice would, but rather as fans believe that athletes do.

The study also revealed that streaky performance was more likely in the midrange of performance (and this same pattern occurred in more than one study, which gives us confidence that these results were not chance flukes). When putting from farther away or throwing at smaller targets, so that success was relatively less likely, or when putting closer in or throwing at larger targets so that success was relatively more likely, performance was less streaky. This may explain, in part, why statisticians have failed to see streaky performance in baseball hitting statistics—baseball hitters are famous for being paid to achieve a very low rate of success.

There are other competitive sports in which situational factors matter less than they do in baseball or basketball, and in these cases, too, evidence of streaky performance has been obtained. One study showed that among horseshoe pitchers who appeared in the World Championships in 2000 and 2001, the chances of a double ringer (players throw the shoes in pairs) were greater after a double ringer than after turns with no or one ringer, so successes and failures came in bunches. Of the sixty-four competitors in those two years, fifty-one were more likely to pitch double ringers after another double than after a non-double. The odds of that happening by chance are less than one in a million.

In the Professional Bowlers Association, another study similarly found that bowlers rolled strikes more often following a strike than following a nonstrike, and that the longer the run of strikes or nonstrikes, the bigger the effect. After one strike, bowlers rolled strikes 57 percent of the time; after one nonstrike, they rolled a strike 56 percent of the time. After four straight strikes, they rolled strikes 61 percent of the time; after four straight nonstrikes, they rolled a strike 49 percent of the time.

Putting a golf ball, throwing a dart, pitching horseshoes, and rolling a bowling ball surely involve different skills than playing baseball; the results of these studies may not generalize to baseball. For one thing, there is a relatively long time between successive at bats for the hitter in baseball. But combined with the potential "fog" in the statistical analyses, these studies should keep us from concluding too quickly that the only cause of hitting streaks and slumps is luck.

Moreover, some more recent statistical studies of baseball have also yielded equivocal results. The authors of the book *Curve Ball: Baseball, Statistics, and the Role of Chance in the Game* present some clever analyses that suggest that the batting records of at least one hitter who was often said to be streaky, Todd Zeile, do seem to be just that. They also present some analyses showing that the Anaheim Angels' pattern of wins and losses in 1998 was more consistent with a model of streaky play than a random model of wins and losses. But they also note that the Zeile analysis may be due to a selection bias—they didn't pick him at random, they picked him because people already thought he was streaky. In any random sample, some small number of players will appear to be streaky, just by chance. The real test would be to see if that pattern repeated itself over the course of Zeile's career. But in the case of the Angels' winning in 1998, there was no selection bias. They looked at the data for all the teams and found evidence of streakiness for more teams than would be expected by chance. Anaheim's streakiness was not even as great as Baltimore's that year.

Finally, players and coaches certainly believe in streaks and slumps. Perhaps this is because people are poor intuitive statisticians—we know from lots of studies that even with formal training, people do not reason well "on the fly" about statistical issues. On the other hand, perhaps it is because the players and coaches are responding to the whole picture, rather than the way that picture is boiled down for the box score. After running a scoreless inning streak to thirty-seven-and-a-third, pitcher Greg Maddux told *USA Today*, "You've got to be lucky when you pitch that many innings and you don't give up a run. I threw probably the best hitter in the game (Vladimir Guerrero) two (bad pitches) and he hit them both at somebody. I didn't get him out, he just hit them at somebody. That's just luck." If players know when luck *is* a factor in a streak, maybe they can also recognize when luck *is not* a factor.

So let's say streakiness may occur after all. At the least, it seems too early to conclude that it does *not* exist. Then, if it exists, what would be the psychology behind it? Every baseball fan has heard the players' ideas. "Hitting is contagious." "Not hitting is contagious." "I just feel really comfortable out there right now." "I just don't feel very comfortable out there right now." "We've got the momentum." "They've got the momentum."

Many, many factors could contribute to fluctuations in mental performance that would in turn cause streaks and slumps. In modeling their data on putting and dart throwing, the researchers found that a wavelike function with a cyclically rising and falling level of performance best accounted for the streaks and slumps they saw in their data. When baseline skill was at a low point in the cycle, slumps were more likely; when it was at a high point, streaks were more likely. Perhaps, they speculated, players' levels of attention, what we would typically think of as their concentration, might wax and wane over time, leading to modest changes in their level of skill.

"Everyone knows what attention is," said William James, the father of American psychology. "It is the taking possession by the mind, in clear and vivid form, of one out of what seem several simultaneously possible objects or trains of thought." Attention can be sharply focused, and elite athletes are exceptionally good at this. The hitter focuses on the pitcher's release point, the pitcher focuses on the catcher's mitt, the fielder focuses on the ball. But attention can also be distracted, and even the best athletes must be susceptible to this at times. The pitcher, for instance, might try to focus his attention on the catcher's mitt, but other "objects or trains of thought" might intrude—crowd noise, a base runner stealing a base, worries about a losing streak, anger at the umpire for a bad call on the previous pitch, pain from an injury—any of these might compete with his desire to focus only on the mitt. Roger Clemens has talked about "seeing the crowd, not just the catcher" when he loses focus. Hundreds of basic laboratory studies of attention also show that responses to stimuli are faster and more accurate with the benefit of focused attention.

Maintaining concentration and attentional focus is an act of will, and research has also shown that there may be a limit to the human exercise of will, and that all kinds of deliberate mental activities push us to that limit. In one study, people did an experimental task after having to resist a tempting plate of chocolate chip cookies: the researchers put the cookies in front of the subjects but asked them not to eat them just yet. As compared with control conditions in which participants did not have to resist the temptation to eat the cookies, performance on the task was poorer when participants had to use their willpower to keep from eating the chocolate. Another study showed that having to focus attention on one thing (like a hitter has to focus on the pitcher's release point) while ignoring another (like, say, how critical the game is for the team's playoff chances) also undermined later task performance. It is no great leap to then suppose that maintaining focus and concentration at one time could impair the ability to do the same thing again at a later time. As good as elite athletes are, there is likely a limit to how long they can maintain their full attention. The ups and downs of the ability to exert the will may account for the cyclic pattern of streaks and slumps. Sports psychologists try to help athletes stem the ebb and flow of concentration and focus. Harvey Dorfman, who has worked with the Oakland A's and Florida Marlins and now works with the clients of agent Scott Boras, and Ken Ravizza, a professor of kinesiology at the University of California at Fullerton who has consulted with the Angels and numerous other sports organizations, each described, in back-to-back articles in *The Sport Psychologist,* the kinds of services they offer to professional baseball players. The emphasis of both programs is on helping the player treat every moment the same:

DORFMAN: Players are helped to develop mental discipline . . . and they are introduced to our task-specific orientation with the focus on the "now"—the next pitch.

RAVIZZA: Consistency is a key skill because many minor league ballplayers could play in the majors if they could handle all the distractions that interfere with performance. Thus a major theme that runs throughout the mental skills training is learning how to play the game one pitch at a time on a daily basis.

Clutch and Choke

SF is 9–3 in its last 12 1-run contests after losing each of its 1st 3 1-run games of year . . . overall, club's 9–6 ledger (.600) in such contests is tied with Arizona (15–10, .600) in NL, behind San Diego (.789, 15–4) and Washington (.682, 15–7) . . .

SF is 6th in NL for runners in scoring position, posting .278 mark (143-for-515) . . . Giants are hitting .324 (48-for-148) with RISP over their last 20 outings . . .

Mike Stadler

> *Giants have had great success with bases loaded, leading NL with*
> *.392 mark (20-for-51) and 5 grand slams . . . SF is just 2 shy of*
> *franchise record for most slams (7, 1951, '54, '70, '98) . . .*

> —*San Francisco Giants Game Notes, June 12, 2005*
> *[ellipses in original]*

The value of a hit, run, out, or other event in a game varies depending on the situation. Home runs mean little if hit late in a 10–0 game. When a pitcher records an out for his team, it increases the chance they will win, but increases it much more when the bases are loaded in the ninth inning than when the bases are empty in the second. Performance in critical, "clutch" situations is the stuff that legends are made of (think Bobby Thomson, Kirk Gibson, Joe Carter, Aaron Boone). Do some players (or teams, as the Giants game notes suggest) perform particularly well in situations like these, and some poorly? Are there clutch or choke players? If so, what is it about their psychology that makes them that way?

Bill James's first example in his "Underestimating the Fog" essay was about clutch hitting. His opinion was that, years of statistical work to the contrary, we should regard as an open question whether or not clutch hitters exist. James and others give more detail on the history of this question than I will here, but the psychological question hinges, to at least some degree, on the statistical one. We need to know whether player performance differs as a function of the importance of a game situation before it makes sense to consider the causes of such differences.

To determine whether or not there is anything more than random variation in clutch or choke hitting, statisticians needed some different tools. The usual baseball statistics like batting average, home runs, and runs scored, and even statistics favored by today's analysts, like OPS (the sum of on-base percentage and slugging percentage) or VORP (Value Over Replacement Player) and the like, are summaries, averaged over all of a player's performance within a given period. To measure clutch hitting, we need to contextualize those statistics by the game situation, which is easy conceptually but difficult in practice. The median number of plate appearances per team per season for the last few years has been about 6250, so there are about 187,500 plate appearances in a major-league season. To figure a player's batting average in clutch vs. nonclutch situations, we need a record of all of those plate appearances and some way to classify each one in terms of its importance. Only relatively recently have such records begun to be available.

The first attempt at an analysis like this was by two brothers, Harlan and Eldon Mills, in 1969. They broke games down into specific situations (e.g., top of the fourth inning, score of 4–2 in favor of the home team, runners at first and third with two out) and analyzed how different outcomes in that situation (e.g., a home run, a pop fly, a hit batter) would affect the ultimate outcome (i.e., did it make a win more, or less, likely?). So if, in a particular situation, the chance that a player's team will win is 62 percent, how does that probability change if the player hits a home run? Or makes an out? If the player's action increased the chances of a win, say, moving it from 62 to 62.6 percent, then that player's Win Points total was credited with an amount corresponding to that 0.6 percent of a win; if the player's action decreased the chances from 62 to 60.9 percent, then his Loss Points total went up accordingly. Offensive and defensive actions (like a pitcher striking out a hitter, or an outfielder dropping a fly ball) also could be coded. The Win Points and Loss Points were then used to compute the Player Win Average, which was the Win Points divided by the total of the Win and Loss Points (this is not the same statistic as Win Shares, which was developed by Bill James, though the spirit is similar).

The Mills brothers' efforts were not rewarded by popular acclaim. In 1970, they published the first edition of *Player Win Averages: A Computer Guide to Winning Baseball Players,* which summarized the 1969 season. It confirmed some of the conclusions made with the conventional statistics: the NL hitter with the highest PWA was Willy McCovey, who won the MVP that year. It also highlighted some performances that were, perhaps, overlooked: the NL pitcher with the highest PWA was Larry Dierker, rather than that year's Cy Young Award winner, Tom Seaver. Unfortunately, that first edition sold so poorly that it was the one and only.

But we are not really talking about clutch ability yet. According to Bill James, the next step was for Dick Cramer, who founded STATS, Inc., to use the PWA data from the 1969 and 1970 seasons to tackle the question of whether or not clutch hitting was a matter of luck, or a trait that some players had and some did not. Cramer reasoned that if there is some ability that players have in varying degrees to perform in the clutch, then clutch hitting ought to be stable from one year to the next like other abilities (the number of home runs a player hit in one year is a pretty good predictor of the number that player will hit the next year). Of course, some luck would be involved, but there ought to be some correlation between clutch performance from one year to the next. Cramer found that there was none; a player might be at the top of the list one year and at the bottom the next. A similar analysis around the same time yielded the same conclusion. There did not appear to be any stable ability for hitting in tight situations.

So the stats in the Giants game notes, which might be taken to suggest that the Giants had demonstrated some "clutch ability," perhaps should not be construed that way. The statistical analyses seem to suggest that there is no clutch ability in Major League Baseball. Yes, the analyses seem to say, David Ortiz and Albert Pujols get big hits, but it is not because they have any special ability for clutch situations. It is just because they are good hitters to begin with.

This conclusion is still not readily accepted. The Elias Sports Bureau's *Baseball Analyst,* for instance, complained in 1988 that "a small group of shrill pseudo-statisticians has used insufficient data and faulty methods to try to disprove the existence of the clutch hitter. But the trends are undeniably apparent except to those who choose not to see." The statistical evidence kept piling up, however. There are now dozens of analyses that suggest that hitting in "clutch" situations is no different than hitting in other situations. Hitters perform in tight, late-game situations about the way they perform in other situations. Joe Sheehan, in an article on the Baseball Prospectus Web site, lays out the current thinking among most baseball analysts:

> In trying to get across the notion that no players possess a special ability to perform in particular situations, the usual line we use is that clutch performances exist, not clutch players. That's wrong. The correct idea is that clutch performances exist, and clutch players exist: *every last one of them.* All major-league players have a demonstrated ability to perform under pressure. They've proven that by rising to the top of an enormous pyramid of players, tens of thousands of

them, all trying to be one of the top 0.1% that gets to call themselves "major leaguers." Within this group of elite, who have proven themselves to be the best in the world at their jobs, there is no discernable change in their abilities when runners are on base, or when the game is tied in extra innings, or when candy and costumes and pumpkins decorate the local GigaMart. The guys who are good enough to be in the majors are all capable of succeeding and failing in these situations, and they're as likely to do one or the other in the clutch as they are at any other time. Over the course of a game, a month, a season or a career, there is virtually no evidence that any player or group of players possesses an ability to outperform his established level of ability in clutch situations, however defined.

If meaningful differences in clutch or choke performance are to be found, the best places to look might be in college baseball or in the minor leagues, before the pool of players has been cut down so that it includes only clutch hitters.

One way to see why we might not be able to detect clutch performance in major-league play is illustrated in the figure. Suppose, as Sheehan suggests, an ability to hit in the clutch, "clutchitude" as it were, exists and that major-league hitters are the cream of the crop in this ability: if we could measure clutchitude directly in all baseball players everywhere, we might get a distribution that looks something like the top panel. You can see that clutchitude varies widely, from low to high, and you can see that this ability is related systematically, but not perfectly (there's always the luck factor) to players' abilities to get hits in tight, late-game situations. We can use a statistical technique called linear regression to draw a line through these points that represents the "best-fitting" model describing the relation between clutch performance and clutchitude. The line essentially says that for every unit of clutchitude we add, we can expect, on average, a given increase in performance in the clutch.

But now let's look just at the major-league players at the top of the distribution, the cream of the crop, as shown in the bottom panel. Notice that this is not every player beyond a certain threshold in clutchitude. The selection process is probably

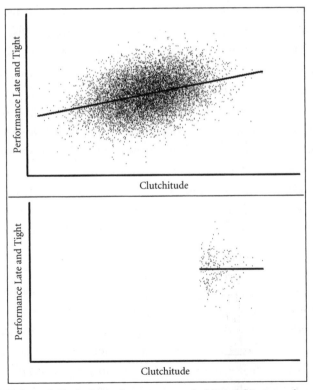

The hypothetical relation between an underlying ability to perform under pressure and actual performance in those situations.

not nearly as good as that (look how many players thought to be "sure things" never pan out when they get their chance in the major leagues). Instead, I set this up so that the likelihood that a player would be included in the "major league" sample increased as clutchitude increased—players far above the clutchitude threshold were almost certain to make it, but players close to the threshold were increasingly less certain to make it. Now if you draw the best-fitting model for this sample, it tells you nothing. The slope of the line is about zero; a player's clutchitude tells you nothing about the player's performance in late and tight situations. (Actually, in this simulated example, the slope was even slightly negative—that is, as clutchitude increased, performance in the clutch actually decreased a very small amount.) Looking at the second figure, we would conclude that there is no relation between clutchitude and performance. Of course, we know that conclusion is crazy, because we know that these players came from a population where clutchitude was very closely related to performance in late and tight situations. This is a statistical problem called "restriction of range"—although there is an underlying relation between clutchitude and performance in late and tight situations, it cannot be seen because we are only looking at a small part of the whole population. This may be part of the murk in James's fog.

Lately, Red Sox slugger David Ortiz has been a bright light in the fog. During one stretch of the 2006 season, it seemed that every morning's sports highlight show featured Ortiz getting another big hit to decide a game. The Elias Sports Bureau passed these statistics to Bill Simmons, aka "The Sports Guy," at ESPN.com: "Since the start of 2005, [Ortiz has] come up 13 times with the chance for a game-ending plate appearance and made an out only once (and he ended up winning *that* game in the 12th inning). . . . He has the most walk-off hits in any four-year span (12, and that doesn't include the three in the 2004 playoffs, which made him the only player in history with three game-ending postseason hits). . . . Since he joined the Red Sox in 2003, he has 15 walk-off hits and the rest of the team has 19 *total.* . . . Since Aug. 1, 2004, Ortiz has hit 21 home runs in 138 at-bats in Late-Inning Pressure Situations (no other player has more than 13)." [ellipses and italics in original] It is hard to be certain about how to categorize Ortiz's performance. On one hand, if you toss several hundred coins twenty times each, a few of them will come up heads eighteen or nineteen or twenty times. In a large sample, it would be strange if no one at all got lucky. Maybe Ortiz is lucky. He certainly has the good fortune to come to bat frequently with runners on base. With Ortiz hitting in front of him, has Manny Ramirez gotten the same number of chances to be a hero?

On the other hand, if there were such a thing as clutch performance, Ortiz is what it would look like. He is one of the game's better hitters to begin with, and it seems he has been consistently "clutch" in the last several years. The numbers The Sports Guy cited seem hard to attribute to chance. Take the statistic that between August 1, 2004, and July 31, 2006, when Ortiz hit the three-run walk-off home run that prompted The Sports Guy's column, Ortiz hit twenty-one home runs in the 138 at bats he had in Late-Inning Pressure Situations. That works out to 6.6 at bats per home run. In the other 1038 at bats Ortiz had during this period, he hit seventy-six home runs, which is 13.7 at bats per home run. To get an idea how unlikely it is that so many home runs would come in those 138 clutch situations, I had a computer repeatedly distribute ninety-seven home runs randomly across 1176 at bats, and then count the number of times that at least twenty-one home runs fell among those 138 Late-Inning Pressure Situations. In a million simulations, twenty-one or more of the home runs came in one of those 138 clutch situations less than 0.3 percent of the time. It is not impossible that Ortiz was merely lucky, but it seems unlikely. Again, though, we have to be wary of selection bias: we picked Ortiz because we knew going in that he had done well in those situations. Just like in the coin-flipping example, seeing one player among hundreds get lucky may not be all that unlikely.

There is an interesting anomaly in Ortiz's amazing run of clutch home runs. Sure he performs especially well in clutch situations, but why doesn't he perform as well in other situations? What's happening early in a game, or when the score is not close, that brings the lesser David Ortiz to the plate? On such occasions during the period we have examined, he was less than half as likely to hit a home run. Perhaps some players need extra pressure to bring out their very best—it might be that they are almost bored by anything else. Or perhaps there is a limit to how often a player can bring that level of mental toughness to bear, and he only does it when it seems to matter most. A clutch player who does better than other players in clutch situations (which Ortiz also seems to do) is one thing, but a clutch player who does better in clutch situations than low-pressure situations? That is not what we usually think of when we think of clutch and is, perhaps, one more reason to be careful about attributing Ortiz's performance, as amazing as it has been, to a special clutch ability. It would seem that there is always plenty of motivation to hit a home run, after all. Hitting them at the rate of one every 6.6 at bats would yield an amazing ninety-one home runs in a six hundred-at-bat season; there is no word to describe the way such a performance would surpass the record.

When all is considered, it would appear that Sheehan is right: there are no discernible differences in clutch hitting ability at the major league level, but only because all hitters are clutch hitters.

Choking may be a more common phenomenon, and the psychological literature probably has a lot more to say about that than it does about clutch performance. Momentary lapses that are too few and far between for a statistical analysis to detect probably do occur from time to time, and sometimes at the worst possible time: late in a game, late in a season, late in a World Series. For one thing, the sample of such games is much smaller, so poor performance in those games could just be a matter of bad luck. If a career .300 hitter goes five for twenty in the World Series for a .250 batting average, did he choke? Likely not—just one more hit and he would have been right at his average. Choking, if and when it happens, is likely so isolated that it would not leave a consistent pattern for a statistical analysis to find. Even so, we can all think of specific occasions when a player or team seemed to choke.

Pick your favorite collapse. Maybe the Cubs against the Marlins in the 2003 National League Championship Series. The series began in Chicago, and the Cubs jumped out to a 4–0 lead in the first inning of the first game, only to give up five in the top of the third. The game was tied 6–6 after six innings, and both teams scored two in the ninth (the Cubs coming up with two in the bottom of the inning to tie the game—no choke there), but the Marlins won it on a Mike Lowell home run in the eleventh. The next three games were pretty much all Cubs. In Game 2, it was 11–0 Cubs before the Marlins finally scored in the sixth, and the Cubs won, 12–3. Game 3 was closer. The Cubs took an early lead, lost it, got it back, lost it again, but finally won the game in the eleventh when Doug Glanville followed a Kenny Lofton single with a triple. Game 4 was another laugher, with the Cubs up 6–0 after four and going on to win 8–3.

So after four games, the Cubs were up 3–1. They lost Game 5, but that was more Josh Beckett's doing than theirs. Beckett threw a complete game two-hit shutout, with eleven strikeouts and only one walk. The Cubs never advanced a runner past first base. But that happens—sometimes a pitcher has a good game. They were still up 3–2 and they were going back to Chicago.

Game 6 opened much the same way Game 5 did, except in reverse. Mark Prior, born in 1980 and in his second year of Major League Baseball just like Josh Beckett, was pitching a beauty worthy of Beckett. Through seven innings, Prior had allowed just three hits and two walks, and had struck out six. There had been some hiccups: in the third inning Mark Grudzielanek made an error and catcher Paul Bako had a passed ball, but no harm had come of those. Having already scored one run in the first inning, the Cubs had runners at first and third with just one out, but scored no more. Since then, they had struck out seven times, and they had hit into two double plays. One of their three total runs had scored on a wild pitch by Marlins pitcher Carl Pavano, who otherwise was keeping the Cubs in check. But the Cubs had the lead and Prior looked to be cruising. The Cubs were (gasp!) six outs away from a World Series, their first since 1945.

If ever there is to be a baseball opera, it must be written about the top of the eighth inning of Game 6 of the 2003 National League Championship Series. By the time the fat lady sang, there had been all kinds of tragedy. Mike Mordecai popped out to left to start the inning. Still cruising, just five outs to go. But then Juan Pierre hit a double. Luis Castillo ran the count to 3–2 and then hit a pop-up foul down the left-field line, near the seats. Left fielder Moises Alou reached the spot quickly and tried to jump and reach over the wall for the catch, but a Cubs fan also tried to make the grab, preventing Alou from catching it. The Cubs argued for fan interference, but that only applies if the fan reaches onto the field of play, not when the player reaches into the stands.

After the episode in left field, Castillo walked on a wild pitch, with Pierre moving to third. The next hitter, Ivan Rodriguez, was down 0–2 quickly, but singled into left, plating Pierre. The Cubs lead was 3–1. The inning looked to be over when Miguel Cabrera hit to shortstop Alex Gonzalez a grounder that looked tailor-made for a double play. Gonzalez was a sure-handed shortstop who made only ten errors in 2003, fewer than the sixteen made by that year's Gold Glove winner, Edgar Renteria. But he muffed the chance, the bases were loaded, and the lead evaporated when (future Cub All-Star first baseman) Derrek Lee doubled.

Kyle Farnsworth relieved Prior and walked Mike Lowell to load the bases, the Cubs hoping for another chance at a double play. But Jeff Conine hit a sacrifice fly to right, and all the runners moved up. Just like that, the Cubs were behind. Farnsworth intentionally walked Todd Hollandsworth to load the bases again, again giving the Cubs a force out at every base if they could get a ground ball. But Mike Mordecai (who had made the first out of the inning, remember) doubled to clear the bases. The Marlins led 7–3. Mike Remlinger relieved Farnsworth, gave up a single for one more run, and then finally got the last out. The Cubs didn't manage a base runner for the rest of the game.

Game 7 did not start well, with the Marlins scoring three in the first, but the Cubs answered with three in the second and two in the third. The Marlins took the lead for good in the fifth with three more runs, and after one more in the sixth and two in the seventh, the Cubs scored one in the bottom of the seventh. But that would be all, and the Marlins, not the Cubs, went to the World Series. The fat lady would have to sing about choking.

Research suggests that choking may emerge from a greater-than-usual self-focus. Pressure of various kinds may increase a person's attention to the mechanical aspects of his performance, to the specific manner in which he performs the sport. Attention to a well-practiced, automatized skill is harmful to performance. This may seem to contradict what was said earlier about how the waxing and waning of attention might account for streaks and slumps in performance, but there is a key difference. In the earlier discussion, the issue was attention or focus on external elements of the situation, like a hitter focusing on a pitcher's release point. The issue here is attention to something internal, like the movement of the hips as the hitter swings the bat. In several studies, conditions that led people to focus on themselves as they performed a manual task have led to poorer performance. Or, if pressure was induced in various ways, such as by making the task competitive or by offering monetary rewards, the same kinds of decrements in performance occurred as when people were induced to focus on themselves.

In one of the virtual reality studies of hitting (described in Chapter 1), as the hitters were attempting to hit pitches in the simulation, a high- or low-pitched tone sounded at a random point sometime during the swing. In a control condition, the hitters just ignored the tone. In another condition, which was designed to take their focus *away from* their swing, they had to say whether the tone was high- or low-pitched. In a final condition, which was designed to put their focus *on* their swing, they had to say whether their bat was moving down or up at the time the tone sounded. For expert hitters (Division I college baseball players), hitting performance was worst in the final condition, when the tone directed their attention to their swing. When the tone directed their attention away from the swing (to the tone itself), their hitting performance was the same as in the condition in which they ignored the tone. (The exact opposite pattern occurred for novice hitters with some, but not extensive, playing experience. When the tone directed attention to the swing, they hit better; when it directed attention away from the swing, they hit worse.)

Another study induced pressure on the hitters to see whether pressure does indeed induce a focus on performance of the skill. After doing some hitting in the simulation, each hitter was told that he would be paired with a partner, and that if he and his partner could collectively increase their number of hits by 15 percent, they would receive twenty dollars. Each hitter was also told that his partner had already completed the test, and that the partner had carried his weight by increasing his hits by 15 percent. Whether the hitter and his partner got the reward or not would be entirely up to him. (This was a ruse—at the end of the experiment, all of the hitters got the twenty-dollar reward.)

When the pressure was on, hitters could better identify the direction their bat was moving when the tone sounded than when there was no pressure. The self-focus hypothesis predicted this result: attention to the mechanics of the swing hurts hitting performance, and pressure to perform well (paradoxically) increases attention to the mechanics of the swing. Other studies have demonstrated similar effects in golf and soccer.

Various kinds of pressures can produce the internal self-focus that leads to choking. Some recent studies suggest that even being subject to stereotyping and related kinds of negative feelings can produce this effect, which researchers have called *stereotype threat*. The stereotype of women holds that they do not do math as well as men. When, before a math test, that stereotype is made salient (creating the threat), women do, in fact, not perform as well as men; when it is not as salient, the difference is much smaller, if not gone altogether. The stereotype of African-Americans is that they are not as smart as whites. When the context makes that stereotype salient, African-Americans do perform less well than whites on an intelligence test; when it is not salient, the two groups perform equally.

In one study, white and black subjects performed a golf putting test under one condition that activated the stereotypical belief that whites are smarter than blacks and that characterized the putting skill as one that required "sports intelligence," in a second condition that activated the stereotypical belief that blacks are better natural athletes than whites and that characterized the putting skill as a test of "natural athletic ability," and in a control condition that made no reference to these stereotypical beliefs and simply presented the study as one of "general sports performance." Compared with their performance in the control condition that evoked no stereotypes, blacks performed about the same in the natural ability context, but their putting scores deteriorated by 23 percent in the sports intelligence context. Whites, in contrast, performed 13 percent worse in the natural ability context than they did in the control condition, but their performance in the sports intelligence condition was about the same as the control condition. Both groups also showed a high increase in the level of anxiety they reported when the stereotype suggested they would perform poorly, blacks in the sports intelligence context, whites in the natural ability context. A similar study had golfers putt at the same time that they listened for a certain word in a series of words spoken to them as they putted. When distracted like this from the concerns of the stereotype, the stereotype threat effect disappeared.

Still another way to induce pressure that leads to this form of choking is to get people to think about failure. Often, it seems, when we try to control our thoughts to achieve a certain outcome, exactly the opposite occurs. In one study, for instance, researchers asked people to hold a pendulum over a platform and to keep it centered there. In one condition, they simply asked them to keep the pendulum steady. In another, they asked them to keep it steady and emphasized that they should not let it move *sideways*. When they measured sideways movement, there was more in the condition that emphasized not moving that way than in the control condition. Asking people to be especially careful not to make a certain error actually made that error more likely. And this effect was exacerbated when people were distracted by having to count backward by thirds from one thousand. A similar result was found in a study of golf putting in which some of the participants repeatedly were warned not to imagine the putt missing when they were preparing their shot.

Thus, for those parts of a skill that require attention, such as aiming a throw (the throwing motion itself is well-practiced and should not be monitored), thinking about the errors we do not want to make may make them more likely. Such thoughts activate, or "prime," the wrong actions. And then worrying makes us check to see if we will make the error we want to avoid; this checking process activates the wrong movement even more.

Think of the famous throwing woes of Chuck Knoblauch or Rick Ankiel. If, in a player's frustration over previous errors, he thinks, "don't throw into the stands" or "don't be wild," he may actually make those outcomes more likely. Being distracted by the pressures that come with media and fan attention may increase the likelihood of those errors still more.

The "curses" that some teams live with may result from a similar kind of effect. Two teams, far beyond all others, have been steeped in the lore of a curse. One, the Red Sox, supposedly cursed for trading Babe Ruth to the Yankees, finally overcame the legend and won it all in 2004. The other, the Cubs, remain baseball's "lovable losers."

The Red Sox were believed to have been cursed when financially troubled Red Sox owner Harry Frazee sold Ruth to the Yankees so that Frazee could finance his Broadway production *No, No, Nanette*. Glenn Stout of ESPN.com recently exploded that myth by showing that the curse lore was invented in 1986 by *New York Times* sportswriter George Vecsey, based in part on historically inaccurate ideas about Frazee. For years, though, few knew and virtually no one acknowledged the true history of the "Curse of the Bambino," and it took on a life of its own. Certainly Red Sox fans were a beleaguered lot who expected to lose. Before the Sox came back from being down zero games to three in the American League Championship Series in 2004, Red Sox fans were again singing, almost in unison, the here-we-go-again song.

The Cubs' curse is more colorful, and perhaps more true, as Steve Gatto details in his book *Da Curse of the Billy Goat*. Though the Cubs had not won a World Series since 1908, the curse evidently began in 1945, when Wrigley Field officials attempted to eject fan William Sianis because Sianis had (inexplicably) brought his pet goat, Murphy, along to Game 4 of that year's World Series. Apparently, Murphy smelled. Sianis prevailed in the initial argument, but was later ejected anyway at the direction of Cubs owner Philip Knight Wrigley. As he was being ejected, Sianis yelled something to the effect of "the Cubs will never win another pennant!" The Cubs lost the game, they lost the World Series, and they have never made it back. Losing is a way of life for Cubs fans, and never was that mind-set in sharper relief than during the collapse in the NLCS in 2003.

Some of the most interesting psychological dimensions of baseball are probably impossible to study directly with any degree of scientific precision and control. Some phenomena are what they are by historical accident, and there is no way to find an appropriate standard of comparison in the historical record. Curses fall into this category. Psychologists seldom appeal to curses as explanations of behavior. Poor management and bad luck seem much more likely causes. But there may be something to curses and jinxes, in that they may become self-fulfilling prophecies of a sort. When members of a group (or team) are, rightly or wrongly, expected to perform poorly, they often do. Stereotype threat creates a self-fulfilling prophecy. If a player lives day in and day out with talk and more talk about failure under pressure, he may, however subtly and unconsciously, try to fight against that belief and, in so doing, turn up that harmful self-focus that undermines his normal level of play.

Part of the miseries experienced by Cubs and Red Sox fans may be due to the perpetuation of stories about jinxes and curses and the continual recounting of all the late-season or late-game collapses that fit that mythology. Players who constantly play with the fear or expectation of another collapse hanging over their heads may, in fact, perform more poorly, but not because of a jinx or curse or a history of close calls and should-have-beens, but because those ideas and constant media and fan attention to them put pressure on the players that in turn leads to harmful self-focus.

Home Field Advantage and Disadvantage

LONG TIME ON THE ROAD: *Today, the Angels conclude a 14-day, 12-game road trip to Chicago White Sox (May 30–June 1; 1–2), Boston (June 3–5; 1–2), Atlanta (June 6–8; 2–1) and New York Mets (June 10–12; 1–1) . . . The club is 5–6 thus far on trip . . .* **The four teams the Angels will face on this trip boast a combined mark of 77–41 at home this season** *. . . Angels finished 10–5 on the road in May and are second in Majors with 20 road victories . . . Halos pitchers own a 3.87 road ERA (304.1 IP—131 ER) overall . . . Angels' road ERA was 2.96 in May (130.2 IP—43 ER) . . .* **Including last season, Angels are 48–28 over last 76 road games** *. . . Halos led AL with club record 47 road wins in 2004.*

—Los Angeles Angels Game Notes, Sunday, June 12, 2005
[ellipses and bold text in original]

Home field advantage is a well-known factor in sports, and baseball is no different: the home team has historically won about 54 percent of the games and scores about half a run more at home on average. In 1989, the statistician for the Texas Rangers, Craig Wright, and Rangers pitching coach, Tom House, who is also a former major-league pitcher, collaborated on *The Diamond Appraised,* a book in which they combined their areas of expertise to address a range of issues in baseball, including the home field advantage. They took turns offering and evaluating a number of potential causes. In Wright's view, about 40 percent of the home field advantage (about 0.2 runs) is due to umpire bias toward the home team. Umpires, he reasoned, feel the pressure from the fans and, presumably unknowingly, bias their calls in that direction. He estimated that about 30 percent is due to "home cooking," that is, sleeping in one's own bed and following a normal daily routine as opposed to the demands of travel, including jet lag. Fitting the player to the ballpark, and vice versa, may account for another 10 percent, he suggests. Teams can select left-handed power hitters for a short right-field fence, or groom an infield to take advantage, or mitigate the disadvantages, of team speed. And another 10 percent may be due to players' familiarity with the ballpark, knowing the outline of the outfield fence or the limits of foul territory, for instance. And finally, he suggests that 5 percent may be the encouragement of the home crowd, and a final 5 percent the strategic edge that comes with batting last. Wright presents some baseball statistics related to each of these factors to support his claims.

The psychological literature supports at least some of these contentions. For example, one study noted that the home field advantage is larger in sports played indoors than in sports played outdoors, which is consistent with the idea that the home crowd is part of the advantage, though the effect would be small in baseball because it is (largely) an outdoor game. Until they lost to the A's in the 2006 playoffs, the success of the Minnesota Twins in their home, the Metrodome, also seemed to lend support to this idea. Another study showed that the longer the visiting team had been on the road and the longer the home team had been at home, the greater the home field advantage, lending some support to the home cooking fraction of the advantage.

Baseball Prospectus has pulled together some data on one of the factors that Wright proposed, the advantage that may come from knowing the ballpark. One article investigated how such knowledge might influence base running. Players playing in their home parks may know better when to take an extra base, going from first to third or second to home, say, on a single, or first to home on a double. The article featured an impressive set of data that yielded both the attempt and success rates for each of these situations over two separate five-year periods. (The results from the two periods correlated highly.) Somewhat surprisingly, there were no substantial differences in either the attempt or success rates of home and visiting teams. No knowledge advantage there.

Another article examined defense statistics and, this time, found some evidence for an advantage for the home team. Using a composite measure of team defense, for the last thirty-four years through 2005, the average ratio of home defense to road defense has *never* been less than 1.0. The difference is not huge—teams play about 1 percent better defense at home than on the road—but adds up to enough that, all other things being equal, teams would have a winning percentage of .508 at home and .492 on the road. That may not seem like much, but remember that the overall home field advantage is .540 to .460. Contrary to Wright and House's 5 percent estimate, it may be that park knowledge accounts for about 20 percent of the home field advantage. Or, it could be that the advantage in defensive performance comes because of home cooking. It is difficult to tease these factors apart unequivocally.

There is a quirky footnote in the literature on home field advantage. Further analyses have since called into a question the idea that the home field was a *disadvantage* for the home team when a World Series championship was imminent, but in 1984, an analysis of World Series play from 1924 to 1982 showed that the home teams in series that went to Game 7 seemed to have a profound disadvantage. In the time frame they examined, the World Series followed the now-familiar pattern of two games at one team's park, three games at the other team's, and then the final two games back at the first team's (if necessary, of course); before that, other patterns were followed (a different pattern was also followed in 1943–1945 because of travel restrictions associated with World War II; a later re-analysis omitted these years). Through 1982, twenty-six World Series went to Game 7. Though the home team's winning percentage in Games 1 and 2 was 60 percent, in Game 7 it was a miserable 39 percent. With home field advantage on the brink of victory, teams seemed much *less* likely to win.

There are two ways to look at this pattern, which the authors of a later analysis called the kinder and darker forms of choking. It could be the anticipation of victory in front of the home crowd that takes the home team off its game. The potential change in self-identity—we're going to be world champions—might cause players to focus their attention on themselves and how wonderful it would feel to win. This in turn distracts the players and leads them to focus too much on skills that they typically would allow to run off automatically, just as self-focus can cause choking as discussed above. Because the home field crowd is invested in that same outcome, this effect is bigger for the home team than for the visitors. This is the kinder form of choking. The darker form would occur when a team fears failure. We can just as easily imagine that the home team, afraid to fail in front of the home fans, is more anxious than the visiting team, and thus performs more poorly.

In Game 6, home teams that were down three games to two had a winning percentage of .727—with their backs to the wall, on the verge of losing the series, the home teams won much more often than would be expected from the usual .540 home field advantage, or even compared with the .600 these teams achieved in Games 1 and 2. When leading three games to two, however, the winning percentage for the home teams was only .375. Imminent success, rather than imminent failure, seemed more of a problem for the home team.

The idea of a home field disadvantage was counterintuitive and quickly gained a lot of media attention and became an accepted part of our understanding of human motivation—these results were often mentioned in psychology textbooks. The idea did not hold up well, however. A follow-up study several years later, which included all seven-game series from 1924 to 1993 (except the World War II years 1943–1945) and the seven-game League Championship series, yielded a different result. In the interim between the two studies, four more World Series went to the seventh game, and the home team won every time (and since 1993, there have been three more seven-game series, and again, all were won by the home team). Home teams were, through 1993, 14–15 in the seventh game of the World Series. Breaking the records down into three time frames (pre-1950, or pre-television), 1950–1968, and 1969–1993 (post-expansion), the authors of the later study turned up the odd fact that in the first and third eras, the home team won Game 7 of the World Series most of the time (they were 6–2 in the pre-TV era and 6–4 in the post-expansion era). In the middle era, somehow, the home team was 2–9.

The most plausible conclusion is that overall, the home team probably has the advantage in the World Series, just like they do during the regular season. But because of the relatively small number of seven-game World Series, the home team's somewhat poor record for a period of years is probably simply due to chance. Overall, since 1980, the team with home field advantage has won twenty of twenty-five World Series.

The Sophomore Slump

BOBBY CROSBY

- *Was placed on the 15-day disabled list on April 6, retroactive to April 5, with stress fractures in his ninth and 10th ribs . . . it was his first career stint on the DL . . . was the A's Opening Day starter at shortstop and went 1 for 2 before leaving the game after striking out in the fourth inning*
- *Batted .337 last June, his best one month batting average in 2004, and now has a .326 (45–135) career average for the month*

—Oakland Athletics Game Notes, Sunday, June 12, 2005

JASON BAY

- *Has started each of his first 60 games*
- *Has gone 4-for-5 in his last two games and is hitting .310 (9-for-29) in 10 games this month*
- *Is hitting .338 (22-for-65) with three HR in his last 20 games*
- *Hit .292 (26-for-89) with two homers in April and .292 (31-for-106) with nine homers in May*

—Pittsburgh Pirates Game Notes, Sunday, June 12, 2005

In mid-2005, the 2004 Rookies of the Year were continuing where they had left off the year before. No sophomore slump for them. Crosby, as you can see, had been hurt early in the year (and he would miss some games late in the year, too), but was hitting .326 with two home runs. By the end of the year, his 2005 statistics would exceed his 2004 statistics—his on-base percentage went up from .319 to .346, slugging percentage from .426 to .456. Bay was hitting .295 with eleven home runs, and would go on to play in all 162 games in 2005, improving right along with Crosby, with his on-base percentage rising from .358 to .402 and his slugging percentage from .550 to .559.

Based on the conventional wisdom, we should be surprised at these performances. Rookies who have outstanding years are expected to endure a slump in their second season. Consistent with the expectation, the previous year's winners, Angel Berroa and Dontrelle Willis, had both seen their performance decline somewhat. And it turns out that, on average, outstanding years *do* tend to be followed by less successful performance.

In April 2005, Aaron Gleeman, writing for hardballtimes .com, looked at the records of all the 114 Rookies of the Year through 2003. Using a variation of Bill James's Win Shares statistic, which measures both the raw performance statistics and how much the player contributes to his team's overall performance, Gleeman determined that 73 of the 114 (64 percent) did, in fact, slump in their sophomore season, relative to their rookie year. Four (3.5 percent) stayed the same. Only a third (37 of 114, or 32.5 percent) of the Rookies of the Year improved to perform even better in their second year. On average, win shares decreased by about 20 percent from the rookie to the sophomore season; the decline was greater for pitchers (33 percent) than it was for hitters (15 percent). And the declines were not trivial, either. More than two-thirds of the players who declined (54) lost more than 25 percent of their win shares from the previous year.

There are several plausible psychological explanations for

the sophomore slump. The player who began one year in relative rookie obscurity might be dazzled by the spotlight that shines on last year's Rookie of the Year—the extra media attention and higher expectations may force him to perform under more pressure than in the first year. Or, it might be that rookies, still untested and with something to prove, are just a bit more motivated, a bit more driven to succeed, and that some of this edge is naturally lost after a player has won his place on the team.

There is also a plausible statistical explanation for the sophomore slump, a phenomenon called *regression to the mean*. Anytime that we measure some statistic that changes over time in a population of individuals and select from the set those individuals with the most extreme scores, and then measure that statistic again at a later time, we can expect that the second measurement for the selected individuals will tend to move from the original extreme score toward the overall average for all individuals in the set. Suppose we take the ten players with the highest batting averages for the month of April 2004 (minimum fifty at bats) and the ten with the lowest averages for the month, and look again at their averages for May. As you can see in the table on page 182, *every one* of the players in the top group sees a decline in his average, and *every one* of the players in the bottom group sees an improvement in his average. As a group, the top hitters in April see their average drop .085 in May, whereas the bottom hitters see theirs improve by .089. Notice, too, that the collective average for all twenty players stays about the same, at .296 in April and .292 in May, and that the May averages of the two groups converge closely on that overall average. (Another factor here is that the sample size is larger in May, and so that month provides a better estimate of the player's "essential" batting average than April does with its smaller sample. But that is part of the point. A sample

		March/April			May		
		H	AB	AVG	H	AB	AVG
L. Ford	MIN	26	62	0.419	31	107	0.290
R. Belliard	CLE	35	84	0.417	25	102	0.245
P. LoDuca	LAD	32	77	0.416	32	98	0.327
S. Casey	CIN	36	87	0.414	40	106	0.377
K. Harvey	KC	25	63	0.397	33	99	0.333
J. Uribe	CWS	24	61	0.393	33	109	0.303
M. Ramirez	BOS	33	85	0.388	33	104	0.317
D. Bautista	ARI	32	85	0.376	29	103	0.282
J. Wilson	PIT	31	84	0.369	39	116	0.336
M. Young	TEX	35	95	0.368	36	120	0.300
Top group average		309	783	0.395	331	1064	0.311
J. Phillips	NYM	11	68	0.162	20	72	0.278
D. Jeter	NYY	16	95	0.168	31	119	0.261
M. Lieberthal	PHI	12	69	0.174	23	87	0.264
A. Gonzalez	FLA	14	77	0.182	24	95	0.253
J. Rollins	PHI	13	71	0.183	30	107	0.280
C. Stynes	PIT	10	54	0.185	12	53	0.226
M. Ensberg	HOU	10	52	0.192	26	80	0.325
B. Williams	NYY	14	72	0.194	26	96	0.271
M. Bellhorn	BOS	12	62	0.194	33	120	0.275
J. Cruz	TB	13	65	0.200	23	87	0.264
Bottom group average		125	685	0.182	248	916	0.271
Average of all players		434	1468	0.296	579	1980	0.292

taken at one moment in time is subject to random variability that, all other things being equal, will "even out" over time.)

Selecting a Rookie of the Year could be a lot like picking the top ten batting averages for April 2004—as a group, the Rookies of the Year are selected because their statistics were highest or near highest among first-year players. When scores are variable over time, as batting averages certainly are, the individuals in a group with the highest measurements at one point in time are likely to see their scores drop when the measure is taken again later, simply because part of the variability in the scores is random. Manny Ramirez is a better-than-average hitter, and so is Derek Jeter. But Ramirez is not a .388 hitter, just as Jeter is not a .168 hitter. Their averages for April 2004 only partly reflected their true abilities—they also reflected the forces of chance.

One study used a larger sample than just Rookies of the Year by including any rookie performance in the top third of the group of rookies. It also looked at how those players performed after their second year, with the idea that there should be a "rebound effect" if the sophomore slump is truly a slump. If the outstanding-rookie play reflects the player's true ability, and there really is a sophomore slump, then performance should return in Years 3, 4, and 5 to the level of Year 1. But if what we see is regression to the mean, then Years 3, 4, and 5 should, on average, remain about like Year 2. The authors of this study regarded their results as "equivocal." Hitters' RBI and pitchers' wins and strikeouts did not change substantially across Years 1 to 5. But RBI and wins are statistics that are heavily influenced by the rest of the team. A hitter has to have runners on base to collect RBI, and a pitcher has to have run support to earn a win. (Remember Roger Clemens in 2005, with a major league–leading 1.87 ERA and a mediocre 13–8 won-loss record? In nine of Clemens's thirty-two starts, the Astros offense was shut out.) The strikeout data did fit the regression to the mean pattern, though not dramatically, dropping from 123 to 115 from Year 1 to Year 2 and averaging 117 in Years 3 to 5. Home runs was the only statistic to show a rebound, but again that was quite small, dropping from twelve to ten in Years 1 and 2 and then averaging twelve again in Years 3 to 5.

Hitters' batting averages and pitchers' ERAs both worsened from Year 1 to Year 2 and declined still more in Years 3, 4, and 5. Batting average dropped from .300 in Year 1 to .276 in Year 2 and then to .269 in Years 3–5; ERA rose from 2.23 in Year 1 to 2.38 in Year 2 and then still more to 2.61 in Years 3–5.

Certainly the preponderance of the evidence seems to rest with the regression to the mean hypothesis. The bottom line? Expect that more often than not, a good rookie year will be followed by a decline in performance. But don't give that any psychological weight. The player simply likely had better-than-usual luck in his first year.

Free Agency, Arbitration, and Being Traded

BELTRAN, CARLOS
> *LAST HOME RUN: June 2, 2005 vs. Arizona (Estes)*
> *HOMESTAND: .256 (10–39, 3-R, 3-2B, HR, 4-RBI, 4-BB, SAC, SF)*
> *LAST HOME RUN: June 2, 2005 vs. Arizona (Estes)*
> *WITH RISP: .291 (16–55), 2-HR, 19-RBI*
> *VS. LHP: .333 (20–60), 1-HR, 6-RBI*
> *VS. RHP: .270 (41–152), 6-HR, 23-RBI*

—New York Mets Game Notes, Sunday, June 12, 2005

We talk about "playing" baseball, but George Will was more correct when he called his book *Men at Work* and not *Men at Play*. At least for the lucky ones, baseball is a job. And the conditions of employment affect performance on the field: salaries, arbitration, free agency, and trades all influence how well these men do their work.

The piles of baseball statistics have been an attractive test bed for psychologists interested in work motivation; both salary and performance data are public and readily available. The common-sense expected result is as obvious as what we know about a rat's behavior in a maze. Find the goal in the maze, get a food reward. Hit more home runs, get a bigger salary. But things are not quite that simple, and competing psychological theories have not always been able to account by themselves for the ways that player salary affects player performance.

The moral side of player contracts, if we can call it that, usually gets the most media attention. Ownership and management are condemned for a lack of fiscal discipline. Players are condemned for being greedy. In 2005, Carlos Beltran was regularly and roundly booed for not living up to the performance fans expected after he signed a seven-year, $119 million deal with the Mets before that season. In 2004, he had hit a combined .265 for the Royals and Astros with a total of 38 HRs. As many have noted, however, it was probably his amazing postseason performance in 2004 that turned Beltran into one of that year's most sought-after free agents: in forty-six at bats, he hit .435 with eight home runs. In 2005, Beltran's power numbers in particular dropped off, and he hit only sixteen home runs. By not hitting his eighth home run until June 16, Beltran took nearly eleven weeks to do in 2005 what he had done in just twelve postseason games in 2004.

Year	Team	AB	Runs	HR	RBI	AVG	OBP	SLG	SB
1998	Royals	14	12	0	7	.276	.317	.466	3
1999	Royals	663	112	22	108	.293	.337	.454	27
2000	Royals	372	49	7	44	.247	.309	.366	13
2001	Royals	617	106	24	101	.306	.362	.514	31
2002	Royals	637	114	29	105	.273	.346	.501	35
2003	Royals	521	102	26	100	.307	.389	.522	41
2004	Royals	266	51	15	51	.278	.367	.534	14
2004	Astros	333	70	23	53	.258	.368	.559	28
2005	Mets	582	83	16	78	.266	.330	.414	17
2006	Mets	510	127	41	116	.275	.388	.594	18

Beltran's downturn was probably no surprise to the authors of a report on the effects of free agency on baseball player performance called "Performance-Undermining Effects of Baseball Free Agent Contracts." The study examined the performance of the thirty-three free agent hitters who, between the 1992 and 1998 seasons, signed new, multi-year contracts of at least $1 million and that provided at least 30 percent more salary than their previous contract. That list of free agents included players like Moises Alou, Barry Bonds, Kenny Lofton, Benito Santiago, and Danny Tartabull. Replicating the basic pattern of results found in several previous studies of baseball free agency (almost all of which focused only on hitters), the researchers found that overall, performance increased somewhat the season before (B1) the player became a free agent relative to the season before that (B2). In the year after the new contract (A1), performance decreased, on average, to levels lower even than observed in year B2. Finally, the second season after signing (A2), performance generally returned to B2 levels.

Of course, this is what happens on average—looking at the case of any one player could yield a different result. Moreover, some of the studies qualify this general pattern somewhat. For instance, one study noted that the increase in salary a hitter may gain in free agency is determined largely by power numbers—reviews of contracts showed that the better the power numbers, the bigger the free agent contract—and that whereas batting average may even drop before free agency, home run rate more closely shows the pattern of an increase in B1, decrease in A1, and recovery in A2. The author argued that this result was consistent with a compromise between two theories. The so-called equity theory would generally predict that would-be free agents, perceiving themselves as undercompensated relative to what they could be earning, would perform less well the season before free agency in order to bring their performance and compensation into what they would believe would be a more equitable balance. On the other hand, expectancy theory would predict that performance would, if anything, improve the season before free agency, by virtue of the player's expectation that his efforts would be rewarded with a hefty new contract. Because batting average mattered less for free agency, and thus had relatively little to do with the player's expectation of future rewards, that might slide to levels more consistent with the player's perception of being underpaid. But hitting for power affected future rewards and, thus, improved.

And why the drop after signing? The researchers offered one general cause for the change in performance and three ways that it might manifest itself. The general idea was that free agent contracts change the player's motivation from relatively internally driven to relatively externally driven. Earlier research had shown that when people are compensated, or compensated more, for doing something that they already enjoy doing, their levels of interest in and motivation for that activity actually decrease. Suppose you regularly keep score when you go to a baseball game, just because you like to, and then someone starts to pay you $20 for every score sheet. Based on this research, we would predict that your motivation and enjoyment for score-keeping would both decrease, because now it would seem like you were doing it for the pay rather than for the simple pleasure. Similarly, a free agent who signs a big contract, even if he was relatively well paid before that, is likely to see playing baseball more as something he does because he gets a big paycheck and less as something he does because he enjoys it. So the general idea is that the player feels he is no longer someone fortunate enough to get paid to do something he loves; he has become an employee, albeit a well-paid one.

One of the possible contributing factors in changing the player's motivation level is the pressure the player experiences as a result of increased expectations and attention from the media and the fans, and from team management and teammates. It is easy to imagine a player "pressing" to justify the big contract. The consensus is that this problem is magnified in New York, where media attention is especially intense, and Beltran's coaches and teammates seem to subscribe to this theory, as shown by their support for him in this news story:

> "It's part of the adjustment for any free agent in New York, trying to play up to expectations and to show other people and themselves that the contract is justified, while trying to play the game relaxed," said Mets hitting coach Rick Down.

Added manager Willie Randolph, "A lot of players try to carry a team, to do too much, which sometimes leads to a little bit of pressing; that's only natural. I've seen a lot of players come through this town, really great players, Hall of Famers, and almost all went through an adjustment."

Mike Piazza is a future Hall of Famer who experienced that adjustment during his first year in New York, after the Mets acquired him in 1998. He told Beltran, "[he should] just have fun with it; it's a great city and obviously there's expectations. But he's a great player, a talented guy, and he can handle it. There's no reason to think he won't be a star here. It just takes time. It's a big switch for him."

Another factor that may contribute here is that the introduction of the reward may undermine a player's feeling of autonomy and free choice and replace it with the feeling that he is being controlled and manipulated. All the extra attention to his performance may give the player the sense that he is only playing to please the people who pay his salary and may take the edge off his motivation to play the game. This seems plausible, but Beltran's play in 2005 does not seem to fit. On August 11, his hustle even got him in big trouble, trouble that would have given him an excuse to take it easy for a little while, but he didn't:

Like two missiles veering horribly off-course, Mike Cameron came charging in from right field, and Beltran from center, and the ensuing, sickening crunch of bone-on-bone was universally deemed one of the worst collisions in baseball history.

Cameron was lucky to have escaped with his life, so terrible were his injuries. Beltran suffered a concussion and a facial fracture. The Mets' playoff dreams were just beginning to percolate, but the All-Star was expected to opt for season-ending surgery, which doctors recommended.

Instead, Beltran quietly refused surgery so that he could attempt to help his team. He chose to play with a broken face.

Beltran missed only four games after the collision, despite the effects of the concussion, which lingered for two weeks. He was having difficulty waking up and feeling off-balance.

Regardless of his injuries, the center fielder continued to hurl himself recklessly after sinking liners. It was an astonishing sight.

Finally, some credence may be due to the familiar line of moral indignation that accompanies a story like Beltran's and says the player was gunning for a big raise before the contract and then got too comfortable—or worse yet, just plain lazy—after signing. The researchers suggest that the reward, because it is so large, may turn the player into a "fat cat" simply by undermining everything that previously motivated him. There is no longer anything more to work for. Though this idea leads us up to the moral high ground, it may be the weakest of the suggestions for why the player's motivation might flag. For one thing, there are other rewards, such as the adulation of fans and the esteem of teammates, batting titles and statistical records, and the chance at postseason play, that might motivate a player to perform well even after signing a blockbuster free agent deal. Major-league baseball players are intensely competitive people—that's how they got to the major leagues in the first place—and there is still a lot to compete for.

Perhaps more importantly, performance rebounds in A2, the second year after the free agent signing. Depending on the structure of the contract, the player likely earns as much, if not more, money in the second and subsequent years of the big contract. He should thus feel as much the "fat cat" in A2 and after as he does in A1. The fat cat theory is not consistent with the rebound typically observed in the free agent's performance.

Another reason to doubt the fat cat theory is that the general trend in player performance, as documented by a study of the 1991 and 1992 seasons, is for players who are overpaid relative to teammates or other players in similar positions to improve their performance rather than let it slide. The relative amount that a player was over- or underpaid as assessed at the beginning of the 1992 season predicted how much the player's performance would improve or decline in the 1992 season relative to 1991. Players who were overpaid tended to improve, and players who were underpaid tended to decline. This finding is additional support for the equity theory already mentioned—in general, the theory predicts that people will match their output to their earnings. If they are underpaid, they will tend to perform less well. But if they are overpaid, performance improves, as if to ward off the perception that the player is behaving like a fat cat. (The authors of the study noted that workers in other fields, perhaps because they are in less visible positions, may have an easier time rationalizing their overpayment, and thus such improvements in performance are not typically observed in other work environments. An overpaid left fielder might hit more home runs next year, but an overpaid middle-management type probably won't shuffle any more paper, or do his shuffling any more efficiently.)

Because players with a new free agent contract are more likely to be overpaid than players who are in the later years of their contracts, the expectation would be that their performance would improve, but instead we first see a decline, and then an improvement. There are all kinds of reasons not to make too much of one case like Carlos Beltran's; numerous idiosyncrasies no doubt also factored into the ups and downs of his performance from 2003 to 2005. For instance, his power production may have declined simply because in 2005 his home games were at Shea, a less hitter-friendly ballpark than Kauffman Stadium or Minute Maid Park. But then what of 2006, when he not only returned to his 2004 level of performance but exceeded it? Even if other factors were at work, Beltran's case illustrates the different ways that motivational factors can influence a player's performance and the relative weakness of the most popular of those notions, the fat cat theory. Fortunately for Mets fans, Beltran followed the typical pattern and, after a brief decline after signing his big contract in 2005, returned in 2006 to his pre-contract level of performance, and then some.

Before players are eligible for free agency, they may at certain times in their early careers seek salary arbitration if they and their team cannot agree on contract terms. The player and his representatives submit a bid for contract terms to an independent arbitrator, as does the team. The arbitrator is bound to select either the player's bid or the team's, and may not split the difference. This situation seems built for equity theorists: it forces the player and the team to compare the player's performance history with that of other players in the labor market and try to divine the fairest estimate of the player's value. Both sides have the opportunity to persuade the arbitrator to accept their reasoning, but because the official may not settle on an intermediate value, the incentives work against their hedging their bid in their own favor. If they move too far from what the arbitrator judges is fair market value for the player, then the other side's bid will win. Thinking in terms of equity theory, few situations could make the player's perception of his value more clear—any discrepancy between that perceived value and his subsequent salary should influence his motivation accordingly.

Somewhat less work has been done on the effects of arbitration on performance, but equity theory, again with the help of expectancy theory, seems to explain players' performance changes before and after salary arbitration. The year before arbitration (B1), player performance improves, and how much it improves is important: the greater the improvement in performance in the pre-arbitration season, the more likely the player is to win the arbitration. Here again, expectancy theory makes sense. Expecting that good performance will be rewarded, performance improves. But then, perhaps, equity takes over. In the year following arbitration (A1), performance drops off for both winners and losers. The losers drop back to about where they were in B2, but the winners slide only about halfway back to that level; their A1 and A2 performance levels fall about halfway between B2 and B1. How much the losers fall may have something to do with the arbitration process. Some of the evidence suggests that the greater the discrepancy between the player's offer and the team's offer, the greater the decline in player performance. And losers are more likely to change teams or leave baseball altogether. Those results fit neatly with equity theory: the more the player perceives that he is underpaid, the sharper the decline in his level of play.

The player has something to say about the outcome of free agency and arbitration. The player has little or nothing to say about being traded, unless he and his team have agreed in the player's contract to limitations on trades, or unless he has ten years of major-league service, the last five with his current team. Several psychological studies of the effects of trades on performance support the conventional wisdom. Players generally know when their team is shopping them around and talking about potential trades with other teams. The pressure and the distraction of that process are commonly thought to wear on the player, and the studies bear that out. When a player is traded during a season, performance tends to be worse than the player's previous career average before the trade, and then returns to normal levels afterward. These effects are not observed when the trade occurs between seasons. It is also commonly believed that players "gear up" when they play against a team that traded them away, and again the data bear this out. Several conditions determined whether this would occur, however, including whether the player had been traded for the first time in his career, whether he had played for a relatively longer time with the trading team, whether he was relatively young at the time of the trade, and whether the player's ability was relatively high. When only one of these conditions was met, this gearing-up effect was relatively small, but if two of the conditions applied, it was bigger, and it was greater still if three or four did.

Steroid Use

In the 2005 season, of course, Rafael Palmeiro tested positive for steroids. Much has been written about the physical effects of

Rafael Palmeiro on Baseball's All-Time Lists			
Category	No.	Rank	Next
Home Runs	559	10th	Reggie Jackson (563)
Extra Base Hits	1176	8th	Frank Robinson (1186)
Total Bases	5305	11th	Frank Robinson (5373)
Doubles	579	14th	Robin Yount (583)
Runs Batted In	1803	16th	Frank Robinson (1812)
Hits	2972	27th	Sam Rice (2987)

steroids and their obvious potential impact on player performance. (However, *Baseball Prospectus* has shown that the seasonal home run rate over the last several years does not
conform to the pattern that the simple notion that steroid use
increases home run hitting would suggest. Things are likely
more complex than that.) Psychologically, less is known. It does
seem fairly clear that administration of testosterone can increase the likelihood of aggressive behavior, hence the commonly used phrase *'roid rage,* but it is much less clear what
other effects there might be. Some claim that testosterone therapy improves mental acuity, but there is very little direct evidence to support that contention.

One argument often heard in the controversy over steroid
use is that while it may help a player hit the ball farther, making contact in the first place still reflects pure talent, unaided
by steroids. The existing literature does little to help us evalu-
ate that claim. Mike Barhke and Charles Yesalis are editors of
Performance-Enhancing Substances in Sport and Exercise, a vol-
ume that digests the state of knowledge about steroids and other
performance-enhancing drugs. Both told me that basically
nothing is known directly about how steroids might influence
psychological performance. Barhke suggested that steroid use
might make a player a bit more aggressive, more likely to
"jump on" a pitch, and might increase confidence. Yesalis was
also not aware of any research that has investigated the link
between steroid use and cognitive enhancement, though he
did say there have long been claims that, for example, the use
of human growth hormone could improve a player's visual
acuity.

We do know—as discussed in the chapter on throwing—
that there is a relation between processing of spatial information

and throwing accuracy. There also appears to be a relation between testosterone levels and spatial ability, but these data are mixed and difficult to interpret conclusively. Spatial abilities are typically measured by tests that require mental manipulation of objects; for example, imaging what an object would look like if rotated, or looking at a diagram of an unfolded object and imaging how the object would appear once folded. One relation between performance on these tests and testosterone is clear: men consistently perform better on average than women.

Looking more closely, one early study demonstrated the usual male advantage on these tests, but also measured androgen (including testosterone) levels in both males and females. Females high in androgen levels (that is, in the range of the males with the lowest levels) performed better on spatial tests than females with low levels. But males with lower levels performed better than males with higher levels. The overall pattern showed that as levels increased from the lowest levels to the highest, performance on tests of spatial ability rose gradually to a peak near where the highest androgen levels were recorded among females and the lowest levels were recorded among males, and then fell off as androgen levels increased to extremely high levels in some males. Both the highest and lowest androgen levels were associated with poorer spatial abilities, with people in the midrange of androgen levels performing the best.

That pattern of results has been replicated in some subsequent studies, including one that took advantage of the annual ebb (spring) and flow (fall) of testosterone levels in males who live in the northern hemisphere to show that spatial ability was better when levels were lower, in the spring. Another showed that the same pattern holds over daily variations in testosterone level, which is higher in the morning, with performance on tests of spatial ability showing corresponding decreases in the morning relative to later in the day. However, no association between testosterone levels and spatial abilities has been observed in some studies, and in still others, the pattern has been reversed altogether, with higher levels of testosterone in males associated with better performance on the test of spatial ability. Of cases where testosterone levels are changed deliberately, rather than merely measured in a sample, one review observed that

> drastically altered testosterone levels yield a coherent picture. In female-to-male transsexuals testosterone has an enhancing, not quickly reversible, effect on spatial ability performance; an opposite effect is reported for male-to-female transsexuals receiving androgen-ablation. In hypogonadal men, visuo-spatial abilities are impaired and most studies report improvement during androgen substitution.

Also, testosterone supplements have been shown to improve spatial ability in older men. The inconsistencies in these results may have come about because the various studies have used different spatial tests, and other aspects of experimental design have varied. Another potential problem is that measurement of steroid levels is sometimes unreliable.

Still, the general pattern that emerges is that over at least part of the range of normally observed testosterone levels, greater testosterone levels lead to higher performance on tests of spatial abilities. And at least some studies show that at the higher end of the range of testosterone levels observed across individuals, or when testosterone levels are relatively high in an individual in which they fluctuate normally, performance may be somewhat depressed. Those changes in testosterone levels due to steroid use may influence psychological abilities relevant to playing baseball, especially (as discussed in Chapter 3) with regard to throwing (and many pitchers have tested positively recently), but perhaps also in relation to any skill that involves spatial perception, which might include hitting.

Depending on the levels of testosterone achieved during steroid use, they may thus improve psychological performance, but it is also conceivable that steroid abuse could actually make hitting a curveball harder, especially since it would raise testosterone levels to an extreme. Recall the experiments with throwing that showed that timing of release was likely based on a spatial model of the throw. If timing of movements during hitting similarly depends on a spatial model, then there may also be some effect on hitting.

Another factor that limits our ability to make firm conclusions is that the studies relating testosterone levels to spatial ability are correlational, rather than controlled, experiments. Conducting controlled studies is problematic because of the obvious concerns about the health of test subjects. Even in relatively low doses, there are concerns that testosterone use may increase risk of prostate cancer and many other health problems. At the levels used by abusers, the dangers are obviously even greater. So though it is likely that our evidence will remain indirect, more will be needed before we can make any definitive judgment about how steroids influence psychological performance on the baseball field.

CHAPTER SIX

Psychology in the Bleachers

On July 24, 2004, a cool, damp, and windy day in Boston, thousands of baseball fans went to Fenway Park hoping to see the Yankees play the Red Sox. It had been raining most of the day, and as the time for the first pitch approached, even though the rain had stopped, it appeared that there would be no game. The few players on the field were not warming up. A tarp covered the infield and puddles covered the tarp. A decision to postpone the game seemed probable, especially given the Red Sox's recent struggles. At the end of May they were tied with the Yankees for first place in the American League East, but after a seven-week swoon they stood nine-and-a-half games behind their bitter rivals.

The weather for the previous night's game had been fine, but the evening was gloomy all the same. The Red Sox had gone up early, but a five-run sixth inning gave the Yankees a 7–4 lead. The Sox scratched their way back even with one run in the bottom of the sixth, one in the bottom of the seventh, and another in the bottom of the eighth. Then, in the top of the ninth, new Yankee third baseman Alex Rodriguez, who as a free agent before the season had been the subject of a bidding war between the Yankees and Red Sox, drove in Gary Sheffield with what would be the winning run. Mariano Rivera closed the bottom of the ninth with just nine pitches. Yankees 8, Red Sox 7.

It looked like the Sox would get a reprieve in the form of a rainout. But just as the Yankees, showered and dressed again in street clothes, were heading back to their bus, they were told that, in fact, the game was to be played. Evidently the Red Sox players had taken a stand and persuaded their management to go on with the game. The decision about whether to interrupt a game because of rain belongs to the umpires, but the decision about whether to start the game belongs to the home team, so the Yankees had to get back off the bus, into their uniforms, and onto the field.

Early in the game, it looked like the Red Sox players might have done better to let the rain have its way. Bernie Williams drove Bronson Arroyo's first pitch deep to center field, where Johnny Damon (still a member of the Sox then) tracked it down just before the wall. Arroyo went on to retire the side in order that inning, but Williams's shot was a sign of things to come. Arroyo made an error allowing A-Rod to reach to open the second, and then Jorge Posada singled and Hideki Matsui doubled, scoring A-Rod. A couple of batters later, Posada scored on a groundout. Just as in the bottom of the first, Yankee pitcher Tanyon Sturtze retired the Sox in order again in their half of the inning. At the end of two it was Yankees 2, Red Sox 0.

The Yankees hit Arroyo hard to start the third inning, too. Williams drove another one deep to the outfield, this time into right-center field for a double. Derek Jeter moved him to third with a single into left field. Gary Sheffield grounded into a double play and Williams scored from third, making it 3–0 and emptying the bases with two out. You have likely seen television footage of what happened next: Arroyo hit Alex Rodriguez on the elbow with a pitch. A-Rod took a step toward the mound, jawing at Arroyo, who was jawing back. Sox catcher Jason Varitek stepped in front of Rodriguez, and umpire Bruce Froemming tried to move in to keep things calm. The move was in vain: A-Rod and Varitek exchanged a few words before Varitek used his catcher's mitt as a boxing glove, landing a punch square in the center of Rodriguez's face.

Predictably, that set off a bench-clearing brawl, but it was not the typical affair. Instead of the usual empty posturing, players were doing some real pushing and shoving, and some were throwing serious punches. In a spinoff away from the main body of the melee, Sturtze put a choke hold on Gabe Kapler, which prompted David Ortiz to take a swing at Sturtze. It's not entirely clear whether that punch landed, but Sturtze came up bleeding at the ear. As the fighting finally subsided and players began returning to the dugouts, Varitek, Rodriguez, Kapler, and Kenny Lofton were all ejected. Clearly, many other players had been fighting, but the umpires apparently were content to eject the two in the middle of the fray and a couple of other players who appeared especially violent. You can imagine Froemming shrugging his shoulders when he later said, "we can't see everything."

In the bottom of the third, the Sox showed some life against Sturtze, who was still pitching for the Yankees. Kevin Millar singled, followed by a Bill Mueller double, which moved Millar to third. They each scored on successive groundouts. At the end of three, it was Yankees 3, Red Sox 2.

The Yankees went in order in the top of the fourth. David Ortiz walked to open the bottom half and at that point Juan Padilla replaced Sturtze, who, it turned out, had hurt his pitching hand in the brawl. A Manny Ramirez double and a Nomar

Garciaparra single plated two more runs. The Sox continued to hit Padilla hard, stroking two more singles and loading the bases before Mueller grounded into a double play. Yankees 3, Red Sox 4.

The fifth inning was uneventful, except that the number of ejections kept pace with the number of innings played: Red Sox Manager Terry Francona was tossed for arguing a call on a force play. Still Yankees 3, Red Sox 4.

The sixth started with an Enrique Wilson single past Bill Mueller at third. Posada then doubled, but was nearly out on Manny Ramirez's throw to second, which probably would have gotten Posada if handled cleanly by Mark Bellhorn. Instead, there were runners at second and third with none out. Matsui next doubled into right, scoring both runners and putting the Yankees back in the lead, 5–4. It looked like that might be all the damage when Sierra popped out and Tony Clark struck out, but then Miguel Cairo singled in Matsui (Yankees 6, Red Sox 4). After Williams singled, Arroyo was lifted for Curtis Leskanic, who walked Jeter and then walked in Cairo by walking Sheffield (Yankees 7, Red Sox 4). Enrique Wilson appeared again and singled for an encore, this time scoring Williams and Jeter and moving Sheffield to third (Yankees 9, Red Sox 4). Posada walked to load the bases again, but Mark Malaska replaced Leskanic and got Matsui looking for a strikeout.

Now it was *really* looking like the Red Sox should have been satisfied with a rainout, but Garciaparra started the bottom of the sixth with a single, and then Trot Nixon walked, chasing Padilla, who was replaced by Paul Quantrill. Millar singled to left to load the bases. Bill Mueller hit a sacrifice fly to center to score Garciaparra (Yankees 9, Red Sox 5). Then Mark Bellhorn doubled to left to score Nixon and move Millar to third (Yankees 9,

Red Sox 6), and Johnny Damon singled to left, scoring Millar and moving Bellhorn to third (Yankees 9, Red Sox 7). Doug Mirabelli struck out, and then Joe Torre replaced Quantrill with Felix Heredia as David Ortiz came to the plate. Ortiz walked to load the bases. And then Manny Ramirez walked, scoring Bellhorn (Yankees 9, Red Sox 8). Scott Proctor replaced Heredia and struck out Garciaparra to end the inning.

That sixth inning took sixty-seven minutes, and saw twenty-two batters, eighty-nine pitches, and ten runs. The Yankees started the inning down 3–4 and ended it up 9–8. It must have looked to Red Sox fans like they were about to fall just short once again, especially when Ruben Sierra opened the seventh inning with a home run and errors by Mueller, Malaska, and Garciaparra on three successive plays loaded the bases with no one out. Amazingly, a fielder's choice, a strikeout, and a soft line drive to Bellhorn at second ended the Yankees half of the inning with no more scoring. Yankees 10, Red Sox 8.

Nixon walked to start the bottom of the seventh, and Proctor balked to move him to second, but there was no more action. The Yankees eighth was uneventful, too, with former Yankee Ramiro Mendoza recording a groundout, a strikeout, and another groundout. The Red Sox eighth started with two quick groundouts by Damon and Mirabelli, but then Ortiz singled. The Yankees brought in closer Mariano Rivera, who threw one pitch and got Manny Ramirez out on a fly to right center. Still Yankees 10, Red Sox 8.

The Yankees were quiet again in the top of the ninth, going in order, and the Red Sox returned to their dugout to face Rivera. Garciaparra got them off to a good start with a double. Nixon flied out to right, taking Gary Sheffield all the way to the wall and moving Garciaparra to third, but it was still an out and only improved the situation marginally. But then Millar singled, scoring Garciaparra. Now things were getting interesting, and the Red Sox put in a pinch runner for Millar. The extra speed would not be required, however, because in the next at bat, Mueller drove a 3–1 pitch over the right-field fence. Yankees 10, Red Sox 11.

Mueller gloried in his big hit, pumping his fist as he rounded the bases, and his team responded by greeting him at home plate, jumping up and down like excited children, hugging and high-fiving one another. The fans responded the same way, arms raised, whooping and hollering, high fives all around. The cheer that went up as Mueller's shot cleared the fence lasted several minutes, and when people did finally begin to leave their seats, they carried that cheer out into the streets. Cars were honking and people were laughing and recalling the ups and downs of the game. The mood of the entire city seemed to have changed.

The fans at that Yankees–Red Sox game were continuing a long American embrace of the game. There have been baseball fans almost as long as there has been organized baseball. As teams and leagues developed in the 1840s and 1850s, so did the interest of people who would participate in the game only as spectators. Witnesses of an 1858 game between All-Star teams from Brooklyn and New York may have been the first paying fans, having shelled out 50 cents each for preparation of the field; by 1868, the top eight teams in the New York area together reaped about $100,000 from ticket sales. Around the same time, newspapers began to carry short summaries of games, and as spectator interest grew, and newspapers realized people would pay to read about baseball, the stories got longer and more detailed and the box score was developed to go with them. Now over 70 million fans attend major-league games each year, for an average of about thirty thousand per game. Another 40 million or so attend minor-league games. What explains our interest—what is the psychology of the baseball fan?

The Drive to the Ballpark

What motivated, for example, 34,501 fans to go to Fenway Park on July 24, 2004, to see the Yankees play the Red Sox? Some were no doubt classic "die-hard" fans whose entire outlook on life would rise with a Sox win and fall with a loss. Some were there more to spend time with family. Some were probably there because they'd been given free tickets and had no other plans that afternoon, others because they were visiting Boston (maybe for the Democratic National Convention, which would be held in the city the coming week).

There are no doubt many other possible motivations, combinations of motivations, and fluid patterns of changing motivations for investing time in baseball—one recent review of the research on why people follow sports or teams or players called the collective mass of studies "chaotic" and another lamented that "little is known . . . about the process of becoming a fan." Consider that one day a fan may be reading box scores on the subway to keep up with the players on his fantasy team and as an escape from the monotony of the daily commute. The next day he may be going to a game because a friend or business connection is in town, and it is their tradition to catch a game if the local team is playing at home. Late in the season, he may be following every minute of every game as his usually hapless team vies for a spot in the playoffs—he is so caught up in the thrill of the chase that he can feel his heart race in late-game pressure situations. During the off-season, he may read scouting reports and follow the news of trades and free-agent signings, just because that is the habit he developed in high school and college, when he and his friends would hang out in front of a game or highlight show on television, arguing with the announcers and one another about a team's prospects, a player's chance of breaking a record, or how long ago a certain manager should have been fired. There are many possible motives for being a baseball fan, but a few emerge from the chaos of studies as especially important.

Love 'Em, Hate 'Em

Fans come to be fans by a process psychologists call socialization, during which an individual learns and adopts a cohesive set of cultural practices and beliefs, as when a young adult enters a profession or an older one enters the world of retirement. For a baseball fan, socialization entails learning the rules, the teams, and the players, choosing a favorite team or a favorite player, adopting habits like celebrating Opening Day and singing "Take Me Out to the Ball Game," and so on.

The mythology of baseball socialization has it that fathers pass love for the game and love for a team on to their sons, and sometimes their daughters. But the myth appears not to hold true. Of four possible "agents" of socialization surveyed in one study— parents, peers and friends, schools, and the community—peers and friends were the most powerful influence, followed by schools, then parents, and then finally community (for males there was a large difference between the level of influence for peers/friends and schools, whereas for females, these agents had approximately equal influence). Although parents may be the *first* agent of socialization, by the time people reach college age their peers and their school have done more to acculturate them into the life of a fan.

Parents are likely to play more of a role, at least in baseball, in determining the team a child first identifies with. Although the most important factor determining how strongly the average fan identifies with a team seems to be the team's success, Americans tend to identify their parents as the strongest influence in initial sports team identification. But context plays an important role; in England, affiliation with a soccer team is determined largely by locality.

Continued identification with a MLB team—like the Yankees or the Red Sox that day in July 2004—seems to be a product partly of locality and partly the team's success. Many fans identify with the geographically closest team, New Yorkers with the Yankees, New Englanders with the Red Sox, for example. For these fans, success matters less; they just root for the local team. For fans who identify with a distant team—imagine a young Virginian who, for whatever reason, became a Red Sox fan in the mid-eighties when they made their run to the 1986 World Series—success matters more. By 2004, that Virginian naturally would be less excited about that late July game with the Red Sox almost ten games out of first place.

But in addition to location and success, many other factors have been studied and found to have some influence on fan motivation, including television exposure, promotions, advertising, escapism, a team's use of technology (like the Internet), the amenities at a stadium or arena, whether the fan played the sport him- or herself, and on and on and on. So again, fans are drawn to a team for many reasons or combinations of reasons.

Fan identification is one of the most studied variables in the psychology of sports fans because it is related to so many of the fans' reactions to and behaviors at the game. Casual fans at the Sox-Yankees game would react one way, while the diehards would react quite differently. Studies have shown that the degree of emotion people feel after a victory or defeat, for instance, depends on their level of identification with the team. And the more highly fans identify with their teams, the more likely they are to be aggressive when the game is over, to show biases against rival fans, even to consider violent or illegal action against their rivals.

In fact, team identification and rivalry may be mutually influential in driving a fan's feelings and behavior: the presence of a strong rival may make it more likely that the fan will identify strongly with his or her favorite team. And some research suggests that fans enjoy their experience at a game even more if the team they love beats a team they hate.

Is there any bigger rivalry in sports than the Yankees and the Red Sox? After the Aaron Boone miracle home run in 2003, and then the Red Sox comeback from a 0–3 hole in the 2004 American League Championship, no other sports rivalry may ever get close. Even before the Varitek-Rodriguez fight, the two teams' shared history was front and center that afternoon in July 2004. The Yankee starting pitcher, Tanyon Sturtze, grew up in Worcester, Massachusetts, and rooted, with his father, for the Red Sox—they attended twelve Red Sox Opening Day games in a row. Sturtze even admitted that he'd had baby pictures taken in a tiny Red Sox uniform. So he was no doubt already familiar with, and had probably himself joined on earlier occasions, the familiar Fenway chant, "Yankees suck, Yankees suck, Yankees suck. . . ." That cheer broke out several times over the course of the game, as early as the first inning and of course in the third inning during the brawl. Sometimes it rose up in response to events in the game, as in the top of the sixth inning when the Yankees retook the lead on Matsui's double. Other times, like in the bottom of the fifth inning after a Johnny Damon single, it rose up seemingly in response to nothing, other than perhaps years of frustration. (Fenway fans even break out into the "Yankees suck" chant when they are not playing the Yankees.) The fans variously booed the Yankees over the course of the game, directing their wrath primarily at Derek Jeter, the Yankees captain and leading symbol of their success, and they booed a fan wearing a Yankees jersey when he caught a foul ball. A clear line had been drawn between "us" and "them."

An interesting sociological theory holds that testosterone plays a key role in the development of various features of our social structure. In animals, testosterone levels are closely related to dominance relationships. When one animal wins a contest for dominance with another, the testosterone levels of the winner increase while the levels of the loser decrease; the animal that has the higher testosterone level to begin with is more likely to win in the first place. Reciprocally, when testosterone levels "surge," the animal gains greater opportunities for reproduction and greater access to resources.

The same pattern holds in competitions between human males, including in physical sports like wrestling and martial arts, but also even in chess and, of all things, coin flipping. In all these cases, the winner's testosterone levels increase, while the loser's decrease. Additionally, increases in status, for instance on graduation from medical school, are associated with increases in testosterone levels, and increases in testosterone levels increase the likelihood of additional future successes. (Females, too, show these kinds of effects; testosterone is the "male" sex hormone, but females have it, too, just in lower levels.)

Such variations in testosterone level are believed to be biologically adaptive. For instance, the changes in the testosterone levels of the winner and loser might decrease the need for subsequent dominance contests. And for the winner, the increase in testosterone levels increases the chances of winning the next encounter as he climbs the social hierarchy. Surges in testosterone may also increase feelings of satisfaction, which help maintain the stability of social relationships and, thus, the overall social order.

In this line of thinking, playing sports has been considered a stand-in or practice for warfare; watching sports, identifying with a team, and sharing that experience with friends may similarly be a by-product of our instinct to prepare for conflict with rival groups. Indeed, one of the significant motivations for being a sports fan is social—in St. Louis it is common to follow the Cardinals because you simply cannot live in the area and not know what is happening with the team; everyone you meet will expect that you can talk about the latest news. Identifying with a team provides a sense of belonging and affiliation with a well-identified group.

At the Yankees-Sox game, fans were united by the "Yankees suck" cheer, but also broke out several times with "Let's go Red Sox, let's go Red Sox." The night before, they had expressed their collective displeasure by booing their team's performance. And the dramatic finish cinched it: people were no longer little knots of two or three or four friends who had come to a ball game together. They belonged to one large group of more than thirty thousand Red Sox fans at the stadium, and an even larger group they knew were rooting for the Red Sox. Anyone motivated by a desire for group affiliation got a season's worth and more.

One implication of the testosterone theory may help explain the high level of interest in sports and the huge role that they play in our society. The hypothesis is that sports play a role in maintaining the social order by producing occasional vicarious surges in testosterone. Just as a surge in the testosterone levels of the winner of a dominance contest produces a feeling of satisfaction, spectators of contests may experience the same increase in testosterone levels and the same increase in contentment.

Researchers have tested this idea by measuring pre- and post-game salivary testosterone levels of fans who, in one case, attended a Georgia vs. Georgia Tech college basketball game (at a neutral site) and, in a second case, watched in a sports bar a 1994 World Cup Soccer Match between Brazil and Italy. In both studies, researchers approached fans and asked for a saliva sample before the game and after the game. The samples were collected within an hour before the games and within a half hour after. Both games were close. The basketball game ended with Georgia winning in the final seconds, and the soccer match ended on a penalty kick after the game was tied at the end of both regulation and overtime.

In both studies, patterns of increasing and decreasing testosterone matched the patterns observed in previous animal and human studies of direct contestants. After the games were over, fans whose teams had won showed increases in testosterone levels relative to pre-game samples, and fans whose teams had lost showed decreases. Because the games were not decided until the last moment, these effects must have occurred relatively quickly. Mueller's home run likely caused a similar ebb and flow of testosterone among the Yankee and Red Sox fans.

Of course, testosterone is also associated with aggression and violence. Although no studies have tested this idea, it seems probable that more highly identified fans are likely to show greater increases or decreases in testosterone levels after their teams win or lose than less highly identified fans. The

Yankees-Sox game was marred not only by the fight on the field, but by several fights in the stands that led to police intervention and arrests. The problems of fan aggression and violence are well known. From heckling and throwing things onto fields and arenas, to fights in the stands and fights with players, to riots before and after games, fans have engaged in all kinds of atrocious behavior.

Like the question of fan motivation in general, the causes of fan aggression and violence are complex and not at all well understood. Consider two statistics: In 1985, after Boston Celtics or Bruins losses, the Boston Garden would sustain about $5000 in damage, but after wins, the toll would be about $500. Another study, of emergency room records in the Washington, D.C., area, showed that women sustained more violent injuries from domestic abuse after Redskins wins than after losses. Losing makes people violent; winning makes people violent. In addition to personality factors, variables such as temperature, crowd size, and alcohol consumption combine to influence the likelihood that a fan will become violent.

Of course, the large majority of baseball fans do not throw things on the field, fight with rival fans, or riot, and it is not at all clear that sports spectating per se makes people violent. Does being a sports fan turn someone not inclined toward aggression and violence into someone who is? Unfortunately, we do not know the answer.

Could It Be We Just Want to Be Entertained?

Why are we baseball fans? Sometimes the simplest answer might be best: baseball is entertaining. By this account, baseball is just another option for filling leisure time, just like watching a movie, listening to music, pursuing a hobby, or hanging out with friends. And of course, the people in charge of the business of baseball work hard to make it entertaining. Announcers try to have a lively, humorous banter. During the Fox broadcast of the Yankees-Sox game, Tim McCarver joked after a shattered bat that those are "ordered in cords" and during the long sixth inning that the game had had "more pitches than an Amway convention."

Indeed, in studies of sports fans, entertainment consistently emerges as a leading motivation. The just-considered group af-filiation motivation also ranks high. These motives are of course not mutually exclusive. Indeed, at least one model of *how* entertaining we find a game suggests that our level of enjoyment depends on our winning and teams we do not like losing. The amount of scoring, the numerous lead changes, and the intensity of the uncertainty about who would win and who would lose the Yankees-Sox game obviously contributed to the entertainment. Fans of either team had plenty of time to feel the satisfaction of seeing their team succeed and their most-hated rivals fail. When the Yankees took the early lead, the love-hate balance tipped one way, then Garciaparra's hit to put the Sox up 4–3 tipped it the other, then Matsui's, and finally Mueller's. Not all games play out this way, of course. It is only that *enough* games like this must occur to satisfy a particular fan's level of motivation.

A third psychological factor, the excitement of the game, the vicarious thrill and tension that spectators often feel, likely also contributes to the game's ability to satisfy the entertainment motive. Psychologists call this *eustress,* the opposite of distress—these situations are stressful, but in a positive way. The Yankees-Sox game was full of eustress. Early in the game, Derek Jeter batted with runners at first and third and no one out, and a bit later Bill Mueller's double would put runners at second and third with no one out—there was plenty of tension in those situations, but nothing compared with what was to come. In the top of the sixth inning, four of the Yankees' runs were scored with two outs—imagine the suspense of seeing one and then another and another and another run score when your favorite team just needs one out to escape. And then in the bottom of that inning David Ortiz batted with two runners on and walked to load the bases for Manny Ramirez, who also walked, bringing up Garciaparra (who, alas, struck out). In the bottom of the eighth, with Ortiz on base, Ramirez came up again, representing the tying run. The Yankees brought in Mariano Rivera—imagine sitting in the stadium watching him warm up. And then there was Nixon's almost-home run in the bottom of the ninth, and finally, finally, Mueller's game-winning shot.

Even the broadcasters' discussion of the Yankees' World Series bonus money over the previous few years could lend some fans a vicarious thrill, thinking of prizes that large. And later, Tim McCarver recalled the double play that ended the fourth inning. The twinge of regret the fans would feel at remembering that moment might be more than most of the players felt, since the players see such situations so often and train themselves to let what is done be done and focus on the next pitch.

Self-Esteem

Another strong motive for many fans' interest in sports is to help boost or maintain their self-esteem. Before the 2004 Red Sox went on to win the World Series, Sox fans were well known for their Curse-of-the-Bambino fatalism, and there was a lot of that attitude on display in the stands before the July 24 game started and during the disasters of the sixth and seventh innings.

But Sox fans may have been a special case until that year's triumph. More generally, psychologists have identified two phenomena that have come to be known as Basking in Reflected Glory (BIRG) and Cutting Off Reflected Failure (CORF). After wins, fans of a team tend to say "we" more in describing the outcome ("we won") and to wear clothes with team colors and logos, whereas after a loss, they tend to say "they" more ("they lost") and not to wear team colors and logos. And later studies have shown that self-esteem changes accordingly. As you would expect, self-esteem is higher after a fan's team wins than after a loss, but the BIRGing and CORFing processes can enhance that effect.

In a study of basketball fans, after a game was over, fans were given a questionnaire that both asked how much they would associate themselves with their team and also measured their self-esteem. For some of the fans, the association question came before the self-esteem test; for others, it came after. Asking the association question first gave the fan a chance to bask in reflected glory by associating with the team or to cut off reflected failure by disassociating from the team. When people are given that chance to bask or cut off before they take the measure of self-esteem, the difference in self-esteem after a win as opposed to a loss is even larger. Moreover, hardcore fans tended to BIRG and CORF more than people who were more casual in their allegiance, perhaps because there is more at stake for the egos of people who identify more with the team.

Social psychologists have now done a lot of work to examine the idea that at least one function served by self-esteem-building processes is to protect us from our innate fear of death. This theory, called Terror Management Theory, has been used to account for a wide variety of self-esteem-related phenomena, including one study that showed that fans who are reminded of their mortality are more likely to engage in tactics similar to BIRGing and CORFing. According to Terror Management Theory, one reason all those fans showed up for that Yankees-Sox game was, at least in part, to help avoid thoughts about their own mortality (although, given the then-typical Sox fan's resignation to losing, we should wonder how going to a Yankees game would help).

The Beauty of It All

Some people are fans because they appreciate the game for the game's sake. We can marvel at Yankee pitcher Scott Proctor's ability to throw a 96mph fastball, or Johnny Damon's ability to turn at the crack of the bat and run down the fly ball that Bernie Williams hit to start the game. During the Fox broadcast, Tim McCarver discussed, with the aid of slow-motion replay, such things as Hideki Matsui's plate coverage and Gary Sheffield's quick hands. These fans also like to think about the strategy of the game and situational tactics, about defensive positioning, the use of relief pitchers, what to do when there are runners on first and third and the runner on first attempts to steal second. Statistics are of obvious interest to these fans, but not just for how the numbers rank teams and players, but also for what they reveal about the underlying nature of the game. These fans appreciate the history of the game—they know not just the current rivalry between the Yankees and the Red Sox, but all the landmark events that brought them to the game. When the PA announcer introduced Fred Lynne to the crowd, fans motivated by the aesthetic side of the game, even the ones too young to have seen Lynne play, knew why he was so appreciated. Those fans were also saving away memories of that day's notable players, Jeter and Ramirez and Ortiz and Rodriguez.

There is a certain kind of satisfaction and happiness that comes with expertise and the ability to appreciate the finer points of some endeavor. As John Stuart Mill wrote in his *Autobiography*, "Those only are happy (I thought) who have their minds fixed on some object other than their own happiness; on the happiness of others, on the improvement of mankind, even on some art or pursuit, followed not as a means, but as itself an ideal end. Aiming thus at something else, they find happiness by the way." This is the motivation of those who are the members of the Society for American Baseball Research, who read Web sites like baseballprospectus.com or journals like *Nine: A Journal of Baseball History and Culture,* and people like you, the reader of this and similar books about the nature of the game of baseball.

Take Me Out to the Ball Game

What turns the fan into a spectator, a ticket holder in the ballpark? Team identification is, perhaps, the most important factor. A general desire for entertainment and social interaction are obviously also major factors in drawing people to ballparks. But social scientists, especially economists, are interested in how various factors moderate that initial interest. Fan behavior, as defined by attendance, can vary dramatically, as anyone can see by watching games played in Shea Stadium and Kauffmann Stadium.

One factor working in favor of both the Yankees and the Red Sox that day was that they both had strong recent winning records. We have already seen that winning teams draw fans; no surprise there. But so do losing teams, although perhaps not in the same numbers. What brings people to buy a ticket for a game when their team is on the skids? One influence may simply be home field advantage: people are more likely to attend a game when a favorable outcome is more certain, and home field advantage makes the home team more likely to win.

Another study analyzed the factors that predict a fan's willingness to buy a hockey ticket to see either the successful Dallas Fire of the Central Hockey League or the sad-sack Fort Worth Breeze of the same league (comparison of two teams from the same league and the same metropolitan area allowed for a measure of control over extraneous variables). For fans of the successful team, the study reported that "winning *is* everything" [emphasis in original]. The variables that related to the likelihood of buying a ticket were the personal relevance of the sport (people responded with "strongly agree" to items like "Hockey is very important to me") and the fan's perception that the team is good (agreeing strongly with items like "This team will win more games this year than most").

For fans of the poorly performing team, as you might imagine, the perception of team quality was not a driving factor in the decision to buy a ticket. Personal relevance was important again, but for these fans, the next most important factor was the fan's perception of the players on the team (as measured by items like "Players on the team have characteristics that others admire"). Fans of losing teams maintain a positive outlook by shifting their focus to other attributes of their favorite team that would make them feel good (they can think, "The team may not be so good, but I like the players").

What about the perennial losers, the Chicago Cubs? How do they maintain such a strong fan base? Liking the players and other aspects of the fan experience turns out to be key. A study of loyal Cubs fans showed that their loyalty stemmed largely from their involvement with the team as children and how much they liked the team and the general experience of being a Cubs fan. Wrigley Field and the near-total coverage of Cubs games on WGN-TV no doubt contributed to that feeling, but the authors of this study argued that those just happened to be resources that the Cubs could exploit to their advantage in helping people enjoy their experiences with the team. They suggested that other teams, using whatever resources they had available, could conceivably create similar loyalty; though, because childhood experience was so important, it would have to be a long-term effort.

Another factor that might influence attendance would be the general level of excitement. Think of the claims of those non-fans who compare watching baseball to watching paint dry. The increase in home run rate and the amount of scoring is often credited with helping baseball regain fan interest after losing it during the 1994–1995 baseball strike. One study supports this, in relation to the American League's introduction of the designated hitter rule in 1973. The gist of the report was that (a) one predictor of attendance in the American League was scoring (more scoring, more fans), (b) the designated hitter rule increases score, and (c) the introduction of the designated hitter rule was, in fact, associated with an increase in attendance at American League ballparks. The report noted one other important fact: scoring did not predict attendance in the National League, and thus, the designated hitter rule would not be expected to raise attendance in that league. They concluded that both the American and National League made the rational economic decision in deciding whether to adopt or not adopt the new rule. Note that the findings of that study showing differences in how AL and NL fans respond to scoring seem no longer to apply: both leagues have since seen increases in scoring, and attendance seems to have increased in response.

Familiarity may be another factor that can influence ticket sales. Every off-season is filled with news of free agent signings—teams often look very different from one year to the next. For successful teams like the Yankees and the Red Sox, turnover often means bringing in a new superstar. For many other teams, it means the loss of players that fans have come to identify with. In a statistical analysis that controlled for the effects of other variables like ticket price, fan income, regional population, and the like, there remained a relation between changes in the lineup and ticket sales; the more changes there were, the more ticket sales declined. However, the study did *not* control for the identities of the new players on the roster. The Yankees had added Alex Rodriguez to their roster before the 2004 season. Presumably adding a player who many regard as the best in the game does not hurt attendance. The observed decline was for the average team.

Familiarity with the ballpark also plays a role in attendance. The flurry of building in the last fifteen or so years has been associated with an increase in attendance, which is consistent with the historical pattern. That pattern also reveals, however, that there is a "honeymoon effect." After a few years, attendance begins to gradually decline. The honeymoon effect is an apt metaphor. Over time, a recent study notes, marital satisfaction starts with an initially high level and gradually declines over a period of ten to fifteen years to a fairly low level, where it remains until late in life when, after perhaps thirty-five to forty years of marriage, satisfaction begins to increase again, perhaps at a time when a couple begins to look back on their life together and focus on fond memories and shared accomplishments. And sure enough, the study found that after satisfaction with a ballpark, as measured by ticket sales, has declined and remained low for many years, it does increase again. Of course, there are relatively few old ballparks left, so it will be some time before we are able to see if this pattern holds.

The Intuitive Fan

We are all amateur psychologists who try to understand the minds and behavior of the players as we watch baseball. We make all kinds of *attributions* about the psychology of others around us, that is, we explain their behavior in terms of other features of the situation. When, during the 2000 World Series, Roger Clemens tossed a piece of Mike Piazza's broken bat across the first-base line as Piazza ran to first, viewers immediately made attributions about Clemens's motivations ("he hates Piazza," "the Yankees are all arrogant," "it's part of his game to try to intimidate the other team," "he's a lunatic," "it's his competitive fire"). Even infants seem to have a rudimentary sense of another person's motivations or intentions, which is one of the reasons many psychologists believe that this "intuitive psychology" that we all practice is an innate drive.

But this intuitive, or "folk," psychology can often be wrong. For example, in reading other people's behavior we often make a classic error called the *fundamental attribution error:* we tend to attribute the causes of another person's behavior more to the person and less to the situation than is appropriate, and more than we do when we think about our own behavior.

This error was discovered by accident. A study had been designed to test the idea that when people perceived someone to be acting of his or her own volition, the individual's behavior would be attributed to personal beliefs and goals; but that when it was clear that the situation was dictating how the person behaved, people would point to external factors as the cause of the individual's behavior. Subjects were to read either a pro-Castro or anti-Castro essay and were led to believe either that the person who had written the essay was free to choose a position on Castro, or that the writer had been compelled to take a position that had been assigned randomly. The subjects were then asked to rate how pro-Castro was each of the writers (not the essays, but the writers).

Of course, as expected, in the condition where subjects believed that the writers had chosen their positions, they rated the pro-Castro writer's pro-Castro feelings as much higher than the anti-Castro writer's. Unexpectedly, they did the same thing in the condition in which the pro- and anti-Castro positions had ostensibly been assigned randomly (although not by as wide a margin as in the other condition). The subjects seemed to believe that the writers' motivations in writing the essays were more internally driven than the situation would dictate. This effect, later termed the fundamental attribution error, has been found in a variety of circumstances and seems to be a general property of how people perceive the actions of others.

In baseball, for instance, we tend to believe that the strikeout is due more to the mastery of the pitcher and less to the law of averages, or the home run is more the pitcher's fault and less due to the wind blowing from behind home plate. Certainly the pitcher plays a role in these situations, but we tend to overemphasize that role and underemphasize the influence of other factors. Similarly, that we attribute a hitting streak or slump to some cause like "seeing the ball better" or "a hitch in the swing" rather than to simple chance variation illustrates the fundamental attribution error. Seeing the ball and controlling the swing are internal forces; luck is external.

The fundamental attribution error is often colored by other

biases. When affected by a *self-serving bias,* for instance, we tend to make attributions in such a way as to cast ourselves in a positive light. So when we succeed, we tend to attribute that success to an internal cause; when we fail, we tend to attribute the failure to an external cause. There are also *positivity* and *negativity biases* in these attributions. We tend to make more internal attributions about the successes of people we like, and external attributions about their failures; we make more external attributions about the successes of people we don't like, and internal attributions about their failures. There can also be *group attribution errors,* which occur when the behaviors of members of one's own group tend to be attributed to internal causes, whereas behaviors of members of other groups tend to be attributed to external causes. And the positivity and negativity biases can apply to groups as well.

Now apply the various attribution errors and biases to the way we talk about baseball games, especially when great rivalries are involved. People will be more likely to make internal attributions about the success of their favorite team (great players making great plays) and external attributions about their team's failures (wind, sun, umpires, or even sometimes the quality of the opposition). If their team has a strong rival (that is, if they are Yankee or Red Sox fans), they will likely exhibit the negativity bias, and blame external factors (Steinbrenner's wealth) for their rivals' success and internal factors (the Yankees suck) for their failures.

These biases were apparent in newspaper and other reports of an especially violent football game between Dartmouth and Princeton in 1951, which prompted a professor at each of the institutions to collaborate on a formal—and now famous—study of the perceptions of fans from each school. During the game, Dartmouth was penalized for seventy yards and Princeton for twenty-five, and there were several plays with offsetting penalties. Princeton star Dick Kazmaier was knocked out early with a broken nose and a concussion. Editorials in the Dartmouth and Princeton student newspapers described two completely different games, with Dartmouth's paper taking the position that the game had been rough, but not unusually so, and Princeton's the position that Dartmouth had played a dirty game. Polling revealed that fan perceptions were similar. Opinion at Dartmouth was mixed, with a minority calling the game "clean and fair" and the rest about evenly divided between "rough and dirty" and "rough and fair." Opinion at Princeton was uniformly in the "rough and dirty" camp; not one person polled at Princeton called the game "clean and fair." In a second part of the study, students at both schools were shown a film of the game and asked to count the infractions they saw as they watched. Dartmouth students observed, on average, 4.3 offenses committed by Dartmouth and 4.4 by Princeton, but Princeton students saw 9.8 offenses by Dartmouth, and 4.2 by Princeton. The professors concluded that "there is no such 'thing' as a 'game' existing 'out there' in its own right which people merely 'observe.' The 'game' 'exists' for a person and is experienced by him only in so far as certain happenings have significances in terms of his purpose. Out of all the occurrences going on in the environment, a person selects those that have some significance for him from his own egocentric position."

Later researchers discovered much the same thing when they took attribution theory out of the laboratory and into the sports pages. They coded quotes from players and coaches about the events and outcomes of a game as internally or externally focused and looked at how many of both kinds of attributions members of a team made. They also looked at attributions made by sportwriters for each team's hometown newspaper. Included in their sample of contests were the games played in the 1977 World Series. There were internal attributions after success (e.g., after the Yankees won Game 4, Yankee manager Billy Martin said of one of his players, "Piniella has done it all"). There were external attributions after failure. (Ron Cey, a Dodger, said, "I think we've hit the ball all right. But I think we're unlucky.") Overall, the study found, consistent with attribution theory, that players and coaches tended to make far more internal than external attributions after a win (by about 80–20 percent) than after a loss (still more internal, but only about 53–47 percent).

Similar examples could be found in the *The Boston Globe* and *The New York Times* after the July 24 game. Both papers featured on their front page the picture of Varitek shoving his catcher's mitt into A-Rod's face. Bob Hohler's and Marc Craig's stories in the *Globe* featured quotes from Boston manager Terry Francona ("You're never out of it if you continue to fight" and, describing the bottom of the ninth, "Trot took a good swing. Manny took a good swing. And one of them [Mueller's] managed to get out") and pitcher Leskanic ("The last 10 days the bullpen has been kind of tired") that attributed Boston's success to internal sources and their difficulties to external ones. In the *Times,* stories by Tyler Kepner and Selena Roberts also illustrated this pattern. Kepner quoted Derek Jeter: "It was a weird game. . . . It was one of those games where the last team that hit was going to win." Roberts wrote that "with a swashbuckler's swipe through Mariano Rivera's devilish cutters, Bill Mueller unleashed a game-winning two-run homer." It was not so much that Mueller took a good swing, as Francona had said, but that he got lucky with a wild swing. Of course, not all of the quotes and not every line in the stories followed this trend. Mariano Rivera told Kepner that he was "disappointed in myself " and that he "should have done better" and Kepner wrote that "three Yankees pitchers buckled in the bottom of the [sixth]."

One of the external factors that we fans seem particularly prone to overlook is chance. Additional psychological processes may contribute to this tendency. Psychologists have studied a number of reasoning *heuristics,* shortcuts that often yield close approximations to an objective analysis but that take much less time and effort, that can sometimes lead us astray. We seem to have a very difficult time distinguishing a random series of events from one that is nonrandom, and similarly have difficulty generating a random sequence of events. One early study reported that when people were asked to judge the likelihood of different sequences of coin flips, the sequences heads-heads-heads-tails-tails-tails and heads-heads-heads-heads-tails-heads are judged to be less likely than heads-tails-heads-tails-tails-heads, even though every single one of the sixty-four possible sequences is *equally* likely to occur if the coin is fair. The first sequence seems to be judged less likely because it is more regular than the prototypical idea of a random sequence—it does not look random. The second sequence seems less likely because a fair coin should produce equal numbers of heads and tails flips, and that sequence is biased five to one in favor of heads. Because people seem to judge the sequences based on how well they represent the prototypical random sequence, this rule of thumb is called the *representativeness heuristic.* We make judgments like this all the time, referring a particular instance of some category back to the prototypical instance of the category.

Two instances of the failure of the representativeness heuristic often appear in discussions about our perceptions of events in sports. One is the "gambler's fallacy," which is the idea that in a sequence of independent events, after a run of one outcome, the other (or another) outcome becomes progressively more likely. In baseball, we often hear that a hitter is "due" because it has been a while since he has had a hit, or had a hit in a particular situation.

The flip side of this is the notion of the "hot hand," the idea that a string of successful outcomes is more likely than usual to be followed by a successful outcome. A manager may select a "hot" hitter or relief pitcher from his bench or bullpen because the expectations of success seem greater than if that player has not had a recent string of success.

There is, of course, an apparent inconsistency in describing these two opposite errors with the same principle. People who fall prey to the gambler's fallacy think that a streak should end, but people who believe in the hot hand think it should continue. But it turns out that people see different contexts differently. A recent study shows that the same underlying sequence of events can lead people to make judgments consistent with the gambler's fallacy or with the hot hand, depending on the context in which the events occur. One context explicitly evoked the idea of randomness because it involved spinning a roulette wheel. People were told that a sequence of one hundred spins resulted in fifty reds and fifty blacks, but that the last four spins had come up red. They were then quite susceptible to the gambler's fallacy; their average estimate that the streak would continue on the next spin was only 12 percent (objectively, of course, black should come up 50 percent of the time, regardless of how many reds have come immediately before).

Another context involved skill—free-throw shooting—and

again depicted a sequence in which both outcomes (a made shot or a miss) had occurred fifty times each over a sequence of one hundred attempts, but in which the last four events were a run of the same outcome (four made shots in a row). In this case, the average estimate that the streak would continue was 56 percent.

A final context involved a competition between two sales-people for total sales in a week. Again, one of them had just won four weeks in a row, though for the last one hundred weeks the total wins for each was fifty. Here, the average judgment of the likelihood that the streak would continue was 66 percent. For-mally, all three contexts presented the same underlying infor-mation (both outcomes occurred fifty times in the last one hundred events, with the string ending with the same outcome four times in a row), but in the context that evoked people's be-liefs about randomness, the gambler's fallacy held sway, and in the contexts that evoked skill and competition, the hot hand belief tended to dominate people's thinking.

It is difficult for fans to think of baseball as a random pro-cess. What happens during a game (or over the course of a sea-son) does not seem *representative* of a random process. One person is trying his damnedest to get on base, and nine people, one in particular, are trying to prevent that. Even though in the preceding chapter we made some allowance for the possibility that there are true streaks and slumps, the sequence of outcomes in baseball remains very close to truly random even if it is not. The simplest understanding of a hitter's chances of getting a hit would be to think of him as a biased coin that will produce an H (for Hit) in proportion to the player's batting average. If he is a .300 hitter, then his chance of getting a hit in *any* at bat is 30 percent, regardless of what he has done in the five or ten or fifty previous at bats. Remember the illustration with the hitter named Cube, who was really just a die who got a hit whenever we rolled a one or a two. There were certainly "streaks" and "slumps" over the course of his simulated season, but they could only have been due to chance.

So statements during Fox's broadcast of the Yankees-Sox game—about Bernie Williams coming to the plate one for three in the game, but hitting .118 in the last fourteen games, or about Matsui coming to the plate in the top of the sixth three for three in the game, with the four, five, and six hitters in the Yankees lineup a collective ten for eleven—appeal to the representativeness heuristic. The broadcasters also noted that the Red Sox had started the season 6–1 against the Yankees, but had lost the last four games against them. These statistics seem anything but representative of a random process—it seems as if Williams had gotten a hit despite being in a slump, that the heart of the Yankees lineup must be particularly hot at the moment, and that the quality of the Red Sox team had somehow changed from early in the season. A run that goes Sox-Sox-Yanks-Sox-Sox-Sox-Sox-Yanks-Yanks-Yanks-Yanks does not appear at all representative of a random process.

The representativeness and other heuristics rely on "the law of small numbers," in contrast with the laws of probability, which depend on the law of large numbers. The size of a sample is very important in probability and statistics. If we toss a coin ten thousand times, it is likely heads will come up very close to 50 percent of the time. But if we toss the coin just twice, the chance that heads will come up around 50 percent of the time is itself only 50 percent. There are four possible combined outcomes of the two tosses (heads-heads, heads-tails, tails-heads, and tails-tails), and each combination of throws is equally likely. So half of the time when we toss a coin twice, the percentage of heads is 50, but 25 percent it is zero, and 25 percent it is a hundred.

Many of the statistics we see in baseball are based on very small samples. There is no better example than the batting average a particular hitter has against a particular pitcher. Unless both the hitter and the pitcher have been in the same league together for a fairly long time, these statistics will almost always be based on only ten or twenty at bats. In twenty at bats, the difference between a .400 batting average and a .250 batting average, which seems huge in the way we usually think about batting averages, is only three hits. Statistically, that difference is virtually meaningless, but it seems more representative of a real difference between hitters than it does of a random process. During Fox's broadcast of the Yankees-Sox game, we heard many statistics based on very small numbers, like Scott Proctor's "outstanding" performance since being recalled from the minors, pitching an inning and a third (an inning and a third!) with two Ks and no runs, or the note early in the game about Tanyon Sturtze's 7.38 ERA at Fenway. Sturtze had pitched at Fenway on several occasions, but his statistics were skewed by a few poor outings (in 2002, he pitched 2.1 innings in Fenway and gave up seven earned runs; in 2003, he threw seven innings and gave up seven earned runs). That is one of the problems with averages based on small samples—they are easily distorted by one or two performances. How predictive was that 7.38 ERA of Sturtze's future performance? Counting the three innings he threw on July 24 and a later relief appearance of two-and-two-thirds innings, he allowed just two earned runs in 2004 (for a 3.86 ERA), and in 2005, he allowed one run in four innings of work at Fenway (2.25 ERA).

A short set of games between two teams reflects the same problems with the short run. Whether it is a normal weekend series during the regular season or the World Series, what happens in such a short period of time is much more subject to the vagaries and vicissitudes of chance than we often think. If one team in the World Series is so much stronger than the other that it has a 60 percent chance of winning any given game (and that is a huge difference in baseball—usually the best teams in a season win around 60 percent of their games and the worst teams win about 40 percent), probability theory tells us that the worse team will still win the World Series around 30 percent of the time. Psychologically, short run statistics can seem important—we tend to judge them as representative of the situation they reflect, though they may well not be. The World Series winner is the best team, right? But of course we know better—any one of the World Series could have turned out entirely differently if the teams had played it over again.

Another common misjudgment is the *illusory correlation*, the tendency to judge that a given event is a good predictor of another, even though the two are not related, or are only weakly related. During the Fox broadcast, Joe Buck read a quote from Bronson Arroyo about his sometimes feeling a bit more comfortable pitching on the road, which was followed by Arroyo's home (1–4, ERA over 5) and away (2–3, 2.83 ERA) statistics. Tim McCarver then speculated about Arroyo having to field requests for tickets when he was at home, that he felt pressure from friends and other people at home, and that pitchers often are able to find a "better rhythm" on the road. And that is the temptation—to see a relation like home-poor/road-good and infer an underlying cause that explains it. (It could be that good pitching causes the feeling or perception that a pitcher is "in a rhythm" rather than the rhythm causing the good pitching.) To their credit, a few minutes later, Fox showed statistics revealing that Arroyo had received the poorest run support of any of the Red Sox pitchers that year, at least partially explaining his won-loss record. And in 2005, his home-road ERAs with the Red Sox were much closer. His 2004 performance was more than likely just a random fluctuation.

It is easy to see how ideas about baseball can take on a life of their own this way. If we begin to think that player X is a clutch hitter, we tend to remember those dramatic, two-out-in-the-bottom-of-the-ninth-inning home runs and forget the times he has struck out with runners in scoring position. If we think pitcher Y is a dominating closer, we remember the number of successive saves he has notched and forget that he always enters the game with no one on base, frequently inherits a lead of two or three runs, and that opposing players actually hit .280 against him.

Memory for some of Barry Bonds's more dramatic home runs may have similarly led people to fear pitching to him too much. One analysis looked at every possible combination of number of outs and the positions of base runners (if any) and found that the number of runs the Giants could be expected to score after the opponent pitched to or walked Bonds was almost always higher if he was walked. The only exceptions were with two outs and first base open. Computers have perfect memories; ours are biased toward more dramatic and emotional events, like losing on a Barry Bonds home run.

The problem is our need to rely on memory to make many of these judgments; our memories are not good enough to provide all the data we need. We can tell the difference between a .300 hitter and a .270 hitter if we have records of their at bats and time to do a little arithmetic. But based only on memory? Over the course of a season, an everyday player will have somewhere between six hundred and seven hundred plate appearances. Assuming all other things are roughly equal, the difference between the .270 and .300 hitters will be a total of eighteen hits (162 and 180, respectively). That's less than a hit per week difference over the course of a season (about twenty-six weeks). It is unlikely that any of us could tell the difference between those hitters based on memory alone. We compensate by relying on heuristics and biases that are efficient and often, but not always, reliable. It is perhaps a bit disconcerting, but also intriguing, to think about how our perception of the game is a product of both what happens on the field and the biased ways in which we perceive it.

AUTHOR'S NOTE

LIKE MANY BASEBALL FANS, I PLAYED LITTLE LEAGUE BALL AND dreamed about making it to the majors. Unfortunately, I reached the limits of my game when pitchers started throwing curveballs, so (again like many fans) I became an avid observer of the sport. I went through a card-collecting phase and pored over the daily box scores. Baseball was my first passion. As a college student I developed a second—cognitive psychology, which is the scientific study of the mind and how it relates to the world.

I thought of my two passions as separate until a random conversation early in my graduate-student days at Purdue University changed my thinking. I was walking down the hall of the psych building one day when I overheard two of my professors in a heated discussion about a recently published academic paper. One of them broke from their conversation and said to the other, "Let's ask Mike." Uh-oh. I had been there only a few weeks and doubted that I had much to say about whatever it was they were debating. I was certainly in no position to weigh in on what might have been some thorny theoretical issue. But then they asked me something like "How much of the variance in the outcome of an at bat does a baseball player's batting average account for?" Not at all what I was expecting, the question was something of a relief since at that stage of my training, I knew more about baseball than about psychology.

I thought it over. Of all the variables that might influence whether a player gets a hit or not in a particular at bat, how much of a factor is the player's batting average? They narrowed it down for me: "Is it a lot, or a little?" I guessed that it was a little, based on what, I cannot remember. That was correct, but the precise answer was still surprising: the player's batting average explains less than 1 percent of what happens in an at bat. On reflection, and after reading the academic paper that had prompted the question from my professors, the answer was not so surprising. After all, most batting averages are somewhere between .250 and .300—a difference of only 5 percent, only twenty-five hits (125 vs. 150) in a five-hundred-at-bat season. As Kevin Costner's character in *Bull Durham* pointed out, that's about one hit per week over baseball's long season. Batting average makes a big difference in the long run, over the course of a season's worth of at bats. But in a situation as isolated as a single at bat, differences in batting averages are too small to have much effect on the outcome. Of course, it is much better if the pinch hitter gets a hit than if he makes an out, but a .250 hitter has almost as good a chance at doing that as a .300 hitter.

Though I was a longtime baseball fan, I had been unaware of the contributions psychological science had made to understanding the sport. And these were not fringe contributions, either: the paper my professors had been talking about appeared in one of the leading professional journals in the field, *Psychological Bulletin*. That paper improved my understanding of the game a little, and changed the way I watched baseball games—in addition to the play-by-play excitement of the game, in addition to the color of the personalities that played it, I began to think about the game as a psychologist, breaking it down into its elements, thinking about factors like motivation and intelligence. That paper from *Psychological Bulletin* focused more on statistics than psychology (psychology, like baseball, makes heavy use of statistics), but it did say something about how to think about the role of the player's ability in the limited situation of a single at bat. It was also the first paper I put in the baseball file I have kept ever since. Over the years, as I was looking for something else in the professional journals, I would occasionally run into another paper related to baseball. Since that occasion at the beginning of my graduate-school years, I have compiled a large collection of research studies on hitting, fielding, and throwing, on what psychological traits are important for baseball, on the ways various factors influence the player's readiness to play the game on any given day, and on the fan's perception of the game. Some of my own research, while not about baseball directly, is also easily applied to baseball. For example, I have done research on implicit learning, which is a form of learning related to what people in sports call "muscle memory," or the instinctive ability to react to particular situations without conscious deliberation, and on automaticity, which is one of the ways that practice can change the performance of a skill from the slow, halting, deliberate way it is performed at first to the fast, smooth, effortless way that it is performed later. All of this research serves to answer the kinds of questions that fascinate baseball fans.

———

I have read many acknowledgments sections and it seems that authors always say something about how much a book depends on the efforts of many people, rather than only them. And now I know how much this is true. I owe a debt of thanks to many people who have encouraged me in this effort and who have helped me come to my own understanding of the psychology of baseball.

I remember well the day that my wife and I were walking with our dogs, talking about different projects I might pursue in a sabbatical I was about to take. I have always had many interests and was not sure which of them to follow. When I mentioned that I had been thinking about *The Psychology of Baseball*, she stopped suddenly and declared, "That's it!" Brandi more than anyone else convinced me that this idea was a good one. She and the rest of my family have been a well of support and encouragement that I have drawn from many times while working on this book.

My friend Steve Weinberg talked me through the process of developing, writing, and shopping a proposal, and he read a first draft. I was lucky then that Susan Arellano, of the Susan Rabiner Agency, saw something in that proposal and helped me shape and refine it and, most of all, helped me begin to find a voice different from the one I've used for years, writing academic journal articles.

At Gotham Books, first Brendan Cahill and then Patrick Mulligan have been enthusiastic readers and gentle but perceptive critics. They helped me continue to move from the academic prose that was my habit into what I hope is now a more engaging description of the psychology of baseball and what that psychology tells us about the game we enjoy so much.

I also want to thank all the researchers who talked to me about their work and friends of friends who made introductions. All the work I write about here was done by other people, and their generosity in talking about it with me was a great help. My brother Jon helped me with some of the mathematics used in the models of fly ball catching. And finally, the students in my winter 2006 Psychology of Baseball class at the University of Missouri–Columbia helped me practice and shape my descriptions of the research as much of the book was being written.

NOTES

INTRODUCTION

xii **Faulty conceptions of physical phenomena** McCloskey, M. (April, 1983). "Intuitive physics." *Scientific American,* 248: 122–130.

xii **Faulty conceptions about disease** Tversky, A., and Kahneman, D. (1973). "Judgment under uncertainty: Heuristics and biases." *Science,* 185: 1124–1131.

xii **Faulty conceptions of behavior** Nisbett, R. E., and Wilson, T. D. (1977). "Telling more than we can know: Verbal reports on mental processes." *Psychological Review,* 84: 231–259.

xii **What makes us happy** Gilbert, D. (2006). *Stumbling on Happiness.* New York: Knopf.

xiii **"Off-field performance inhibitors"** Dorfman, H. A. (1990). "Reflections on providing personal and performance enhancing consulting services in professional baseball." *Sport Psychologist* 4: 341–346.

xiii **Sosa's corked bat** Adair, R. K. (2002). *The Physics of Baseball* (3rd Edition). New York: HarperCollins.

CHAPTER ONE

2 **Sturm's streak** Seidel, M. (1988). *Streak: Joe DiMaggio and the Summer of '41.* New York: McGraw-Hill, p. xvi.

3 **Yankees in 1941** Creamer, R. W. (1991). *Baseball in '41.* New York: Viking Penguin.

5 **Ted Williams** Montville, L. (2004). *Ted Williams.* New York: Doubleday.

9   **Detailed analysis of swings** Shaffer, B., Jobe, F. W., Pink, M., and Perry, J. (1993). "Baseball batting: An electromyographic study." *Clinical Orthopaedics and Related Research* 292: 285–293; Welch, C. M., Banks, S. A., Cook, F. F., and Draovitch, P. (1995). "Hitting a baseball: A biomechanical description." *Journal of Orthopaedic & Sports Physical Therapy* 22: 193–201.

11   **Study of cricket** McLeod, P. (1987). "Visual reaction time and high-speed ball games." *Perception* 16: 49–59.

13   **Study with infrared light** Bahill, A. T., and LaRitz, T. (1984). "Why can't batters keep their eyes on the ball?" *American Scientist* 72: 249–253.

16   **Effect of Ruth's cancer on his vision** Voisin, A., Elliott, D. B., and Regan, D. (1997). "Babe Ruth: With vision like that, how could he hit the ball?" *Optometry and Vision Science* 74: 144–146.

17   **Scaling-by-ball-size method** Bootsma, R. J., and Peper, C. E. (1992). "Predictive visual information sources for the regulation of action with special emphasis on catching and hitting." In Proteau, L., and Elliott, D., eds., *Vision and Motor Control*. Amsterdam: North-Holland, pp. 285–314.

18   **"Looming" and the size of objects** Some of the mathematics involved in this calculation were worked out in a bad science fiction novel from the 1950s called *The Black Cloud*, by the otherwise accomplished astronomer Sir Fred Hoyle. The black cloud in question was looming from deep space at planet Earth. To predict the imminent collision, one of the astronomers in the novel uses the same analysis that these researchers relied on in some of their calculations.

19   **Virtual pitch study** Gray, R. (2002a). "Behavior of college baseball players in a virtual batting task." *Journal of Experimental Psychology: Human Perception and Performance* 28: 1131–1148.

21   **Varied pitch speed study** Bahill, A. T., and Karnavas, W. J. (1993). "The Perceptual Illusion of Baseball's Rising Fastball and Breaking Curveball." *Journal of Experimental Psychology: Human Perception and Performance* 19: 3–14.

21   **Performance and perception of tasks** Jacoby, L. L., Allan, L. G., Collins, J. C., and Larwill, L. K. (1988). "Memory influences subjective experience: Noise judgments." *Journal of Experimental Psychology: Learning, Memory, and Cognition* 14: 240–247.

22   **Dart-throwing and perception** Wesp, R., Cichello, P., Gracia, E. B., and Davis, K. (2004). "Observing and engaging in purposeful actions with objects influences estimates of their size." *Perception & Psychophysics* 66: 1261–1267.

22   **Steep hills and perception** Bhalla, M., and Proffitt, D. R. (1999). "Visual-motor recalibration in geographical slant perception." *Journal of Experimental Psychology: Human Perception and Performance* 25: 1076–1096.

25   **Limits to "filling-in"** This simple demonstration was developed by neuropsychologist V. S. Ramachandran and is described along with several others in his 1998 book *Phantoms in the Brain*. New York: William Morrow & Company. (In his book, Ramachandran relates how he has gotten so good at putting objects into his blind spot that he amuses himself at boring meetings by "beheading" other attendees by aligning their heads with his blind spot. The brain is good, but it cannot conjure up a replacement for a missing face.)

26   **Theory on rising fastballs** McBeath, M. K. (1990). "The rising fastball: Baseball's impossible pitch." *Perception* 19: 545–552.

30   **Virtual-reality hitting experiment** Gray, R. (2002b). "Markov at the bat: A model of cognitive processing in baseball batters." *Psychological Science* 13: 542–547.

35   **Sign-stealing by Giants** Prager, J. H. (January 31, 2001). "Giants' 1951 Comeback, The Sport's Greatest, Wasn't All It Seemed—Miracle Ended With 'The Shot Heard Round the World'; It Began With a Buzzer—'Papa's' Collapsible Legacy." *Wall Street Journal*, p. A1; Neyer, R. (February 13, 2001). "It ain't cheatin' if you don't get caught." http://espn.go.com/classic/s/neyer_on%20_shot.html.

36   **Ben Sheets and tipping pitches** Verducci, T. (October 10, 2001). "Learning curve." *Sports Illustrated* 95(13): 74–87.

36   **Virtual-reality experiment** Gray (2002a), op. cit.

36   **Experiment on baseball seams** Hyllegard, R. (1991). "The role of baseball seam pattern in pitch recognition." *Journal of Sport & Exercise Psychology* 13: 80–84.

37   **Flicker and baseball seams** Bahill, A. T., Baldwin, D. G., and Venkatewaran, J. (2005). "Predicting a baseball's path." *American Scientist* 93: 218–225.

39   **Virtual-reality experiment** Gray (2002b), op. cit.

CHAPTER TWO

42   **The Catch** Hano, A. (1995). *A Day in the Bleachers: The 50th Anniversary of "The Catch."* Cambridge, MA: Da Capo Press.

47   **Catching while wearing eye patch** Michaels, C. F., and Oudejans, R. R. D. (1992). "The optics and actions of catching fly balls: Zeroing out optical acceleration." *Ecological Psychology* 4: 199–222.

49   **Estimating where a ball will land** Saxberg, B. V. H. (1987). "Projected free fall trajectories: I. Theory and simulation." *Biological Cybernetics* 56: 159–175.

50   **Study changing ball size and effects of gravity** Oudejans, R. R. D., Michaels, C. F., Bakker, F. C., and Dolné, M. A. (1996). "The relevance of action in perceiving affordances: Perception of the catchableness of fly balls." *Journal of Experimental Psychology: Human Perception and Performance* 22: 879–891.

50   **Estimating landing spot while standing still** Todd, J. T. (1981). "Visual information about moving objects." *Journal of Experimental Psychology: Human Perception and Performance* 7: 795–810.

51   **Simple collision model** Example based on Pollack, H. N. (1995). [Letter]. *Science* 268: 1681.

52   **Chapman's model** Chapman, S. (1968). "Catching a baseball." *American Journal of Physics* 36: 868–870.

54   **Acceleration as a cue** Todd, J. T., op. cit.

54   **Study on changes in acceleration** Babler, T. G., and Dannemiller, J. L. (1991). "Role of image acceleration in judging landing location of free-falling objects." *Journal of Experimental Psychology: Human Perception and Performance* 19: 15–31.

57   **McBeath's model** McBeath, M. K., Shaffer, D. M., and Kaiser, M. K. (1995). "How baseball outfielders determine where to run to catch fly balls." *Science* 268: 569–573.

57   **Braking and collisions** Fajen, B. R. (2005). "The scaling of information to action in visually guided braking." *Journal of Experimental Psychology: Human Perception and Performance* 31: 1107–1123.

61   **Ability of a robot to catch** Sugar, T., and McBeath, M. (2001). "Robotic modeling of mobile ball-catching as a tool for understanding biological interceptive behavior." *Behavior and Brain Sciences* 24: 1078–1080; Suluh, A., Sugar, T. G., and McBeath, M. K. (2001). "Spatial navigational principles:

Applications to mobile robots." *Proceedings of the 2001 IEEE International Conference on Robotics and Automation* 2: 1689–1694.

62   **Ability of dogs to catch** Shaffer, D. M., Krauchunas, S. M., Eddy, M., and McBeath, M. K. (2004). "How dogs navigate to catch Frisbees." *Psychological Science* 15: 437–441.

62   **Curved optical trajectories** McLeod, P., Reed, N., and Dienes, Z. (2001). "Toward a unified fielder theory: What we do not yet know about how people run to catch a ball." *Journal of Experimental Psychology: Human Perception and Performance* 27: 1347–1355.

62   **Chasing uncatchable balls** Shaffer, D. M., and McBeath, M. K. (2002). "Baseball outfielders maintain a linear optical trajectory when tracking uncatchable fly balls." *Journal of Experimental Psychology: Human Perception and Performance* 28: 335–348.

63   **The GOAC theory** McLeod, P., and Reed, N. (in press). "The Generalised Optic Acceleration Cancellation Theory of Catching." *Journal of Experimental Psychology: Human Perception and Performance.* Interview with Mike McBeath, March 28, 2005.

64   **Amount of information in optical image** Oudejans, R. R. D., Michaels, C. F., Bakker, F. C., and Davids, K. (1999). "Shedding some light on catching in the dark: Perceptual mechanisms for catching fly balls." *Journal of Experimental Psychology: Human Perception and Performance* 25: 531–542.

67   **Study with LCD glasses** Oudejans, R. R. D., Michaels, C. F., Bakker, F. C., and Dolné, M. (1996). "The relevance of action in perceiving affordances: Perception of catchableness of fly balls." *Journal of Experimental Psychology: Human Perception and Performance* 22: 879–891.

69   **Novices vs. experts at catching balls** Oudejans, R. R. D., Michaels, C. F., and Bakker, F. C. (1997). "The effects of baseball experience on movement initiation in catching fly balls." *Journal of Sports Sciences* 15: 587–595.

CHAPTER THREE

83–4   **Biomechanical study of pitching** Fleisig, G. S., Andrews, J. R., Dillman, C. J., and Escamilla, R. F. (1995). "Kinetics of baseball pitching with implications about injury mechanisms." *The*

American Journal of Sports Medicine 23: 233–239; Sabick, M. B., Torry, M. R., Young-Kyu, K., and Hawkins, R. J. (2004). "Humeral torque in professional baseball pitchers." *The American Journal of Sports Medicine* 32: 892–898.

86   **Spatial relations and the brain** Geary, D. C. (1996). "Sexual selection and sex differences in mathematical abilities." *Behavioral and Brain Sciences* 19: 229–284.

87   **Early appearance of gender difference in throwing** Thomas, J. R., and French, K. E. (1985) "Gender differences across age in motor performance: A meta-analysis." *Psychological Bulletin* 98: 260–282.

87   **Spatial abilities and gender** Geary, D. C. (1998). *Male, Female: The Evolution of Human Sex Differences*. Washington, DC: American Psychological Association.

87   **Study on boys' throwing** Kolakowski, D., and Malina, R. (197x). *Nature* 251: 410–412.

89   **Throwing and the vertical direction** Jardine, R., and Martin, N. G. (1983). "Spatial ability and throwing accuracy." *Behavior Genetics* 13: 331–340.

90   **Evolution and enjoyment of throwing** Darlington, P. J. (1975). "Group selection, altruism, reinforcement, and throwing in human evolution." *Proceedings of the National Academy of Sciences* 72: 3748–3752.

91   **Throwing and planning** Calvin, W. H. (1993). "The unitary hypothesis: A common neural circuitry for novel manipulations, language, plan-ahead, and throwing?" In Gibson, K. R., and Ingold, T. (eds.). *Tools, Language, and Cognition in Human Evolution*. Cambridge, UK: Cambridge University Press, pp. 230–250; Calvin, W. H. (2004). *A Brief History of the Mind: From Apes to Intellect and Beyond*. New York: Oxford University Press. See also Joseph, R. (2000). "The evolution of sex differences in language, sexuality, and visual-spatial skills." *Archives of Sexual Behavior* 29: 35–66.

91   **Hunting as means to impressing females** Geary (1996), op. cit.

93   **Optimal throwing movement** Hore, J. (1996). "Motor control, excitement, and overarm throwing." *Canadian Journal of Physiology and Pharmacology* 74: 385–389; Hore, J., Watts, S., and Vilis, T. (1992). "Constraints on arm position when pointing in three dimensions: Donders' law and the Fick gimbal strategy." *Journal of Neurophysiology* 68: 374–383; Hore, J.,

Watts, S., and Martin, J. (1996). "Finger flexion does not contribute to ball speed in overarm throws." *Journal of Sports Sciences* 14: 335–342; Hore, J., Watts, S., and Tweed, D. (1996). "Arm position constraints when throwing in three dimensions." *Journal of Neurophysiology* 72: 1171–1180.

93   **Seaver's advice** Seaver, T., and Lowenfish, L. (1984). *The Art of Pitching*. New York: William Morrow and Company.

94   **Timing of the release** Hore, J., Watts, S., Martin, J., and Miller, B. (1995). "Timing of finger opening and ball release in fast and accurate overarm throws." *Experimental Brain Research* 103: 277–286.

94   **Window of time for releasing ball** Jegede, E., Watts, S., Stitt, L., and Hore, J. (2005). "Timing of ball release in overarm throws affects ball speed in unskilled but not skilled individuals." *Journal of Sports Sciences* 23: 805–816.

94   **Window for MLB pitchers** Hore, J., Timmann, D., and Watts, S. (2002). "Disorders in timing and force of finger opening in overarm throws made by cerebellar subjects." *Annals of the New York Academy of Sciences* 978: 1–15.

94   **Causes of throwing errors** Hore, J., Watts, S., and Tweed, D. (1996). "Errors in the control of joint rotations associated with inaccuracies in overarm throws." *Journal of Neurophysiology* 75: 1013–1025.

95   **Accuracy in darts** Smeets, J. B., Frens, M. A., and Brenner, E. (2002). "Throwing darts: timing is not the limiting factor." *Experimental Brain Research* 144: 268–274.

95   **Slow speed of dart throws** McNaughton, S., Timmann, D., Watts, S., and Hore, J. (2004). "Overarm throwing speed in cerebellar subjects: effect of timing of ball release." *Experimental Brain Research* 154: 470–478.

96   **Study on throwing to different heights and distances** Watts, S., Pessotto, I., and Hore, J. (2004). "A simple rule for controlling overarm throws to different targets." *Experimental Brain Research* 159: 329–339.

96   **"Perturbing" the throwing motion** Hore, J., Ritchie, R., and Watts, S. (1999). "Finger opening in an overarm throw is not triggered by proprioceptive feedback from elbow extension or wrist flexion." *Experimental Brain Research* 125: 302–312.

97   **Speed of throwing motion** Hore, J., O'Brien, M., and Watts, S. (2005). "Control of joint rotations in overarm throws of

different speeds made by dominant and nondominant arms."
Journal of Neurophysiology 94: 3975–3986.

98   **Velocity of fingers at release** Hore, J., and Watts, S. (2005).
"Timing finger opening in overarm throwing based on a spatial
representation of hand path." *Journal of Neurophysiology* 93:
3189–3199.

99   **Instructional book** Bennett, B. (1999). *101 Pitching Drills*.
Champaign, IL: Coaches Choice Books.

99   **Wrist flexion** Debicki, D. B., Gribble, P. L., Watts, S., and Hore, J.
(2004). "Kinematics of wrist joint flexion in overarm throws
made by skilled subjects." *Experimental Brain Research* 154:
382–394.

99   **"Back forces" and the wrist** Hore, J., Watts, S., and Tweed, D.
(1999). "Prediction and compensation by an internal model for
back forces during finger opening in an overarm throw."
Journal of Neurophysiology 82: 1187–1197; Hore, J., Watts, S.,
Leschuk, M., and MacDougall, A. (2001). "Control of finger
grip forces in overarm throws made by skilled throwers."
Journal of Neurophysiology 86: 2678–2689.

101   **Effect of schema on thought** Posner, M. I., Snyder, C. R. R, and
Davidson, B. J. (1980). "Attention and the detection of signals."
Journal of Experimental Psychology: General 109: 160–174.

101   **Brain imaging of imagination** Kosslyn, S. M., Thompson, W. L.,
Klm, I. J., and Alpert, N. M. (1995). "Topographical representa-
tions of mental images in primary visual cortex." *Nature* 378:
496–498.

CHAPTER FOUR

113   **Reaction time among players and nonplayers** Paull, G., and
Glencross, D. (1997). "Expert perception and decision making
in baseball." *International Journal of Sport Psychology* 28:
35–56.

113   **Reaction time in AA Southern League** Classé et al. (1997).
"Association between visual reaction time and batting, fielding,
and earned run averages among players of the Southern
Baseball League." *Journal of the American Optometric
Association* 68: 43–49.

114   **Visual abilities of MLB players** Laby, D. M., et al. (1996). "The
visual function of professional baseball players." *American
Journal of Ophthalmology* 122: 476–485.

114   **Pulfrich Phenomenon** http://dogfeathers.com/java/pulfrich.html.

115   **MLB players and the Pulfrich Phenomenon** Hofeldt, A. J., and Hoefle, F. B. (1993). "Stereophotometric testing for Pulfrich's phenomenon in professional baseball players." *Perceptual and Motor Skills* 77: 407–416.

115   **Dynamic visual acuity** Banks, P. M., Moore, L. A., Liu, C., and Wu, B. (2004). "Dynamic visual acuity: A review." *The South African Optometrist* 63: 58–64.

115   **Eye dominance and hitting** Adams, G. L. (1965). "Effect of eye dominance on baseball batting." *Research Quarterly* 36: 3–9; Portal, J., and Romano, P. E. (1988). "Patterns of eye-hand dominance in baseball players." *New England Journal of Medicine* 319: 655–656.

116–7 **Study on handedness** Grondin, S., Guiard, Y., Ivry, R. B., and Koren, S. (1999). "Manual laterality and hitting performance in Major League Baseball." *Journal of Experimental Psychology: Human Perception and Performance* 25: 747–754.

125   **Winslow's test** William Winslow agreed to share a copy of the test, which is protected by copyright, and to let me include sample items associated with each of the eleven traits, on the condition that I would not reveal any of the questions relating to accuracy and objectivity.

129   **AMI test as reliable predictor of success** Peetoom, G. A. (1987). "Predicting success in professional baseball with the Athletic Motivation Inventory." Ph.D. dissertation, University of Mississippi.

129   **AMI scores of recreational and college players** Hightower, J. [1973; cited in Bowie, B. G. (1989). "Predicting success in the draft of the National Hockey League using the Athletic Motivation Inventory." Doctoral dissertation, University of Mississippi.]. "A comparison of competitive and recreational baseball players on motivation." Master's thesis, Louisiana State University, Baton Rouge, Louisiana.

131   **University of California study on SAT** http://www.ucop.edu/news/sat/research.html.

134   **Rob Neyer on team chemistry** For just a few examples, see http://espn.go.com/mlb/columns/neyer_rob/1372319.html; http://sports.espn.go.com/mlb/columns/story?columnist neyer_rob&id=1719173.

http://sports.espn.go.com/mlb/columns/story?columnist-neyer_rob&id=1584461.

135   **Recent reviews of personality research** Bazana, P. G. , and Stelmack, R. M. (2004). "Stability of personality across the life span: A meta-analysis." In Stelmack, R. M. (ed.). *On the Psychobiology of Personality: Essays in Honor of Marvin Zuckerman,* pp. 113–144; Caspi, A., Roberts, B. W., and Shiner, R. L. (2005). "Personality Development: Stability and Change." *Annual Review of Psychology* 56: 453–484.

CHAPTER FIVE

146   **Odds on DiMaggio's streak** Short, T., and Wasserman, L. (1989). "Should we be surprised by the streak of streaks?" *Chance* 2: 13.

147   **Study of basketball streaks** Gilovich, T., Vallone, R., and Tversky, A. (1985). "The hot hand in basketball: On the misperception of random sequences." *Cognitive Psychology* 17: 295–314.

150   **Streaks in putting and dart-throwing** Gilden, D. L., and Wilson, S. G. (1995). "Streaks in skilled performance." *Psychonomic Bulletin & Review* 2: 260–265.

151   **Streaks in horseshoes** Smith, G. (2003). "Horseshoe pitchers' hot hands." *Psychonomic Bulletin & Review* 10: 753–758.

151   **Streaks in bowling** Smith, G., and Dorsey-Palmateer, R. (2004) "Bowlers' hot hands." *The American Statistician* 58: 38–45. See also Frame, D., Hughson, E., and Leach, J. C. (2004). "Runs, regimes, and rationality: The hot hand strikes back." http://leeds-faculty.colorado.edu/hughsone/workingpapers/bowl.pdf.

154   **Limits to maintaining will** Baumeister, R. F., Bratslavsky, E., Muraven, M., and Tice, D. M. (1998). "Ego depletion: Is the active self a limited resource?" *Journal of Personality and Social Psychology* 74: 1252–1265; Schmeichel, B. J., Vohs, K. D., and Baumeister, R. F. (2003). "Intellectual performance and ego depletion: Role of the self in logical reasoning and other information processing." *Journal of Personality and Social Psychology* 85: 33–46.

157   **Mills brothers** For the full story of the Mills brothers' work, see Schwarz, A. (2004). *The Numbers Game: Baseball's Lifelong Fascination with Statistics.* New York: St. Martin's Press.

158–9 **Clutch and choke hitting** Recently, another study of clutch hitting (Fuld, E. [May 19, 2005]. "Clutch and choke hitters in Major League Baseball: Romantic myth or empirical fact." Unpublished manuscript.) introduced a new "importance index" for measuring the importance of different game situations. After conducting a series of analyses, this study concluded that clutch hitters do, in fact, exist, though there have not been many of them. Using a strict statistical criterion, in fact, only two players in the years 1974–1992 were clearly "clutch" hitters: Eddie Murray and Bill Buckner. Several other players, including Frank Duffy, Alan Trammell, Denny Doyle, and Rickey Henderson, also emerge as clutch hitters under one set of assumptions or another. The study also looked for evidence of choke hitters. Some candidates for that unfortunate category did emerge, but none who met relatively strict statistical criteria, so it would appear that there have been very few, if any, choke hitters in Major League Baseball.

The study's approach was systematic and thorough—it used different combinations of various assumptions—and tried to address potential flaws in earlier attempts to measure clutch hitting. Still, I was left with some doubts. The aim of these analyses is to identify players who, if they exist, have some intrinsic characteristic that makes them a clutch (or choke) hitter. Yet, when the careers of the various players were broken down by season, many of them showed up on both lists. Murray and Buckner both played sixteen of the seasons in the sample, and both emerged as clutch hitters in nine of the sixteen seasons, but as choke hitters in two other seasons. Craig Reynolds, who had thirteen seasons in the sample, emerged as a clutch hitter seven seasons and a choke hitter four seasons. If clutch hitting is an intrinsic ability, it seems to me such wide fluctuations would be unlikely.

168 **Choking and greater-than-usual self-focus** Baumeister, R. F. (1984). "Choking under pressure: Self-consciousness and paradoxical effects of incentives on skilled performance." *Journal of Personality and Social Psychology* 46: 610–620.

168 **Virtual reality study** Gray, R. (2004). "Attending to the execution of a complex sensorimotor skill: Expertise differences, choking and slumps." *Journal of Experimental Psychology: Applied* 10: 42–54.

169   **Pressure in golf and soccer** Beilock, S. L., Carr, T. H.,
       MacMahon, C., and Starkes, J. L. (2002). "When paying
       attention becomes counterproductive: Impact of divided versus
       skill-focused attention on novice and experienced performance
       of sensorimotor skills." *Journal of Experimental Psychology:
       Applied* 8: 6–16.

170   **"Stereotype threat"** For a brief review of this literature, see
       Stone, J., Sjomeling, M., Lynch, C. I., and Darley, J. M. (1999).
       "Stereotype threat effects on Black and White athletic perfor-
       mance." *Journal of Personality and Social Psychology* 77:
       1213–1227; See also Steele, C. M., and Aronson, J. (1995). "Stereo-
       type threat and the intellectual test performance of African
       Americans." *Journal of Personality and Social Psychology* 69:
       797–811; Steele, C. M. (1997). "A threat in the air: How stereo-
       types shape intellectual identity and performance." *American
       Psychologist* 52: 613–629.

170   **Putting study with black and white subjects** Stone et al., op. cit.

171   **Putting while distracted** Beilock, S. L., Jellison, W. A.,
       McConnell, A. R., and Carr, T. H. (June 2003). "When negative
       stereotypes lead to negative performance outcomes:
       Understanding the stereotype threat phenomenon in
       sensorimotor skill execution." Paper presented at the North
       American Society for the Psychology of Sport and Physical
       Activity. Savannah, Georgia. Cited in Beilock, S. L., and
       McConnell, A. R. (2004). "Stereotype threat and sport: Can
       athletic performance be threatened?" *Journal of Sport & Exercise
       Psychology* 26: 597–609.

171   **Pendulum study** Wegner, D. M., Ansfield, M., and Pilloff, D.
       (1998). "The putt and the pendulum: Ironic effects of the mental
       control of action." *Psychological Science* 9: 196–199.

171   **Study of putting in which participants were warned not to
       miss** Beilock, S., Afremow, J. A., Rabe, A. L., and Carr, T. H.
       (2001). " 'Don't Miss!' The debilitating effects of suppressive
       imagery on golf putting performance." *Sport Psychology* 23:
       200–221.

175   **Home field advantage in indoor vs. outdoor sports** Schwartz, B.,
       and Barsky, S. F. (1977). "The home advantage." *Social Forces*
       55: 641–661.

175   **Length of home stand and home field advantage** Courneya, K. S.,
       and Carron, A. V. (1991). "Effects of travel and length of home

stand/road trip on the home advantage." *Journal of Sport & Exercise Psychology* 13: 42–49.

176   **Home field advantage and base running** Click, J. (August 16, 2004). "How parks affect baserunning: Looking for the home-field advantage." http://www.baseballprospectus.com/article.php?articleid=3347.

176   **Home field advantage and defense** Click, J. (November 3, 2005). "Homeland defense." http://baseballprospectus.com/article.php?articleid=4583.

176–7 **Home field advantage in Game 7 of World Series** Baumeister, R. F., and Steinhilber, A. (1984). "Paradoxical effects of supportive audiences on performance under pressure: The home field disadvantage in sports championships." *Journal of Personality and Social Psychology* 48: 1447–1457.

177   **"Kinder and darker forms of choking"** Schlenker, B. R., Phillips, S. T., Boniecki, K. A., and Schlenker, D. R. (1995) "Championship pressures: Choking or triumphing in one's own territory?" *Journal of Personality and Social Psychology* 68: 632–643.

186–8 **Performance and free-agent contracts** Sturman, T. S., and Thibodeau, R. (2001). "Performance-undermining effects of baseball free-agent contracts." *Sport Psychology* 23: 23–36; Lord, R. G., and Hohenfeld, J. A. (1979). "Longitudinal field assessment of equity effects on the performance of major league baseball players." *Journal of Applied Psychology* 64: 19–26; Duchon, D., and Jago, A. G. (1981). "Equity and the performance of major league baseball players: An extension of Lord and Hohenfeld." *Journal of Applied Psychology* 66: 728–732; Harder, J. W. (1991). "Equity theory versus expectancy theory: The case of major league baseball free agents." *Journal of Applied Psychology* 76: 458–464.

188–9 **Beltran story** Cwelich, L. (October 12, 2005). "No questions about Beltran's effort: Switch-hitting slugger leaves everything on the field." mlb.com.

191   **Doubts about "fat cat" theory** Werner, S., and Mero, N. P. (1999). "Fair or foul? The effects of external, internal, and employee equity on changes in performance of Major League Baseball players." *Human Relations* 52: 1291–1311.

193   **Performance before and after arbitration** Bretz, R. D., and Thomas, S. L. (1992). "Perceived equity, motivation and

final-offer arbitration in Major League Baseball." *Journal of Applied Psychology* 77: 280–287; Hauenstein, M. A., and Lord, R. G. (1989). "The effects of final-offer arbitration on the performance of major league baseball players: A test of equity theory." *Human Performance* 2: 147–165; Sommers, P. M. (1993). "The influence of salary arbitration on player performance." *Social Science Quarterly* 74: 439–443.

193–4 **Psychological studies on trades** Bateman, T. S., Karwan, K. R., and Kazee, T. A. (1983). "Getting a fresh start: A natural quasi-experimental test of the performance effects of moving to a new job." *Journal of Applied Psychology* 68: 517–524; Jackson, J. M., Buglione, S. M., and Glenwick, D. S. (1988). "Major League Baseball performance as a function of being traded: A drive theory analysis." *Personality and Social Psychology Bulletin* 14: 46–56; Kopelman, R. E., and Pantaleno, J. J. (1977). "Rejection, motivation and athletic performance: Is there a traded player syndrome?" *Perceptual and Motor Skills* 45: 827–834; Nicholson, C., McTeer, W., and White, P. (1998). "The effects of changing teams on the performance of Major League Baseball players." *Journal of Sport Behavior* 21: 92–100.

194 **Trades during the season and effect on performance** Kopelman, R. E., and Pantaleno, J. (1977). "Rejection, motivation and athletic performance: Is there a traded player syndrome?" *Perceptual and Motor Skills* 45: 827–834.

195 **Home run rate and steroids** Silver, N. (March 30, 2005). "2005—Setting the stage." http://www.baseballprospectus.com/article.php?articleid=3881.

195 **Testosterone and aggression** Pinna, G., Costa, E., and Guidotti, A. (2005). "Changes in brain testosterone and allopregnanolone biosynthesis elicit aggressive behavior." *Proceedings of the National Academy of Sciences* 102: 2135–2140; Zitzmann, M., and Nieschlag, E. (2001). "Testosterone levels in healthy men and the relation to behavioural and physical characteristics: facts and constructs." *European Journal of Endocrinology* 144: 183–197.

195 **Steroids and mental acuity** Pearson, H. (2004). "A dangerous elixir?" *Nature* 431: 500–501.

196 **Spatial abilities and androgen levels** Shute, V. J., Pellegrino, J. W., Hubert, L., and Reynolds, R. W. (1983). "The relationship between androgen levels and human spatial abilities." *Bulletin of the Psychonomic Society* 21: 465–468; Gouchie, C., and Kimura, D. (1991). "The relationship between testosterone levels and cognitive ability patterns." *Psychoneuroendocrinology* 16: 323–334.

196   **Spatial abilities and seasons** Kimura, D., and Hampson, E. (1994). "Cognitive pattern in men and women is influenced by fluctuations in sex hormones." *Current Directions in Psychological Science* 3: 57–61.

196–7   **Spatial abilities and time of day** Moffat, S. D., and Hampson, E. (1996). "A curvilinear relationship between testosterone and spatial cognition in humans: Possible influence of hand preference." *Psychoneuroendocrinology* 21: 323–337.

197   **No association between testosterone and spatial abilities** Halari, R., et al. (2005). "Sex differences and individual differences in cognitive performance and their relationship to endogenous gonadal homroes and gonadotropins." *Behavioral Neuroscience* 119: 104–117.

197   **High levels of testosterone and spatial abilities** Hooven, C. K., Chabris, C. F., Ellison, P. T., and Kosslyn, S. M. (2004). "The relationship of male testosterone to components of mental rotation." *Neuropsychologia* 42: 782–790.

197   **Transexuals and spatial abilities** Zitzmann, op. cit.

197   **Testosterone supplements and spatial abilities** Cherrier, M. M., et al. (2001). "Testosterone supplementation improves spatial and verbal memory in healthy older men." *Neurology* 57: 80–88.

197   **Measurement of steroid levels** Pearson, op. cit.

198   **Testosterone and health risks** Pearson, op. cit.

CHAPTER SIX

205   **State of studies on fan behavior** Funk, D. C., and James, J. (2001). "The Psychological Continuum Model: A conceptual framework for understanding an individual's psychological connection to sport." *Sport Management Review* 4: 119–150; Jacobson, B. (2003). "The social psychology of the creation of a sports fan identity: A theoretical review of the literature." *Athletic Insight* 5(2). http://www.athleticinsight.com/Vol5Iss2/FanDevelopment.htm.

206   **Fathers passing on game to sons** Hall, D. (1985). *Fathers Playing Catch with Sons: Essays on Sport (Mostly Baseball).* New York: North Point Press. Note that Hall shatters the myth about fathers socializing their sons into the game. It was his father *and* mother whom he listened to games with, and "the sound of baseball grew louder" when he married his wife, Jane, who was a baseball fan, too.

206   **Daughters and baseball** Goodwin, D. K. (1997). *Wait Till Next Year: A Memoir.* New York: Touchstone.

206   **Influence of "agents" of socialization** Wann, D. L., Melnick, M. J., Russell, G. W., and Pease, D. G. (2001). *Sport Fans: The Psychology and Social Impact of Spectators.* New York: Routledge.

207   **Parents and team identification** Wann, D. L., Tucker, K. B., and Schrader, M. P. (1996). "An exploratory examination of the factors influencing the origination, continuation, and cessation of identification with sports teams." *Perceptual and Motor Skills* 82: 995–1001.

207   **Locality and team identification** Jones, I. (1997). "A further examination of the factors influencing current identification with a sports team, a response to Wann et al. (1996)." *Perceptual and Motor Skills* 85: 257–258.

207   **Team success and identification** Wann et al. (2001), op. cit.

207   **Other reasons for identification** Funk & James (2001), op. cit. Jacobson (2003), op. cit. Wann et al. (2001), op. cit.

208   **Emotional level and identification level** See for example Wann et al. (2001).

208   **Enjoyment level and rivalry** Zillmann D., and Paulus, P. B. (1993). "Spectators: Reactions to sports events and effects on athletic performance." In Singer, R. N., Murphy, M., and Tennant, L. K. (eds.). *Handbook of Research on Sport Psychology.* New York: Macmillan, pp. 600–619.

209   **Testosterone and social structure** Kemper, T. D. (1990). *Social Structure and Testosterone.* Piscataway, NJ: Rutgers University Press.

210   **Sport as stand-in for warfare** Geary, D. C., and Flinn, M. V. (2002). "Sex differences in behavioral and hormonal response to social threat": Commentary on Taylor et al. (2000). *Psychological Review* 109: 745–750.

211   **Research on salivary testosterone levels** Bernhardt, P. C., Dabbs, J. M., Fielden, J. A., and Lutter, C. D. (1998).

"Testosterone changes during vicarious experiences of winning and losing among fans at sporting events." *Physiology & Behavior* 65: 59–62.

212 **Domestic abuse and Redskins wins** Wann et al. (2001), op. cit.

213 **Sports as simply entertainment** Wann et al. (2001), op. cit.

213 **Enjoyment dependent on team performance** Zillman, D., Bryant, J., and Sapolsky, B. S. (1989). "Enjoyment from sports spectatorship." In Goldstein, J. H. (ed.). *Sports, games, and play: Social and psychological viewpoints* (2nd ed.). Hillsdale, NJ: Erlbaum, pp.241–278.

215 **BIRG and CORF** Cialdini, R. B., Borden, R. J., Thorne, A., Walker, M. R., Freeman, S., and Sloan, L. R. (1976). "Basking in reflected glory: Three (football) field studies." *Journal of Personality and Social Psychology* 34: 366–375; Cialdini, R. B., and Richardson, K. D. (1980). "Two indirect tactics of image management: Basking and blasting." *Journal of Personality and Social Psychology* 39: 406–415; Snyder, C. R., Lassegard, M., and Ford, C. E. (1986). "Distancing after group success and failure: Basking in reflected glory and cutting off reflected failure." *Journal of Personality and Social Psychology* 51: 382–388; Wann, D. L., and Branscombe, N. R. (1990). "Die-hard and fair-weather fans: Effects of identification on BIRGing and CORFing tendencies." *Journal of Sport and Social Issues* 14: 103–117; More recently, see Bizman, A., and Yinon, Y. (2002). "Engaging in distancing tactics among sports fans: Effects on self-esteem and emotional responses." *Journal of Social Psychology* 142: 381–392.

215 **Terror Management Theory** Greenberg, J., Pyszczysnki, T., and Solomon, S. (1986). "The causes and consequences of the need for self-esteem: A terror management theory." In Baumeister, R. (ed.). *Public Self and Private Self.* New York: Springer-Verlag, pp. 189–212.

217–8 **Home field advantage and attendance** Kochman, L. M. (1995). "Major League Baseball: What really puts fans in the stands?" *Sport Marketing Quarterly* 4: 9–11.

218 **Study on hockey fans** Fisher, R. J., and Wakefield, K. (1998). "Factors leading to group identification: A field study of winners and losers." *Psychology & Marketing* 15: 23–40.

218–9 **Study on Cubs fans** Bristow, D. N., and Sebastian, R. J. (2001). "Holy cow! Wait 'til next year! A closer look at the brand loyalty of Chicago Cubs baseball fans." *The Journal of Consumer Marketing* 18: 256–273.

219 **Attendance and the designated hitter** Domazlicky, B. R., and Kerr, P. M. (1990). "Baseball attendance and the designated hitter." *The American Economist* 34: 62–68.

220 **Lineup changes and attendance** Kahane, L., and Shmanske, S. (1997). "Team roster turnover and attendance in major league baseball." *Applied Economics* 29: 425–431.

220 **Familiarity with ballpark and attendance** McEvoy, C. D., Nagel, M. S., DeSchriver, T. D., and Brown, M. T. (2005). "Facility age and attendance in Major League Baseball." Unpublished manuscript.

221–2 **Study on Castro positions** Jones, E. E., and Harris, V. A. (1967). "The attribution of attitudes." *Journal of Experimental Social Psychology* 3: 1–24.

222 **"Fundamental attribution error"** Ross, L. (1977). "The intuitive psychologist and his shortcomings: Distortions in the attribution process." In Berkowitz, L. (ed.). *Advances in Experimental Social Psychology* (vol. 10). New York: Academic Press, pp. 173–220.

223–4 **Dartmouth and Princeton game** Hastorf, A., and Cantril, H. (1954) "They saw a game: A case study." *Journal of Abnormal and Social Psychology* 49: 129–134.

224–5 **Attribution theory and sport quotes** Lau, R. R., and Russell, D. (1980). "Attributions in the sports pages." *Journal of Personality and Social Psychology* 39: 29–38.

226 **Study on coin flips** Tversky, A., and Kahneman, D. (1974). "Judgment under uncertainty: Heuristics and biases." *Science* 185: 1124–1131.

227 **Study on roulette wheel** Burns, B. D., and Corpus, B. (2004). "Randomness and inductions from streaks: 'Gambler's fallacy' versus 'hot hand.'" *Psychonomic Bulletin & Review* 11: 179–184.

231 **Worse team winning the World Series** Mosteller, F. (1952). "The World Series Competition." *Journal of the American Statistical Association* 47: 355–380.

232 **Pitching to Barry Bonds** Baseball Prospectus. (May 17, 2004). "When to pitch to Barry." *Sports Illustrated*, p. 57.

INDEX

Index

Index